Scaling the Secular City

Scaling the Secular City

A Defense of Christianity

J. P. Moreland

BAKER BOOK HOUSE
Grand Rapids, Michigan 49516

Copyright © 1987 by Baker Books
a division of Baker Book House Company
P.O. Box 6287, Grand Rapids, MI 49516-6287

ISBN: 0-8010-6222-5

Library of Congress Catalog Card Number 87-70626

Thirteenth printing, September 1998

Printed in the United States of America

For information about academic books, resources for
Christian leaders, and all new releases available from
Baker Book House, visit our web site:
http://www.bakerbooks.com

To my **mother** and **father,**
who created the space
for me to find
the One in whom we live
and move and have our being

A wise man scales the city of the mighty
And brings down the stronghold in which they trust.
[Prov. 21:22]

Contents

Foreword

C. S. Lewis once wrote: "To be ignorant and simple now—not to be able to meet the enemies on their own ground—would be to throw down our weapons, and to betray our uneducated brethren who have, under God, no defense but us against the intellectual attacks of the heathen. Good philosophy must exist, if for no other reason, because bad philosophy needs to be answered."

Scaling the Secular City is not just another apologetics book. This is a fresh, up-to-date defense of the Christian faith by a bright mind. J. P. Moreland musters new arguments, tackles new problems, and reveals penetrating insight as he gives reasons for the historic Christian faith. His rich background in philosophy, science, and theology is manifest in the helpful way he operates on the borders of these disciplines. His insights into the contemporary philosophical issues make him one of the ablest young apologists in America.

This book not only will help the average Christian, but also will challenge the best scholars. It is another good example of the renaissance of classical apologetics in a day that refuses to either capitulate to the philosophical skeptics or give a reason for our hope.

Norman L. Geisler

Acknowledgments

It is a great delight for me to acknowledge several people who have helped me in preparing the present work. Four thinkers bear special mention. I want to thank Josh McDowell for first introducing me to the joy and importance of apologetics. Norman L. Geisler has been a constant source of encouragement and his writings and life have been a consistent role model of courage in contending for the Christian faith. William Lane Craig has given me several suggestions on earlier drafts of this manuscript and his writings have influenced much of my thinking. Finally, I owe more than I can mention to my friend and philosophical mentor Dallas Willard. His gracious spirit and tenacious mind have been inspiring.

Several people helped me with the preparation of the manuscript: Rich Tucker, Gloria Matarazzo, Kathy Fesmire, Mary Garland Considine, Richard Loper, and Ron Scheller. Their labor made my task easier. Allan Fisher at Baker has been a delight to work with. In addition, my friends Bill and Patty Roth, Klaus and Beth Issler, Greg and Debbie Kappas, Walt and Marty Russell, Tim and Bobbi Smick, Jim and Jeanie Duncan, Jim and Carol Dethmer, and John Glenn, have been especially helpful to me.

Finally, I thank God for my wife, Hope, and my little girls, Ashley and Allison. Anyone who engages in the rigors of apologetics and philosophy runs the risk of becoming dry and out of touch with the emotional side of life. These wonderful women in my life have loved me dearly during this project. My love for them is the sine qua non of my life.

Introduction

In recent years there has been a noticeable increase in the number of intellectuals who embrace historic Christianity as a rational worldview. In philosophy, at least seven journals are produced by Christian theists and in 1978 the Society of Christian Philosophers was formed. This society includes several hundred professionally trained philosophers who embrace some form of the Christian faith. In science, there has been a crisis in the neo-Darwinian version of evolutionary theory, and sociologists and philosophers of science have raised objections which have called into question the truth claims and rationality of science as a discipline. The American Scientific Affiliation and the Creation Research Society list among their members several hundred professional scientists who believe that real facts of science and the Christian faith are compatible. In New Testament studies there has been a clear movement since the 1960s toward a more conservative view of the New Testament materials.

Taken by themselves, the trends listed do not prove that Christianity is true or even rational. But these trends do point to the fact that a number of thinkers believe that secularism is an inadequate view of the world and that a rational apologetic can be given for historic Christianity. This volume is a work in Christian apologetics which attempts to state and defend some of the arguments which support the rationality of the Christian faith.

It is important for the Christian community to engage in apologetics for at least four reasons. First, Scripture commands us to defend the faith and gives us several examples of such activity. Genesis 1 does not merely assume the existence of the God of the Bible, but attempts to refute ancient Near Eastern concepts of deity by arguing that there is one God and that he created everything. The Old Testament prophets often appealed to the facts of history, prophecy, creation, or providence to reason with other nations. In the New Testament, Jesus authenticated his own credentials by urging people to consider his works. He met honest questions with evidence, as is seen in his encounter with Thomas. In Acts, Paul reasoned with unbelievers and gave evidence for the gospel by appealing to creation and the facts surrounding Jesus' life and resurrection. Jude 3 and 1 Peter 3:15 explicitly command us to contend for the faith by giving a rational answer to those who question our faith. Scripture does warn us against using *bad* philosophy (Col. 2:8) and thinking that philosophy alone can illumine the content of the gospel or lead someone to faith (1 Cor. 1:18-25). But such warnings do not militate against the practice of good apologetics.

Second, apologetics can help remove obstacles to faith and thus aid unbelievers in embracing the gospel. Certainly the Holy Spirit must be involved in drawing men to Christ. But a preacher is not absolved of the responsibility of preparing his sermon just because the Spirit must apply the Word of God to the lives of his listeners. In the same way, ambassadors for Christ are not excused from the responsibility of defending the gospel. The Spirit can use evidence to convict men of the truth of the proclamation.

Third, apologetics can strengthen believers in at least two ways. For one thing, it gives them confidence that their faith is true and reasonable; therefore, apologetics encourages a life of faith seeking understanding. Further, apologetics can actually encourage spiritual growth. A person's ability to grow in Christ is in some measure dependent on what that person is able to see in the Scriptures and the world around him. Some people cannot see patterns in a great work of art even though they are staring at the canvas, because they have not been trained to see those patterns. Similarly, some people cannot see God at work in the world or understand and appropriate certain features of the Bible because they have not been trained to see those patterns. Instead, they view the world through secular glasses. Their subconscious structures cause them to interpret events and statements in ways which stifle growth. Apologetics can focus attention on some of those secular structures, call them into question, and release the self to view the world in a way more compatible with a Christian worldview.

Fourth, apologetics can contribute to health in the culture at large. For example, the last several years have witnessed an upsurge in the formation of bioethics committees. This in turn has raised in the culture at large questions about the objectivity of value, the reality of life after death, and so on. When believers promote their faith because it is true and rational, they contribute to a general cultural perception which sees that moral and religious issues are not mere matters of private taste, but rather are areas where truth and rational argument are appropriate. And they remove the religious dimension of such discussions from the private arena of personal opinion to the public arena of rational discussion.

This book is an attempt to defend the thesis that the Christian God does in fact exist and that it is rational to believe that he does. But what does it mean to say that such a belief is rational? Two senses of rationality are relevant to this question. A belief *P* can be rational in the sense that it is a rationally *permissible* belief. A belief *P* is permissible in case believing *P* is just as warranted as believing not-*P* or suspending judgment regarding *P* in light of the evidence. A belief *P* can also be rational in the sense that it is a rationally *obligatory* belief. A belief *P* is obligatory if believing *P* has greater warrant than believing not-*P* or suspending judgment regarding *P* in light of the evidence. In my view, the evidence in this book contributes to making the belief that the Christian God exists at least permissible and, I would argue, obligatory.

In chapters 1–4, several arguments are offered for the existence of a personal God. Chapter 1 describes the kalam cosmological argument, supports that argument with scientific and philosophical lines of reasoning, and considers objections. Chapter 2 centers on issues which cluster around the design argument. Several types of design are discussed, three forms of the argument are presented, and objections are considered. Chapter 3 attempts to argue for God from the existence of finite minds by first establishing that substance dualism is a defensible solution to the mind/body problem and, second, by arguing that minds do not come into existence from nothing or emerge from matter. Chapter 4 argues that the existence of God is the best solution to the question of the meaning of life.

Chapters 5–6 present a case for the deity and resurrection of Jesus of Nazareth. Chapter 5 offers five general lines of evidence for the claim that the New Testament documents are reliable historical sources about Jesus. Chapter 6 examines the evidence for the empty tomb, the resurrection appearances, and four important features of the early church. The chapter closes with a brief examination of the role of Hellenistic influences on the New Testament picture of the resurrection of Jesus.

Chapters 7–8 focus on objections raised against Christian theism. In chapter 7 the relationship between science and Christianity is analyzed. The realism/antirealism debate is surveyed, limits to science are discussed, five models of integration between science and theology are presented, and the main philosophical, theological, and scientific issues in the creation/evolution debate are described. Chapter 8 concludes the book by analyzing four key issues: the visibility of God, the charge that belief in God is a psychological projection, the value of religious experience, and the nature of five different forms of ethical relativism.

I have tried to write an intermediate-level work that is aimed at those who want a serious discussion of apologetic issues without having formal training in philosophy. A number of good works in apologetics are written at a popular level. There are also a number of very technical works in the philosophy of religion and New Testament studies which are accessible only for the professional scholar. This work is an attempt to provide a treatment of some central apologetic themes at a level somewhere between the two. Beginners in apologetics will find much of value; professional philosophers and theologians will also benefit from some of the material, especially the resources in the notes. The book can also be given to an interested unbeliever. Each chapter is self-contained, and someone could be encouraged to read a particular chapter in light of his specific questions and needs. I have tried to list several resources for further study so the reader can do more work on a topic of interest.

The conclusion contains a summary of the arguments offered in each chapter. The reader may wish to turn there first for an overview of the structure of the book.

1

The Cosmological Argument

One of the most important arguments for God's existence is the cosmological argument. It has had a tarnished yet sturdy history and, like the Bible, it has outlived most of its critics. The argument gets its name from the Greek word *kosmos*, which means "world" or "universe." The argument generally begins with the existence of the world or some part of it and seeks to establish the existence of a necessary Being who causes the existence of the world.

Actually, there are three very different forms of the cosmological argument. This is important to keep in mind, since in many cases critics will raise what they believe to be objections against the cosmological argument in general. Their objections, even if successful, often work against only one form of the argument.

The three forms of the cosmological argument are the Thomist argument, the Leibnizian argument, and the kalam argument. Since the main burden of this chapter is to state and defend the kalam cosmological argument, I will mention only briefly the other two forms. This is not to imply they are not valuable. Both of them are good arguments. But the kalam argument has not received the attention it deserves, so this chapter will center on stating and defending it.

The Thomist Argument

The Thomist argument receives its name from Saint Thomas Aquinas (1225–1274). It begins by asserting the existence of finite, contingent beings. These would be beings which could have not existed and thus are dependent for their being on something else. Finite beings owe their current existence either to an infinite regress of other dependent beings or to a necessary Being, one which could not cease to exist if it does in fact have existence. An infinite regress of finite beings does not cause the existence of anything.[1] Adding another dependent being to a chain of dependent beings does not ground the existence of the chain. To say that it does is like saying one could get an orange by adding an infinite number of apples to a basket of apples. Adding apples to apples does not yield an orange; adding dependent beings to dependent beings does not yield a necessary Being. The current existence of all finite beings is caused or grounded by the existence of a necessary Being, and this being is God.

Three features of the argument are central. First, proponents must spell out what it is to be a dependent being; this is done by appealing to what is called the essence/existence distinction. A being's essence is its whatness or nature and its existence is its thatness (that it is). Proponents argue that one cannot move from a finite thing's essence to its existence. By contemplating Fido's dogness it does not follow that Fido really exists. If he does exist, being must be given to his essence.

Second, the nature of the infinite regress used in the argument is important. The regress of beings does not go back through time, but is current or simultaneous. Third, the nature of God as a necessary Being is crucial. God is necessary in a metaphysical sense. This is sometimes put by saying

---

1. The Thomist argument turns on a distinction between a per se regress and a per accidens regress, the former being the one used in the argument. See Patterson Brown, "Infinite Causal Regression," in *Aquinas: A Collection of Critical Essays*, ed. Anthony Kenny (Notre Dame: University of Notre Dame Press, 1976), pp. 214–36.

that God is necessary de re. It is not a logical contradiction to deny God's existence. Rather, if God exists he exists necessarily. He could not have not-existed.

There are a number of contemporary advocates of the Thomist argument. Two of them are Norman L. Geisler and Bruce R. Reichenbach.[2]

The Leibnizian Argument

The Leibnizian cosmological argument receives its name from the philosopher Gottfried Wilhelm Leibniz (1646–1716). It begins by asking the question "why is there something rather than nothing?" Why does anything at all exist? It then uses the principle of sufficient reason (for anything that exists, there must be some reason, some purpose or rational context, why it exists rather than not exists) to argue for the existence of an intrinsically intelligible or self-explanatory being—God—whose existence is logically necessary. This is sometimes put by saying that God's existence is necessary de dicto. That is, it would be a logical contradiction to deny the proposition *God exists*.[3]

Two issues are important for this argument. First, why should anyone believe in the principle of sufficient reason? It may hold on a limited basis. For example, if I take my car to the garage to have it fixed, I would certainly think it odd for the mechanic to tell me that there is no reason why it does not work. He may not *know* the reason, but surely there is one. But does the principle hold with regard to the universe as a whole? Could not one agree with atheist Bertrand Russell and simply say that the universe is just there and that is all? There is no explanation. I do not find Russell's response satisfying, but in any case, the principle of sufficient reason, at least as it applies to the universe as a whole, is a key issue in the Leibnizian argument.

The second important issue involves whether or not any being's existence is logically necessary. Is it a contradiction to deny the existence of any being? Deciding this question requires, among other things, a discussion of the ontological argument and its relationship to the cosmological argument. A recent proponent of this form of the cosmological argument is Richard Taylor.[4]

2. Norman L. Geisler, *Philosophy of Religion* (Grand Rapids: Zondervan, 1974); Bruce R. Reichenbach, *The Cosmological Argument: A Reassessment* (Springfield, Ill.: Charles C. Thomas Publishers, 1972).

3. See Geisler, *Philosophy of Religion*, pp. 180–81.

4. Richard Taylor, *Metaphysics*, Foundations of Philosophy series, 2d ed. (Englewood Cliffs, N.J.: Prentice-Hall, 1974). The Leibnizian form of the cosmological argument had a significant influence on Thomists. See John Edwin Gurr, *The Principle of Sufficient Reason in Some Scholastic Systems, 1750–1900* (Milwaukee: Marquette University Press, 1959).

The Kalam Argument

The kalam cosmological argument gets its name from the word *kalam*, which refers to Arabic philosophy or theology. The kalam argument was popular among Arabic philosophers in the late Middle Ages. Christian philosophers during that period did not generally accept the argument, perhaps due to the influence of Aquinas, who, following Aristotle, rejected it.[5] A notable exception was Saint Bonaventure, a contemporary of Aquinas, who argued extensively for the soundness of the kalam argument.[6]

In recent years, there has been a small but growing number of thinkers who have defended this line of reasoning.[7] But without doubt, the most thorough and articulate advocate of the argument has been William Lane Craig.[8]

Statement of the Kalam Argument

Overview

Consider the following diagram offered by Craig:[9]

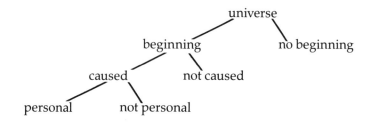

The kalam argument presents a number of dilemmas. First, the argument states that the universe either had a beginning or it did not. If it had a

---

5. In 529 the Christian philosopher John Philoponus tried to show that Aristotle's views regarding infinity and the beginning of the universe were internally inconsistent. See Richard Sorabji, *Time, Creation, and the Continuum: Theories in Antiquity and the Early Middle Ages* (Ithaca, N.Y.: Cornell University Press, 1983), pp. 210–24. However, in the late medieval period, most philosophers followed Aquinas.

6. See Bernardino M. Bonansea, "The Impossibility of Creation from Eternity According to St. Bonaventure," *Proceedings of the American Catholic Philosophical Association* 48 (1974): 121–35.

7. For example, see the widely used introductory text, Ed L. Miller, *Questions That Matter: An Introduction to Philosophy* (New York: McGraw-Hill, 1984), pp. 254–63.

8. I am deeply indebted to several of Craig's writings, among which are these: *The Cosmological Argument from Plato to Leibnitz*, Library of Philosophy and Religion series (New York: Barnes and Noble, 1980); *The Existence of God and the Beginning of the Universe* (San Bernardino, Calif.: Here's Life, 1979); *Apologetics: An Introduction* (Chicago: Moody, 1984); "Philosophical and Scientific Pointers to Creatio ex Nihilo," *Journal of the American Scientific Affiliation* 32 (March 1980): 5–13; "Professor Mackie and the Kalam Cosmological Argument," *Religious Studies* 20 (1985): 367–75.

9. Craig, "Philosophical and Scientific Pointers," p. 5.

beginning, then this beginning was either caused or uncaused. If the beginning was caused, the cause was either personal or not personal. The burden of the argument is to establish one horn of each dilemma, and in so doing, to argue for the existence of a personal Creator. Thus, the argument attempts to show that there had to be a beginning to the universe which was caused by a personal Being.

In order to defend the argument, a premise must be established at each dilemma. Here are the major premises of the argument:

1. The universe had a beginning.
2. The beginning of the universe was caused.
3. The cause for the beginning of the universe was personal.

Set Theory

Before we attempt to establish these premises, it is important to distinguish between two kinds of infinity—a potential infinite and an actual infinite. The distinction goes back to Aristotle, but it has been made more precise in recent years by modern set theory.

Although some mathematicians distinguish between a class and a set, for our purposes it will suffice to use the two terms interchangeably. A *set* refers to a collection of objects called the members or elements of the set. For example, the set A, composed of my two children, Ashley and Allison, would be represented as follows:

$$A = \{\text{Ashley, Allison}\}$$

Similarly, the set B, composed of all the even integers from one to ten, would look like this:

$$B = \{2, 4, 6, 8, 10\}$$

Now we need to define the notion of a *proper subset*. A set C is a proper subset of a set D if and only if there is no member of C that is not a member of D, but there is a member of D that is not a member of C. Thus, the following set $A1$ is a proper subset of A:

$$A1 = \{\text{Ashley}\}$$

and $B1$ is a proper subset of B:

$$B1 = \{2, 4\}$$

If a set C is a proper subset of a set D, then C is a part of D or is contained in D, but not vice versa.

Before we can consider potential and actual infinites, one more set theoretic notion is important. This is the notion of the *identity conditions for a set*. Consider "two" sets, A and B, which are in fact the same set. Two sets, A and B, are identical if and only if each member of A is a member of B, and each member of B is a member of A. A set is defined by its membership. Two sets which have all and only the same members are really identical. There is an important implication from this fact. A set cannot change members by addition, subtraction, or any other way, and still be the same set. Once it adds or loses a member, it is no longer the same set. Sets and the properties which are true of them do not change. A set is considered timelessly and does not grow, decrease, or change through time.

Actual Infinity

We can now begin to consider the difference between an actual and a potential infinite by first studying some properties of infinite sets. According to Charles C. Pinter in *Set Theory*, "a finite set is one which 'has n elements,' where n is a natural number [one of the integers 1, 2, 3, . . .], and an infinite set is one which is not finite."[10] A finite set has a definite number of elements which can be specified by counting the number of members in the set and assigning the appropriate number to that set. Thus, our set A had $n = 2$ elements, and B had $n = 5$.

An infinite set is very different from this. In order to see this, we need to define two notions: denumerability and one-to-one correspondence.[11] There is a *one-to-one correspondence* between two sets, A and B, if and only if the members of A can be paired with the members of B such that each member of A is paired with exactly one member of B and each member of B is paired with exactly one member of A. In other words, A and B have the same number of members. This is called having the same cardinal number.

Now assume one could form the set of all the natural numbers (e.g., 1, 2, 3, . . .). A set is *denumerable* if and only if it can be put in a one-to-one correspondence with the set of all the natural numbers. The set of all the natural numbers and all other denumerable sets (those with the same number of members as the set of natural numbers) is what we are calling an actual infinite. The set of natural numbers is usually given the name ω, and the cardinality of this set—the number of members in it—is called $\aleph_0$ (aleph nought).

An actual infinite is a set considered as a completed totality with an ac-

10. Charles C. Pinter, *Set Theory* (Reading, Mass.: Addison-Wesley, 1971), p. 138.

11. In addition to Pinter, see Geoffrey Hunter, *Metalogic: An Introduction to the Metatheory of Standard First Order Logic* (Berkeley: University of California Press, 1971), pp. 4–41; Abraham Fraenkel, *Abstract Set Theory* (Amsterdam: North-Holland Publishing Company, 1961), pp. 4–65.

tual infinite number of members. Among the most prominent of the definitions for an actual infinite set A are these two:

A is actually infinite if A has a denumerable subset.

A is actually infinite if A can be put into one-to-one correspondence with a proper subset of itself.

Consider two sets, E and F. E is the set of all the natural numbers. F is the set of all the even numbers. Which set has more members? You might be inclined to say that E has twice as many members as F. But according to infinite set theory, both sets have the same number of members, $\aleph_0$. This can be seen by putting the two sets into one-to-one correspondence with one another:

$E=0\ \ 1\ 2\ 3\ 4\ 5\ \ 6\ \ 7\ \ldots$
$F=0\ \ 2\ 4\ 6\ 8\ 10\ 12\ 14\ldots$

F is a part of the whole, E. But since F and E are actual infinites, they are equal.

From the preceding discussion, several properties of actual infinites emerge. First, an actual infinite is a timeless totality which neither increases nor decreases in the number of members it contains. Second, a proper subset or part of an actual infinite can be put into one-to-one correspondence with (be made equal to) that actual infinite, as seen in E and F. This contrasts with a finite set, which *cannot* be put into one-to-one correspondence with one of its proper subsets. In finite sets, the whole is always greater than any of its proper parts.

Third, the following theorems could be proved of actually infinite sets: $\aleph_0 - 1 = \aleph_0$, $\aleph_0 + 1 = \aleph_0$, $\aleph_0 - n = \aleph_0$, $\aleph_0 + n = \aleph_0$, and (where n is any natural number), $\aleph_0 \cdot \aleph_0 = \aleph_0$. In addition, one can add or subtract denumerably many members from an actual infinite set and not change the number of members in the set! One interesting implication of these theorems has been stated by Geoffrey Hunter: "The number of points in infinite space of $\aleph_0$ dimensions is the same as the number of points on a line a billionth of an inch."[12]

Potential Infinity

In contrast to an actual infinite stands the notion of a potential infinite. The idea of a potential infinite is not a set theoretic idea at all, but occurs,

12. Hunter, *Metalogic*, p. 41.

among other places, in discussions about infinitesimal calculus. Perhaps you have seen this statement:

$$\lim_{n \to \infty} 1\backslash n = 0$$

As mathematician Abraham Fraenkel puts it, this statement "asserts nothing about [actual] infinity (as the ominous sign seems to suggest) but is just an abbreviation for the sentence: 1\n can be made to approach zero as closely as desired by sufficiently increasing the positive integer n."[13]

A potential infinite has three important properties relevant to our discussion. First, a potential infinite increases its number through time by adding new members to the series. Second, a potential infinite is always finite. A potential infinite can increase forever and it will never become an actual infinite. Adding one more member to a finite set, no matter how often this is done, will simply result in a larger finite set. Third, since a potential infinite is always finite, at no time will the finite set formed from the members of the series traversed at that moment be equal to one of its proper subsets.

This digression into the features of actual and potential infinites has been necessary because these features will play an important role in using the kalam cosmological argument to argue for the existence of God.

Defense of the Kalam Argument

Premise 1: The Universe Had a Beginning

The first premise we need to defend is the one stating that the universe had a beginning. Four general considerations can be raised which support this premise.[14] Two of these considerations are philosophical and two are scientific in nature.

The Nonexistence of an Actual Infinite

Puzzles with an Actual Infinite   The first argument is this: An actual infinite cannot exist. A beginningless temporal series of events is an actual infinite. Therefore, a beginningless temporal series of events cannot exist. It seems clear that if one claims that there was no beginning to the universe, then this is equivalent to saying that there have been an actual infi-

---

13. Fraenkel, *Abstract Set Theory*, p. 6.
14. See Craig, *Apologetics*, pp. 75–93.

nite number of past events in the history of the universe. If these events are collected into a set, this set would have a cardinality of $\aleph_0$; that is, it would have an actual infinite number of members.

It does not seem possible for an actual infinite to exist in the real world. In order to prove this, we can assume that it *is* possible for an actual infinite to exist and try to show that this assumption implies unreasonable consequences. And since these consequences seem to be false, the assumption which led to them must be rejected.

Certain examples can be given which show that an actual infinite which exists in the real world leads to unacceptable consequences and that thus there is no such thing as a really existent actual infinite. Craig offers the following case.[15] Imagine a library with an actually infinite number of books. Suppose further that there is an infinite number of red books and an infinite number of black books in the library. Does it really make sense to say that there are as many black books in the library as there are red and black books together? Surely not. Furthermore, I could withdraw all the black books and not change the total holdings in the library. Let us also assume that each book has an actual infinite number of pages. There would be just as many pages in the first book in the library as there are in the entire, infinite collection. If someone read the first book, she would read just as many pages as someone who read every page of every book in the library!

Consider a second example offered by Russell.[16] The example is about a person, Tristam Shandy, who writes his autobiography so slowly that it takes him a whole year to write about just one day of his life. If he lives an actually infinite number of days, he will allegedly be able to complete his autobiography. This is because the set of all the days in his life can be put into one-to-one correspondence with the set of all his years. But does this really make sense? It would seem that the longer he lives the further behind he would get.

I take as a final example an illustration offered by Saint Bonaventure.[17] Suppose that the past is an actual infinite number of events. Now for each yearly revolution of the sun, there are twelve revolutions of the moon during the same period. No matter how far back one goes, the number of lunar revolutions would be twelve times that of the sun. But if they have been revolving on their courses for an actual infinity, then a paradox results. The number of lunar revolutions would be equal to the number of solar revolutions. But this seems to be absurd. How could this be the case if the lunar revolutions occur twelve times more frequently than the solar revolutions?

15. Craig, "Philosophical and Scientific Pointers," pp. 6–7; see also G. J. Whitrow, "On the Impossibility of an Infinite Past," *British Journal for the Philosophy of Science* 29 (1978): 39–45.

16. Cited in Fraenkel, *Abstract Set Theory,* p. 6.

17. See Bonansea, "Impossibility of Creation from Eternity," p. 122.

Something has gone wrong here, and it is the admission of an actual infinite into the real world.

These puzzles illustrate some unreasonable consequences which follow if actual infinites really exist. The properties of an actual infinite create the problems. After all, it does not seem reasonable to affirm that the number of points on a line a billionth of an inch long is equal to the number of points in an infinite space of $\aleph_0$ dimensions.

Three Objections to the Puzzles   In spite of the intuitive appeal of the puzzles, some philosophers have not been persuaded by them. Three major objections have been raised against this way of attacking the reality of an actual infinite. First, some have argued that the mere presence of infinite set theory in mathematics is enough to dispel these puzzles. The fact that there is such a thing as infinite set theory—and this theory includes the properties attacked by the puzzles listed—shows that the language and theory of infinite sets are coherent and we must adjust our view of the world accordingly.

This objection does not succeed. The mere presence of a generally accepted theory in mathematics says nothing, by itself, about anything in the real world of entities. For example, it is well known that there are at least three different and internally consistent geometries of space. Euclidean space is built on the axiom that through a given point not on a straight line, exactly one line can be drawn parallel to the straight one. Two other geometries of space can be formed if this axiom is replaced by one saying that either more than one line or no line could be drawn. These are called Lobachevskian and Riemannian geometries respectively. But it does not follow from the mere presence of these three geometries of space that actual space in the real world fits all three.

One simply cannot move from the mathematical to the real without further argument. There is a major debate in the philosophy of mathematics over exactly what mathematics is about. Three major schools are involved in this debate.[18] The first school is the nominalist school, which contains within it those who call themselves formalists. This school denies the existence of numbers or, indeed, any abstract entities. There are no mathematical entities which mathematical statements refer to and which make mathematical statements true. Mathematical systems are merely internally consistent, formal languages generated by a set of formation rules, and mathematical systems have no ontological implications, that is, no implications for the way the world is.

18. See Stephen F. Barker, *Philosophy of Mathematics* (Englewood Cliffs, N.J.: Prentice-Hall, 1964), pp. 56–81; Paul Benacerraf and Hilary Putnam, eds., *Philosophy of Mathematics: Selected Readings* (Englewood Cliffs, N.J.: Prentice-Hall, 1964); Paul Benacerraf, "Mathematical Truth," *The Journal of Philosophy* 70 (November 1973): 661–79; Pinter, *Set Theory*, pp. 1–20.

A second school is the intuitionist or constructivist school of mathematics. This school holds that mathematics is about activities or concepts in mathematicians' minds. A mathematical object exists only if it can be constructed in the mind. Intuitionists deny the existence of an actual infinite, since no one can actually construct such a set in the mind.

The third school is the Platonist or realist school, which is the position I favor. This school holds that mathematical entities really exist in the world. For example, mathematical realists hold that numbers exist. Some say they are substances, some properties, still others sets. It is only the Platonist in mathematics who believes there are straightforward ontological implications from mathematical theories. But even a Platonist could deny the existence of an actual infinite. He could be a Platonist about finite sets but deny Platonism about infinite sets if he were persuaded by the puzzles raised against infinite sets.

Therefore, the mere presence of a mathematics of infinite sets does little to show that an actual infinite really exists in the world. This follows only if one is a Platonist of a certain sort. So this objection does little to counter the puzzles raised against an actual infinite.

A second objection has been raised against the puzzles which criticize the actual infinite. Fraenkel states that the attitude of some philosophers about the existence of an actual infinite "may be explained by their adherence to the classical principle *totum parte maiuis* (the whole is greater than a part). This principle in its proper meaning is, however, limited to the domain of finite sets. . . . Its invalidity in the domain of infinity is just characteristic of the latter."[19]

Fraenkel's point is this. The puzzles raised against an actual infinite all turn on a problematic feature of infinite sets: a part of the set can be equal to the whole. In finite sets two principles apply. First, the whole is greater than any of its parts. Second, two sets are equal if there is a one-to-one correspondence between their members. But in infinite sets only the second principle applies. My puzzles fault infinite sets for violating the first principle. But this is simply faulting infinite sets for not being finite sets. In infinite sets a part can equal the whole and that is all there is to it.

This objection has some force. Consider a parallel case. Realists and nominalists disagree over the existence of entities called universals (e.g., redness, humanness, wisdom). Universals are entities that can be in more than one place at the same time.[20] Nominalists object to universals on the

19. Fraenkel, *Abstract Set Theory*, p. 20. See also J. L. Mackie, *The Miracle of Theism* (Oxford: Clarendon Press, 1982), pp. 92–95.

20. Actually, this definition of universals is incorrect, since a proper one makes no reference to place. But the one given in the text is adequate for my purposes. For more on this issue, see J. P. Moreland, *Universals, Qualities, and Quality-Instances: A Defense of Realism* (Lanham, Md.: University Press of America, 1985), pp. 1–35.

grounds that it is impossible for something to be in more than one place at the same time. Realists rightly respond by pointing out that this objection fails because it faults a universal for not having the properties of a particular. The realist response is like the one raised by advocates of the actual infinite. They argue that the puzzles I have raised fault an actual infinite for not having the properties of a finite set.

But consider a second case. Suppose one were to argue that there is no such thing as a square circle because the attributes of such an entity are internally contradictory. A defender of the existence of a square circle might respond by saying that it is inappropriate to use the criterion of internal consistency for internally contradictory entities because this judges them by an inappropriate criterion—internal consistency—which should be applied only to internally consistent entities.

I do not believe this response would work. One would still be justified in rejecting square circles for two reasons. First, the concepts *square* and *circle* are no longer functioning in a clear, normal way. If they were, then it would seem intuitive that these attributes could not be conjoined in one object. They seem to exclude each other. Second, the defender of the square circle has not given us reasons which are sufficient to warrant overturning our basic intuitions about reality.

In the realist/nominalist debate things are different. The realist *does* give a number of reasons for justifying the existence of universals. And he also is able to offer a broad understanding of existence which justifies the acceptance of entities which can be located in several places at the same time.

It seems that the defender of an actual infinite is more like the defender of square circles than the defender of universals. He argues that one should accept the principle that a part can be equal to a whole and thus the puzzles should be rejected. The defender of the kalam argument says that a whole is greater than any of its parts and thus the puzzles argue against the existence of an actual infinite. There do not seem to be sufficient, independent reasons for accepting an actual infinite with its unusual properties. As has been pointed out, the mere presence of the mathematics of infinity is insufficient, and I know of no other reason which sufficiently justifies acceptance of infinite sets. Further, the lack of justification becomes more troublesome when we realize that terms like "part," "add," or "subtract" are being used in such an odd way in connection with the actual infinite that this usage should be rejected because it lacks sufficient justification. How can something still be a part of a whole if it equals that whole? How can members be "added to" or "subtracted from" a set without increasing or decreasing its members?

It would seem, then, that this second objection fails to remove the force of the puzzles against the actual infinite. But a third objection to the puzzles has been raised recently by Richard Sorabji.[21] Sorabji tries to show how terms like "addition," "subtraction," and "part" can be given clarity when they are applied to actual infinites. If this can be done, argues Sorabji, then the puzzles do not succeed in casting doubt on the existence of an actual infinite. This is because the principle that a part can be equal to its whole can be sufficiently clarified so that it no longer appears troublesome.

Sorabji asks us to imagine two lines extending from the present moment infinitely far into the past. One line contains an actual infinite number of days; the other an actual infinite number of years. Says Sorabji, "I can now explain the sense in which the column of past days is not larger than the column of past years: it will not *stick out beyond the far end of* the other column, since neither column has a far end."[22]

Sorabji goes on to argue that one can "add" members to each collection without making that collection larger. But how can one add members to a collection without making it larger? What does addition mean in this case? He says that one infinite can be larger than another in the sense that it contains more members (i.e., it contains all the members of the other actual infinite and some more besides). For example, the set of natural numbers contains all the members in the set of all even numbers and it contains additional members besides the even numbers. But, Sorabji argues, containing additional members *besides* another set does not mean it contains members *beyond* that other set. Neither set will be beyond the other—it will not "stick out beyond the far end" of the other set. Sorabji's defense of the actual infinite boils down to his illustration of the two infinite lines and his beyond/besides distinction.

The distinction between beyond/besides is not clear, however, and it appears to be a distinction without a difference. It means that one infinite set can have members besides another infinite set without having members beyond it. There are two problems with Sorabji's suggestion. First, I cannot conceive of a line extending an actual infinite distance without an end. Asserting the existence of such a line is begging the question here, since it is precisely such a state of affairs that is being debated. Second, suppose that the two lines, one with an infinite number of days and one with years, really did exist side by side. Then it would be possible to divide the lines into equal segments and pair them up one-to-one. Each year segment on the second line would be placed side by side with a day segment on the first line. But how could this be? There would be 365 more day segments than year segments. Furthermore, if one added a year to the second line, then this would amount to adding one segment to the line. But then one

21. Sorabji, *Time, Creation, and the Continuum*, pp. 217–18.
22. Ibid., p. 217.

would have to add 365 more segments to the first line. How could it be that one line would not extend beyond the other in such a situation? Denying that the lines have ends simply begs the question.

Sorabji does not really clarify the notion of an actual infinite. He merely asserts its existence by setting up the example the way he does. But the problematic puzzles appear all over again. It would seem, then, that none of the three objections removes the force of the puzzles that have been raised against the actual infinite. It does not seem that an actual infinite could exist. But since a beginningless series of events is an actual infinite, then a beginningless series of events is impossible. The universe must have had a beginning.

The Impossibility of Traversing an Actual Infinite

Statement and Support of the Argument   There is a second argument for the fact that the universe had a beginning. Let us assume that someone has not been persuaded by our first argument against the existence of an actual infinite. This second argument works even if an actual infinite is possible. It states that if there is an actual infinite, it must occur, as it were, all at once. It can be put as follows: It is impossible to traverse (cross) an actual infinite by successive addition. The temporal series of past events has been formed by successive addition. Therefore, it cannot be actually infinite. But since it is not infinite, it must be finite (i.e., it must have a first term). And this is what we mean by saying the universe had a beginning.

This second argument, therefore, can grant the existence of an actual infinite. But it does not grant that such an infinite could be traversed.

Several reasons can be offered for the contention that an actual infinite cannot be traversed by successive addition. The first is an argument from the nature of causal sequences.[23] Consider any event: for instance, a helicopter passing overhead. This event is caused by another event which preceded it in time—the pilot got in the vehicle. In order for any event to take place, the entire chain of its causal antecedents must have already occurred and be actual. Otherwise, a necessary precondition for the last member in the chain (the event under consideration) would not have occurred and the rest of the chain would not have occurred either (since its existence depends upon this necessary precondition).

Now the present moment has as its ultimate chain of causal antecedents the entire history of the cosmos. If any past event has not already been actualized, then the present could not have occurred. This means that the past is actual and contains a specifiable, determinate number of events. This chain of events must have had a first member. Without a first member,

---

23. This argument was first suggested to me by Dallas Willard.

there would be no second, third, or nth member in the chain where the nth member is the present event. A causal sequence leading up to an event must have a first member and a determinate number of members in the sequence, since the entire sequence is already actual. But an infinite succession of past events would not have a determinate number of members nor would it have a first member. So if the past is actually infinite, the present moment could not have been caused; that is, it could not have come to be.

Consider a second argument. It is impossible to count to infinity. For if one counts forever and ever, he will still be, at every moment, in a place where he can always specify the number he is currently counting. Furthermore, he can always add one more member to what he has counted and thereby increase the series by one. A series formed by successive addition is a potential infinite. Such a series can increase forever without limit, but it will *always* be finite. This means that the past must have been finite. For the present moment is the last member of the series of past events formed by successive addition. And since one cannot reach infinity one at a time, then if the past was actually infinite, the present moment could not have been reached. For to come to the present moment, an actual infinite would have to have been crossed.

Third, suppose a person were to think backward through the events in the past. In reality, time and the events within it move in the other direction. But mentally he can reverse that movement and count backward farther and farther into the past. Now he will either come to a beginning or he will not. If he comes to a beginning, then the universe obviously had a beginning. But if he never could, even in principle, reach a first moment, then this means that it would be impossible to start with the present and run backward through all of the events in the history of the cosmos. Remember, if he did run through all of them, he would reach a first member of the series, and the finiteness of the past would be established. In order to avoid this conclusion, one must hold that, starting with the present, it is *impossible* to go backward through all of the events in history.

But since events really move in the other direction, this is equivalent to admitting that if there was no beginning, the past could have never been exhaustively traversed to reach the present. Counting to infinity through the series 1, 2, 3, . . . involves the same number of steps as does counting down *from* infinity to zero through the series . . . , -5, -4, -3, -2, -1, 0. In fact this second series may be even more difficult to traverse than the first. Apart from the fact that both series have the same number of members to be traversed, the second series cannot even get started. This is because it has no first member!

A beginningless universe has no first member. Before any event in the history of the cosmos, there has already transpired an actual infinite number of events. So no matter how far back one goes in one's mind, one is no closer to traversing the past than before he began counting—even if he counts back through an infinite number of events (which is impossible). In light of such a beginningless infinite series, neither the present, nor tomorrow, nor *any* moment in the past could be reached.

Fourth, the best way to solve Zeno's paradoxes is to deny the possibility of traversing an actual infinite. Zeno of Elea (born 489 B.C.) was a pre-Socratic Greek philosopher who offered puzzles to show that motion and plurality are incoherent notions. Against motion Zeno offered two puzzles which criticized motion as a continuous phenomenon and two puzzles which criticized motion as a discrete phenomenon. We will consider just one of the puzzles—the paradox of the race course. Consider a runner who begins at some point A and who wishes to reach another point B. In order to do this, he must first reach the midpoint between A and B. But before he can reach this midpoint, he must reach the midpoint of the midpoint. In order to move from any point to any other point, a runner must traverse an infinite number of points and this is impossible. Thus motion is an illusion.

Since we all know motion does occur, something must be wrong with Zeno's puzzle. What is it? From the time of Aristotle, the basic solution to Zeno's puzzles has been to distinguish between a potential and an actual infinite. Zeno would be correct if one had to traverse an actual infinite in order to get from one point to another. But the infinite of his puzzle is a potential infinite only. No matter how often one divides the line between A and B into midpoints, one will have only a finite number of points to traverse. If one had to traverse an actual infinite in going from A to B, then motion would be impossible. Similarly, if one had to traverse an actual infinite to come to the present moment, that could not be done either. But the past is only finite.[24]

Objections to the Argument   These arguments present a strong case for the fact that the universe had a beginning. Nevertheless, some have tried to defend the possibility of traversing an actual infinite by criticizing the arguments presented. Four major criticisms have been raised. First, Wallace Matson has argued that one cannot traverse an actual infinite in finite time. But given an infinite amount of time one could accomplish this task.[25] But Matson's statement is inaccurate. The problems with traversing an actual infinite have nothing to do with how much time one has. The problems focus on the nature of an actual infinite itself. All Matson has done is

24. For a helpful treatment of Zeno's puzzles, see Max Black, "Achilles and the Tortoise," *Analysis* 11 (March 1951): 91–101.

25. William Lane Craig, "Wallace Matson and the Crude Cosmological Argument," *Australasian Journal of Philosophy* 57 (June 1979): 163–70.

to postulate one actual infinite to resolve problems with another actual infinite. He posits, as it were, a time above time. But this merely begs the question at issue. And it does not solve the problems with traversing an actual infinite. It merely shifts those problems from one actual infinite to another.[26]

Second, William Wainwright and J. L. Mackie argue that the objections assume an infinitely distant beginning. But, they argue, there is *no* beginning, not even one infinitely far away. Thus, if a person goes back mentally through the cosmos, she will never reach a point that is infinitely far away. She will always be at a point which is a finite distance away from the present, and thus that distance will be traversable.[27]

This objection seems to me to be very weak. For one thing, the defender of the kalam argument does *not* assume an infinitely distant beginning to the universe to generate his puzzles against traversing an actual infinite. Rather, he—not Wainwright or Mackie—takes the actual infinite seriously. If the past is actually infinite, then there is no beginning at all. It is precisely this lack of a beginning that causes most of the problems. If there were no beginning, then reaching the present would be like counting to zero from negative infinity. As Craig points out, this is like trying to jump out of a bottomless pit. One could get no foothold in the series to even get started, for to get to any point, one *already* has to have crossed infinity.[28] Furthermore, I agree with Mackie that if one goes back in time one never reaches a point an infinite distance away. But this proves that the past was finite. For if the past had been infinite, then Mackie has just shown that no matter how far back one goes, he could never *in principle* traverse the past. This is equivalent to saying that all the events in an infinite past could not be crossed to reach the present, since the number of events traversed is not a function of the direction one takes in traversing them.

Third, some have argued that it may be impossible to count *to* infinity, but it is possible to count down *from* infinity. But this objection seems patently absurd. For one thing, the number of members in both series is the same. Why would one be easier to cross than the other? Second, assume that someone had been counting toward zero from negative infinity from eternity past. If a person goes back in time from the present moment, he will *never* reach a point when he is finishing his count or even engaging in the count itself. This is because at every point, he will have already had an infinity to conduct the count. As Zeno's paradox of the race course points out, the problem with such a situation is not merely that one cannot com-

---

26. Black has shown that the difficulty with traversing an actual infinite is not related to having enough time. See "Achilles and the Tortoise," pp. 96–101.

27. William Wainwright, review of *The Kalam Cosmological Argument* by William Lane Craig, in *Nous* 16 (May 1982): 328–34; Mackie, *The Miracle of Theism*, p. 93.

28. See Craig, *Apologetics*, pp. 79–81.

plete an infinite task; one cannot even start an infinite task from a begin-ningless situation. For one could never reach a determinate position in the infinite series which alone would allow the series to be traversed and ended at zero (the present moment).

These comments should help to clarify a response to a fourth objection offered by Sorabji.[29] He argues that the criticisms raised against traversing an actual infinite all turn on comparing traversing a series to counting the series and that this is a bad comparison. According to Sorabji, counting differs from traversing in one important respect: counting assumes a start-ing point. Counting through an infinite series would be impossible, for it involves a starting point. Traversing an infinite series would not be impos-sible, for it would involve no starting point.

But this objection also fails. First, Max Black has shown that the criti-cisms against traversing an actual infinite have nothing to do with count-ing. Counting is merely an act with a start and a finish, and thus traversing an infinite number of counts, or any other kind of events, would be subject to the same criticisms; these criticisms are based on the nature of the actual infinite, not on the nature of counting.[30] Second, the main point of the com-parison between counting and traversing is not that one has a starting point and the other does not. Rather, both involve the successive formation of a series. Third, if traversing an infinite differs from counting through an infinite in that the former has no starting point but the latter has one, then this makes traversing an infinite even worse than counting through it. It does not make the situation better.

In order to see this, consider the following. Sorabji seems to be claiming that one cannot count from one to infinity because such a series has a start-ing point in the number one, but one can traverse an infinite series because it has no beginning. But does it help one to count to positive infinity if, instead of starting at one, he is told he must count from a beginningless negative infinity? How does this help? Using the word *traverse* instead of *count* cannot cover up the problem. In this latter case, one could not even reach the number one, much less positive infinity.[31]

It seems, then, that it is impossible to traverse an actual infinite. And since a beginningless series of past events would be an actual infinite, then such a series—given that we have reached the present moment—must be

29. Sorabji, *Time, Creation, and the Continuum,* pp. 219–24.

30. Black, "Achilles and the Tortoise," p. 95.

31. Sorabji also argues that counting is not analogous to traversing in that the former has two termini (when the count begins and when it ends) and the latter has only one terminus (when the traversing ends at the present moment). But this makes traversing an actual infinite less plausible, not more plausible. Whatever else it means to finish an act of traversing an infinite, finishing would certainly come after start-ing such an act. But how does it help to say that one cannot start to traverse a beginningless series of past events? In such a case, one could never reach a particular point in the series to get going to the next point. This makes the task worse than counting, not better.

impossible. The universe had a beginning. I now turn to two scientific arguments which establish that the universe had a beginning.

The Big Bang Cosmology

In the late 1920s, astronomer Edwin Hubble discovered a phenomenon known as the red shift—light from distant galaxies is shifted toward the red end of the spectrum. This indicates that the universe is expanding. Galaxies are moving away from one another much like dots on the surface of an inflating balloon. This discovery has led to what is now known as the big bang theory of the origin of the universe.[32]

The big bang theory includes two important features. First, the universe as we know it began from a large explosion some fifteen billion years ago and has continued to expand ever since. Second, the original configuration of the big bang was a state of "infinite" density where all of the mass, energy, space, and time were contained in a single mathematical point with no dimensions. These two features jointly imply that the universe sprang into existence from nothing a finite time ago. As scientist Robert Jastrow puts it, "What is the ultimate solution to the origin of the Universe? The answers provided by the astronomers are disconcerting and remarkable. Most remarkable of all is the fact that in science, as in the Bible, the world begins with an act of creation."[33]

The major rival cosmology at present is called the oscillating universe model. This model holds that the universe has gone through an infinite number of expansions and contractions and will continue to do so into the future. The main debate between this model and the big bang model as I have represented it here is the question of whether or not there was just one initial expansion.

Several factors indicate that there was only one initial expansion and the explosion which caused it was an absolute beginning to the universe of mass/energy and space-time. First, there is no known mechanism to explain how all the mass of the universe could converge simultaneously, reconvene into a dimensionless mathematical point, and bounce back into a new expansion with 100 percent efficiency. The second law of thermodynamics states that there is no such thing as a 100 percent efficient perpetual-motion machine. Second, even if such a mechanism could be conceived, there could not have been an actual infinite number of past cycles because of the problems with an actual infinite. Third, if the universe is going to contract into another point, then the only thing that will draw

---

32. For introductory treatments of the big bang theory, see John Polkinghorne, *The Way the World Is: The Christian Perspective of a Scientist* (Grand Rapids: Eerdmans, 1984), pp. 7–16; John Wiester, *The Genesis Connection* (Nashville: Nelson, 1983), pp. 17–45; Paul Davies, *God and the New Physics* (New York: Simon and Schuster, 1983), pp. 9–57.

33. Cited in Wiester, *The Genesis Connection*, p. 24.

the matter of the universe back together is gravity. The strength of the gravity in the universe is a function of the density of the mass in the universe. According to Craig, the universe would need to be at least twice as dense as scientists currently hold it to be for it to reach a point of expansion and then contract again.[34] The universe appears to be open; that is, there was one and only one explosion. The universe had a beginning.

One objection should be considered briefly. The objection goes back to Immanuel Kant and has been raised several times since.[35] The idea of an absolute beginning to time is inconceivable, for one can always ask what happened before the first moment. And to answer this, one must postulate a time before time, which is absurd. So the notion of a first moment in time is incoherent.

Most theists—at least those who hold that God is timeless—respond by saying that the first event was not the first moment *in* time, but the first moment *of* time. There was no time before the first moment. Whatever existed "prior" to the first moment was timeless and immutable. And when we use the word *prior* here, we do not mean temporally prior to time, but outside time altogether. God existed "prior" to the first moment in that he was—and is—timeless. This may be mysterious and inspiring, but it is not incoherent and contradictory.

Some have thought that the idea of God existing "prior" to the first moment is like saying something is north of the North Pole, which is absurd. But it should now be evident what is wrong with this comparison. If something exists north of the North Pole, it is still being treated as a thing existing at a spatial location. But when the theist says that God exists "prior" to the first moment, she is not treating God as a thing existing at a temporal location. So the analogy breaks down.

The Second Law of Thermodynamics

The Argument   Thermodynamics is an exact science which deals with energy. The second law of thermodynamics is one of the most fundamental, best-established laws in all of science. The second law involves a concept known as entropy (S). Entropy can be understood in terms of energy, disorder, or information. The second law states that the entropy of the universe (or any isolated system therein, where an isolated system is one which has neither mass nor energy flow in or out of the system) is increasing. Put differently, the amount of energy available to do work is decreasing and becoming uniformly distributed. The universe is moving irreversibly toward a state of maximum disorder and minimum energy.

---

34. Craig, *Apologetics*, p. 86.

35. See Ernan McMullin, "How Should Cosmology Relate to Theology?" in *The Sciences and Theology in the Twentieth Century,* ed. A. R. Peacocke (Notre Dame: University of Notre Dame Press, 1981), pp. 36–38.

An example may be helpful. Suppose someone enters a room and discovers a cup of coffee which is still warm. He would be able to tell that it had not been there forever; in fact, given the right information, he could even calculate how long it had been cooling off. The second law states that the cup will cool off and the temperature of the room will move toward a state of uniform temperature distribution.

Consider a second example. If someone opens a bottle of perfume in a room, the perfume will leave the bottle and disperse in such a way that it will become uniformly distributed throughout the room. The second law tells us that neither of these examples should happen in reverse order. It is highly improbable that a cup in equilibrium with the temperature of the room will suddenly become hot. Similarly, a room full of perfume evenly distributed will not suddenly change spontaneously in such a way that the perfume will all go into an empty bottle.

Applied to the universe as a whole, the second law tells us that the universe is wearing down irreversibly. It is heading toward a state of maximum disorder and uniform energy distribution. The sun will burn up and all other localized sources of energy will burn up as well. But since a state of maximum entropy has not yet been reached, the universe has not been here forever. If the universe had already undergone an infinite past, it would have reached such a state by now. As theoretical physicist Paul Davies puts it: "If the universe has a finite stock of order, and is changing irreversibly towards disorder—ultimately to thermodynamic equilibrium—two very deep inferences follow immediately. The first is that the universe will eventually die, wallowing, as it were, in its own entropy. This is known among physicists as the 'heat death' of the universe. The second is that the universe cannot have existed forever, otherwise it would have reached its equilibrium end state an infinite time ago. Conclusion: the universe did not always exist."[36]

It would seem, then, that the second law implies a beginning to the universe when the universe was, as it were, wound up and energy and order were put into it.

Two Objections   Two major objections have been raised against this kind of argument from the second law.[37] First, it has been argued that the universe is infinite and, therefore, the argument does not work. The universe could be infinite in two ways relevant to this objection: either it is infinite in extension and in the matter/energy already present in it, or it is finite but there is a constant creation of new energy from an infinite source

36. Davies, *God and the New Physics*, p. 11.

37. *Encyclopedia of Philosophy*, s.v. "Entropy," G. J. Whitrow; Craig, *The Existence of God*, pp. 66–69; Robert E. D. Clark, *The Universe: Plan or Accident?* (Grand Rapids: Zondervan, 1949), pp. 26–42.

of energy or from nothingness. This objection runs aground on the problems already raised with an actual infinite. Furthermore, the most widely accepted current understanding of the universe is one which views it as finite and not infinite. And there is no scientific evidence for continuous creation of matter or energy, even if such a notion could be squared with the highly rational principle that something cannot come from nothing without a cause.

A second objection has been offered by G. J. Whitrow: "It would seem that not only is it difficult to formulate the concept of entropy for the whole universe but also that there is no evidence that the law of entropy increase applies on this scale."[38] In other words, the second law of thermodynamics is clearly defined for each and every segment of the universe, but it has no clear meaning when applied to the universe as a whole.

This objection seems to involve a misunderstanding of the different relationships between parts and wholes and a corresponding distinction between two kinds of properties.[39] Consider an apple. It seems correct to say that the weight of the apple is identical to the sum of the individual weights of all the apple's ultimate parts. If one could weigh all the atoms in the apple, their combined weight would simply *be* the weight of the apple. In this case the property known as the weight of the apple is called an additive property. It is not an existent reality over and above the sum of the individual weights of the apple's parts.

Now consider the wetness or redness of the apple. These properties are called emergent properties when viewed diachronically (through time) or supervenient properties when viewed synchronically (at a given time). The redness of the apple is a genuinely new property which is not a property of any of the apple's ultimate parts. Atoms have no color.

In the case of additive properties, it is not wrong to ascribe to a whole a property which belongs to its parts. This is because the property of the whole *just is* the sum of the individual properties. The weight of an apple just is the sum of the weights of all the parts of the apple. If all the parts of a table were brown, then the brownness of the table would be identical to the brownness of each part taken collectively.

When it comes to emergent properties, things are different. A part may have a property not possessed by the whole (e.g., each atom in an apple is constantly in motion but the apple itself is stationary). On the other hand, the whole may have a property not possessed by any of its parts (e.g., the apple is red, sweet, and wet but none of its atomic parts have these properties).

---

38. Whitrow, "Entropy," p. 529.

39. See Keith Campbell, *Metaphysics: An Introduction* (Encino, Calif.: Dickenson, 1976), pp. 25–58; R. Harré, *The Philosophies of Science* (Oxford: Oxford University Press, 1972), pp. 140–67.

Entropy is a property which is defined for and true of each and every part of the universe. There is no evidence whatever that there is a region of the universe where the second law does not apply. Laws of science are universals and the denial of this fact is question-begging.[40] Either entropy is an additive property and is true of the universe taken as a whole, or the universe is a whole which has emergent properties not possessed by its parts. Specifically, entropy would hold for parts of the universe but not for the universe as a whole.

Let us take the second horn of the dilemma first. If the universe is an entity which has emergent properties over and above the properties of its parts, then certain implications follow which seem damaging to atheism—especially that form of atheism motivated by scientism (the view that only what science says is real and true *is* real and true). The "universe" becomes an entity which seems to be immutable, outside space and time, self-existent, and nonphysical. At the very least, the "universe" must be treated as a nonphysical reality beyond the laws of science, since one of the most fundamental laws of science—the second law—does not apply to it. I see no reason to think that any other scientific law would apply to the "universe" in this sense. But now the "universe" becomes a nonphysical reality which can be described and discussed only metaphysically. It is beyond the world of science. In fact, the "universe" now possesses certain attributes that classical theists would ascribe to God, and the atheist has come perilously close to holding to the existence of God—or a Being very much like him—and simply calling him the "universe." But no atheist would want to say that his debate with a theist is merely semantic.

The best way, then, for the atheist to escape the conclusion that God exists is to deny that the second law applies to the universe taken as a whole. But the atheist pays a big price for this move and it may be in this case that the result is not worth the cost.

But what about the other horn of the dilemma, which views entropy as an additive property? This seems to be a more reasonable view. Imagine that space is divided up into a number of volumes of side r. Each volume would be r^3. The second law of thermodynamics would be clearly definable for such a volume and would be true of that volume. The second law is definable for and true of each and every finite volume in the universe, regardless of where that volume is or how large r is. There is no section of the universe which exists anywhere that cannot be represented by a volume like r^3. Therefore, the second law applies to each and every part of the universe without remainder. There is no region of the universe that escapes the second law. But since volume is an additive property—the vol-

40. For more on the nature of universals, see Moreland, *Universals, Qualities, and Quality-Instances;* D. M. Armstrong, *Universals and Scientific Realism,* 2 vols. (Cambridge: Cambridge University Press, 1978).

ume of the universe is identical to the sum of all the individual volumes r^3—then the entire universe is subjected to the second law. There is no fallacy in moving from each part of the universe to the whole universe. It is up to the objector to specify some region of the universe where the second law does not apply. If there is no such region, then each and every volume of the universe and all the physical entities contained in those volumes are subject to the second law.

Premise 2: The Beginning of the Universe Was Caused

Since the universe began to exist, it would seem that the most reasonable view to take would be that the first event was caused. The principle that something does not come from nothing without a cause is a reasonable one. This is especially true with regard to events. Events have a definite beginning and end, and do not happen without something causing them. By contrast, God does not need a cause, since he is neither an event nor a contingent being. He is a necessary Being and such a being does not need a cause. In fact, it is a category fallacy to ask for a cause for God since this is really asking for a cause for an uncaused being.

The first event, then, needs a cause, for unlike God, it was not a necessary being and it had a beginning and an end. Some have objected to this line of reasoning, however, and have maintained that it is not true to maintain that all events need a cause. Usually this objection makes an appeal to certain features of quantum mechanics. Quantum mechanics, according to this objection, shows that there is an ultimate indeterminacy in nature at the subatomic level. The law of cause and effect does not hold, events occur without a cause, and entities come into existence from nothing.

Two things can be said about this objection. First, not all philosophers and physicists are agreed as to how to interpret quantum mechanics. A number of thinkers, including those who adhere to the Copenhagen school of thought, argue that the laws and theoretical entities of quantum mechanics should be treated in nonrealist terms. This involves taking the statements of quantum mechanics as statements about our knowledge (or language) of reality, and not about a mind-independent reality itself. Thus, nature is not really indeterminate; we just do not know—perhaps cannot know—the underlying causes of quantum phenomena (if it makes sense in the Copenhagen view to even talk about a mind-independent realm of reality underlying the world we observe).

Second, even if one interprets quantum mechanics along realist lines (quantum theory states, at least approximately, the way the world is), it does not follow that events above the subatomic level do not have causes. Even if one grants that a photon of light can pop into existence from a "quantum ghost" (sheer nothingness which underlies every thing), it does not follow that the first event did not need a cause. Even if one can make statements like the one about quantum ghosts intelligible, and I personally doubt that this is possible, macroevents still have causes. When an apple falls something caused it. When an event as massive as the big bang occurred, something caused it. It is an unwarranted extrapolation to argue from the microlevel to the macrolevel.

It could be argued that the origin of the universe *was* a quantum phenomenon at the microlevel and, therefore, the first event could have occurred without a cause since it was not a macroevent. Two things can be said in response to this. First, I have already pointed out that there is no agreed-upon interpretation of quantum mechanics. In particular, most seem to take quantum mechanics in nonrealist terms. Our knowledge of reality at the quantum level may be probabilistic and not deterministic, but that does not mean no causes operate at that level. It means only that we have no ability to predict them with certainty.

Second, in the absence of a clear consensus on quantum interpretation, it seems reasonable to hold to the well-established law of cause and effect. Surely the burden of proof is on those who deny that law, and if quantum theory can be understood in a way which preserves the law of cause and effect, then that interpretation of quantum theory is preferable for that reason.

Nevertheless, some maintain the plausibility of the assertion that the universe came from nothing without a cause. Isaac Asimov asserts that just as $0 = +1 + (-1)$, so nothingness may have spawned equal-sized globs of positive and negative energy. Davies makes a similar statement: "There is a still more remarkable possibility, which is the creation of matter from a state of *zero* energy. This possibility arises because energy can be both positive and negative."[41]

In order to see what is wrong with these statements, we need to investigate two issues: identity and predication, and the ontological status of nonbeing. First, let us consider identity and predication by looking at two sentences.[42]

1. Socrates is the teacher of Plato.
2. Socrates is white.

Sentence 1 expresses an "is" of identity. Socrates is identical to the teacher of Plato. Identity is a relation which is reflexive (A is identical to itself), symmetrical (if A is identical to B, then B is identical to A), and tran-

41. Davies, *God and the New Physics*, p. 31. For a survey of eight different interpretations of quantum physics, see Nick Herbert, *Quantum Reality: Beyond the New Physics* (Garden City, N.Y.: Doubleday, Anchor Books, 1985), pp. 16–29.

42. See Moreland, *Universals, Qualities, and Quality-Instances*, pp. 168–72.

sitive (if A is identical to B, and B is identical to C, then A is identical to C). If A and B are identical, then whatever is true of A is true of B and vice versa.

Sentence 2 expresses an "is" of predication. Socrates is not identical to whiteness. Whiteness is a property which Socrates *has*. Whiteness is predicated of Socrates. Predication is a different relation than identity. For example, predication is not transitive. If Socrates is white, and white is a color, then it does not follow that Socrates is a color.

One important feature of predication is relevant to our discussion. A cannot be predicated of B if B does not exist, except, perhaps, in thought only. Socrates could not really *be* white if Socrates did not exist. Predication is a relationship that a property has to a substance (or event or bare particular) which obtains only when the property and the substance really exist.

Next, let us consider the ontological status of nonbeing. Nonbeing (i.e., nothingness) does not exist. Nonbeing is not some shadowy mode of reality. Nonbeing has no properties and causes nothing; in short, it is a pure lack of existence. When someone says that something comes from nothing, this cannot mean that nonbeing was the efficient or material cause of that something. Nonbeing is not some shadowy stuff from which something is made.

This is sometimes put by saying that negative properties do not exist. There is a difference between negation (the simple denial of existence) and the positive assertion of the existence of nonbeing. An apple has a number of properties: redness, roundness, sweetness. When we deny that an apple has squareness we are denying the existence of a property in the apple. We are not asserting that, in addition to redness, the apple has the negative property of not-squareness.[43]

We are now in a position to expose the problems inherent in the statements by Asimov and Davies. Suppose we have a container with ten protons and ten electrons. The total charge of the container is zero. The positive charge of each proton is a property predicated of that proton. The same is true of the negative charge of the electron (unless negative here is taken as some sort of privation). If one separated the protons from the electrons and put them into two different containers, one would have a positively-charged container and a negatively-charged container. But the positive and negative charges would not come from nothingness. It is simply that the total charge of the original container was zero because the positive charge was equal to the negative charge.

If a state of zero energy is conceived of as a state of affairs where the total amounts of positive and negative energy are equal, then when the positive

---

43. For helpful discussions of negative properties and existence, see Armstrong, *Universals and Scientific Realism,* Vol. 1 pp. 19–29; Reinhardt Grossmann, *The Categorial Structure of the World* (Bloomington: Indiana University Press, 1983), pp. 402–16; Richard M. Gale, "Negation and Non-Being," *American Philosophical Quarterly Monograph Series,* no. 10, ed. Nicholas Rescher (Oxford: Basil Blackwell, 1976).

and negative energy becomes separated, this is not a case of something coming from nothing. It is merely a case of separation.

If a state of zero energy *is* conceived of as nothingness, then *it* does not exist. Nothingness has no nature and thus it has no exigency or internal striving toward the production of *any* state of affairs, much less one where positive and negative energy is balanced. Nothingness might just as well have produced ten unicorns and five pens. Nothingness is not an entity which has an equal amount of positive and negative properties which comprise the stuff for the production of a specific state of affairs. Nothingness has no properties whatever, and it is not identical to an existent state of affairs where the positive and negative charge, or the positive and negative energy, is equal. The latter contains some sort of stuff (protons and electrons or energy); the former contains nothing.

It is, then, a mistake to use language like that of Asimov and Davies. Such talk seems to say that nonbeing is identical to an existent state of affairs with positive and negative properties. But nothingness is just that, and nothingness has no nature, causal powers, or tendencies toward anything whatsoever.

One suspects that at bottom, the assertion that the universe came from nothing without a cause is a mere assertion without support; a sort of ungrounded logical possibility which provides the atheist with a last-ditch effort to avoid the existence of a first Cause. Atheist B. C. Johnson asserts that "if time might have been nonexistent [prior to the first event], then so might causality. The universe and time might have just popped into existence without a cause."[44] Such a view is a logical possibility, but one which is most likely metaphysically impossible, and in any case, one without sufficient reasons. There is no reason to deny what we experience as true every day. Events have causes. So did the first one.

Premise 3: The Cause for the Beginning of the Universe Was Personal

The first event was caused either by something personal or by something impersonal. Prior to the first event—where prior means "ontologically prior," not "temporally prior"—there was a state of affairs which can be described by the following: there was no time, space, or change of any kind.

It is hard to conceive of such a state of affairs in physicalist terms (i.e., in terms of matter and energy). But let us grant that such a state of affairs could exist.

44. B. C. Johnson, *The Atheist Debater's Handbook*, Skeptics Bookshelf series (Buffalo: Prometheus, 1981), pp. 70–71.

In this state of affairs, either the necessary and sufficient conditions for the first event existed from all eternity in a state of immutability or they did not. If they did not, then the coming-to-be of those conditions was the first event. One can then ask about the necessary and sufficient conditions for *that* event. No matter how far back this regress goes, the coming-to-be of any set of necessary and sufficient conditions for a further event will itself be an event. And it will be an event which becomes a part of the series of past events which occurs *after* the first event—unless, of course, it is the first event itself.

It seems, then, that the only way a physicalist understanding of the beginning of the universe can avoid the first event being uncaused is to say that the necessary and sufficient conditions for the first event existed from all eternity in a timeless, changeless state. These conditions for some reason or other gave rise to the first event.

The problem with this scenario is this. In the physical universe, when A is the efficient cause of B, then given the presence of A, B obtains spontaneously. If the necessary and sufficient conditions for a match to light are present, the match lights spontaneously. There is no deliberation, no waiting. In such situations, when A is the efficient cause of B, spontaneous change or mutability is built into the situation itself.

The only way for the first event to arise spontaneously from a timeless, changeless, spaceless state of affairs, and at the same time be caused, is this—the event resulted from the free act of a person or agent. In the world, persons or agents spontaneously act to bring about events. I myself raise my arm when it is done deliberately. There may be necessary conditions for me to do this (e.g., I have a normal arm, I am not tied down), but these are not sufficient. The event is realized only when I freely act. Similarly, the first event came about when an agent freely chose to bring it about, and this choice was not the result of other conditions which were sufficient for that event to come about.

In summary, it is most reasonable to believe that the universe had a beginning which was caused by a timeless, immutable agent. This is not a proof that such a being is the God of the Bible, but it is a strong statement that the world had its beginning by the act of a person. And this is at the very least a good reason to believe in some form of theism.

2

The Design Argument

There can be little doubt that the most popular argument for God's existence is the design argument, also called the teleological argument.[1] The argument was introduced in ancient Greece and was also em-

---

1. Thomas McPherson has shown that the argument has been called both the argument *from* and the argument *to* design. This in turn depends on what one takes design to be. I will simply use the phrase *the design argument* and specify the different kinds of design used. See Thomas McPherson, *The Argument from Design* (London: Macmillan, 1972), pp. 6–13.

ployed by medieval philosophers, among them Thomas Aquinas. It flourished in the seventeenth and eighteenth centuries, especially in England, where the argument was restated by William Paley (1743–1805) and in two famous series of volumes, the Boyle Lectures and the Bridgewater Treatises. In the nineteenth and twentieth centuries, the design argument has fallen into disfavor among philosophers and scientists, due in large measure to the criticisms leveled against it by David Hume, Immanuel Kant, and Charles Darwin.[2] In recent years, the design argument has attracted a growing number of supporters, and it has once again moved to center stage in arguments for and against the existence of God.

Actually, it is a misnomer to talk of *the* design argument. One burden of this chapter will be to show that there is a family of arguments which differ in form and in the sort of design they utilize, but which deserve to be called design arguments nonetheless. In this chapter different kinds of design will be described; different forms of the argument will be discussed; objections to the design arguments will be stated and criticized.

Different Kinds of Design

Design as Order

Some proponents of the design argument describe design as order, pattern, or regularity.[3] The universe as a whole, and certain aspects within it, confronts us as an orderly, arranged *universe*. (It is surely possible that reality might have been a chaos.) Three different kinds of order have been utilized. First, some have defined order as *qualitative sequences*. For example, colors come in qualitative sequences where they are arranged in a spectrum. Similarly, sounds, tastes, textures, and other qualities come in orderly arrangements where the members of the sequence are arranged in a patterned way and not chaotically.

Second, some have characterized order as *regularities of spatial compresence*. Here, order is seen in patterns of spatial arrangement at some point in time. Manmade examples of this are towns with all their roads at right angles to each other or a section of books in a library arranged in alphabetical order. Examples in nature abound. From the spatial arrangement of the parts of the human eye to the uniform distribution of galactic clusters, the universe is filled with regularities of spatial compresence.

2. All three continued to have respect for the design argument. Hume in particular felt that some form of theism is more reasonable than naturalism, given the presence of design in the world.

3. See Brian Davies, *An Introduction to the Philosophy of Religion* (Oxford: Oxford University Press, 1982), pp. 50–51, 58–61; McPherson, *The Argument from Design*, pp. 7–8; Richard Swinburne, "The Argument from Design," *Philosophy* 43 (July 1968): 199–212.

Third, Richard Swinburne defines order as *regularities of temporal succession*.[4] Here, order is seen in the simple patterns of behavior in physical objects. The temporal sequence of notes in a song or the movements of a dancer's body would be examples of temporal sequences due to human intelligence. Natural examples are easy to find. For example, objects behave in accordance with the laws of nature. The paths of heavenly bodies follow regular temporal sequences in accordance with laws of gravity and motion. Organisms grow in certain sequences. Regularities of succession are all-pervasive. Simple natural laws govern almost all successions of events.

Swinburne gives the following argument for using design as temporal succession:

> Almost all regularities of succession are due to the normal operation of scientific laws. But to say this is simply to say that these regularities are instances of more general regularities. The operation of the most fundamental regularities clearly cannot be given a normal scientific explanation. If their operation is to receive an explanation and not merely to be left as a brute fact, that explanation must therefore be in terms of the rational choice of a free agent.[5]

Swinburne argues that the free choice of a rational creature is the only way, other than normal scientific explanation, of accounting for natural phenomena. If letters are scribbled in the sand one can use either explanation to account for this fact. But scientific explanation merely replaces one regularity with another one, so in the end one is left with broad scientific laws which govern temporal successions. Why should we accept these broad regularities as evidence for a rational agent instead of treating them as brute givens without an explanation? Swinburne answers that we can explain some temporal regularities by appealing to rational agency and that the other regularities cannot be explained except in this way. For example, the temporal succession of notes in a song or movements of a dancer's body can be explained by an appeal to a rational agent singing the song or dancing. Similarly, the celestial harmony of movement in the universe is due to laws which came from a rational agent.

Design as Purpose

A variety of differences exists among those who have used design as purpose. Four distinctions will help us flesh out these differences. First, one can distinguish between a plan or intention on the one hand, and a

4. Swinburne, "The Argument from Design," pp. 200–206.
5. Ibid., p. 204.

purpose, goal, or end on the other hand. Suppose someone is looking at a table and reasons as follows: I know where the wood came from (the trees in the forest), but where did the design come from? A table may have a certain shape or arrangement of parts which may, in turn, have a purpose (to eat on). This arrangement of parts reflects a plan in the mind of the builder of the table. Or consider a watch. A watch is a complex whole consisting of several parts which interact together to achieve an end, recording the time. This arrangement of parts reflects a plan in the mind of the watch's designer.

So design may refer to the orderly arrangement of parts in the object itself and the fact that they work together for some goal or end. Here design is used as *purpose*. Or design may refer to the plan or blueprint in the mind of the maker of the object. Here design is used as *plan*. It can be argued that purpose is an evidence of a plan.[6] Just as the purpose of a watch (the complex interaction of several different kinds of parts to achieve the end of keeping the time) is evidence for a plan in the mind of a designer of the watch, so the purpose of the eye (the complex interaction of several different kinds of parts to achieve the end of seeing) is evidence for a plan in the mind of a designer of the eye.

A second distinction involves two different ways of taking design as purpose. First, one can take purpose as beneficent order.[7] Here the emphasis is on the fact that things move toward ends and these ends are good and valuable. Several features of the world work together to promote human life (e.g., the presence of plant life, oxygen, the human heart which can pump blood through the body). Time and time again, when a new disease is discovered, a cure is available and waiting to be found. In fact, this happens so often that we assume that, given enough time, we will find cures for disease. The world is such that cures will be found.

Others take purpose as nonbeneficent order.[8] Here emphasis is placed on the mere fact that things in the world strive toward certain ends, and those ends may be value neutral. Usually, things in the world come from other things of the same kind—trees from trees, tomatoes from tomatoes. This is especially true of complex entities (e.g., living organisms). When a

6. Aristotle was the first philosopher to give detailed treatment to ends or final causes. He felt that entities with heterogeneous parts (composite parts which are not uniform among themselves) had to be explained by final causes toward which those parts moved. For a treatment of Aristotle's final cause, see Richard Sorabji, *Necessity, Cause, and Blame: Perspectives on Aristotle's Theory* (Ithaca, N.Y.: Cornell University Press, 1980), pp. 155–81; Etienne Gilson, *From Aristotle to Darwin and Back Again: A Journey in Final Causality, Species and Evolution*, trans. John Lyon (Notre Dame: University of Notre Dame Press, 1984).

7. C. Stephen Evans, *Philosophy of Religion*, Contours of Christian Philosophy series (Downers Grove: Inter-Varsity, 1985), pp. 59–63.

8. Two books which list a number of examples of this kind of design are James E. Horigan, *Chance or Design?* (New York: Philosophical Library, 1979), and Robert E. D. Clark, *The Universe: Plan or Accident?* (Grand Rapids: Zondervan, 1949).

complex entity (e.g., a watch) radically originates from parts which are not like it, this origination is due to intelligent intervention. Thus, the mere presence of cooperation of parts toward an end is evidence of intelligent design, regardless of whether that end is valuable. For example, nature usually takes the simplest, most efficient means to achieve an end. Chemical compounds will react to form the most stable state of affairs possible. Electric charges will seek the most uniform distribution possible. Given the proper circumstances, an acorn will become a mature oak tree.

A third distinction is made between an action and the result of an action.[9] The act of striking a golf ball can be seen as evidence of a plan or intention in the player's mind. Likewise, the presence of the ball five inches from the cup may also be used to infer a plan in someone's mind. Both actions and the results of actions can be used in the design argument. But the former is more direct, since one can see someone doing something and it is usually easier to determine the presence of a plan. It is easier to attribute the ball near the cup to chance (someone accidentally dropped it) than it is to attribute the golf swing to an unintentional series of movements. In this regard, many religious believers offer evidence of divine intention in the events of world history (God's plan for Israel) or in the events of their personal lives (provision, instruction, opportunities for ministry). But both actions and the results of actions can be appealed to in the design argument.

Finally, design as either purpose or plan may involve biological or nonbiological examples. The circulatory system and the eye would be examples of the former. Cosmological examples (the freezing point of water, the properties of carbon, the uniform distribution of charge) and psychological or spiritual examples (answers to prayer, a message coming to someone just when he needs it, the formation of Israel as a nation) are examples of the latter.

Design as Simplicity

Both the unity of the world and its simplicity have impressed some as evidence that the world is a result of a single, rational, efficient mind. A major assumption of science is that when one is confronted with a variety of complex phenomena, one should seek to find an underlying unity which reduces that complexity to simplicity. Such an assumption is behind the current drive to find a grand unified theory, a theory which unifies the four basic forces of nature (electromagnetism, gravity, the strong and weak nuclear forces) into one simple theory.[10]

9. McPherson, *The Argument from Design*, p. 23.
10. Paul Davies, *God and the New Physics* (New York: Simon and Schuster, 1983), pp. 144–76.

It is a fact that the phenomena of nature have been simplified time and again (i.e., shown to be the result of an underlying, unifying phenomenon), and the theories of science often exhibit a breathtaking simplicity. For example, movement as diverse as an apple falling and a galaxy rotating can be explained by the simple laws of motion expressed by Isaac Newton. But why should the world be simple? Why should it be a unity? Why should the laws describing it be simple? The belief that the world could be explained by using a principle of simplicity arose in conjunction with medieval theism in which the world was likened to a text. When an author writes a text, the simplest explanation of his words is usually correct. Furthermore, it is a sign of intelligence to be able to communicate something in simple terms, or for that matter, to be able to design a machine in a simple way. The fact that the world exhibits unity and simplicity is taken as evidence that behind it stands a designer who made it in a simple, efficient, and unified way.

Design as Complexity

Hand in hand with design as simplicity is the notion of design as complexity. The more we discover about the universe, the more we find that it is incredibly complex and intricate. For example, the organic compounds in living organisms come in four groups: carbohydrates, lipids, proteins, and nucleic acids. These compounds exhibit a staggering complexity in their composition as well as a precise intricacy in their relationships with each other. DNA is an extremely complex molecule which contains a very specific arrangement of parts.

When one realizes that the world exhibits such complexity and that at the same time this complexity can be expressed in simple terms, then this can be seen as evidence of an intelligent designer. It is one thing for a simple phenomenon to be capable of being simplified. It is another thing to find simple unity where there is complex diversity.

Design as Beauty

Generally, two different orders of beauty are used in the design argument: the beauty of the world itself and some of its aspects, and the beauty of the theories which accurately describe the world and some of its aspects. Consider the former. Several features of the world manifest beauty: a sunset, fall in Vermont, the human body, the Rocky Mountains, the singing of birds. Two things can be said about these examples. First, they all exhibit real, objective beauty. Space does not allow for a defense of the objectivity of beauty. Suffice it to say that if one denies the objectivity of beauty, then this sort of design will not be of use in arguing for a designer.[11] Second, the beauty in the examples cannot be accounted for in terms of survival value, natural selection, and the like. For one thing, some of the examples (the Rocky Mountains) are not biological organisms. Further, even when one considers biological organisms (the human body) it is not clear that the *beauty* of those organisms is related to their survival. Since science does not deal with value qualities (aesthetic or moral) in its descriptions of the world, then beauty as an aesthetic property is not a part of evolutionary theory.

In short, some would argue that the beauty of the world and many of its aspects points to the existence of a grand Artist. The second kind of beauty used in the design argument is beauty as a property of scientific theories about the world. Philosophers of science have often pointed out that one of the criteria for a true (or rational) scientific theory is its elegance or beauty. Stanley L. Jaki points out that Albert Einstein and Erwin Schrödinger were guided by the conviction, borne out by previous scientific discoveries, that a good scientific theory would safeguard the beauty of nature and would itself be formally or mathematically beautiful.[12]

Beautiful theories or systems of thought which are mere inventions get their beauty from the superior human intellect which formed them. Similarly, beautiful theories, which are discovered and which accurately reflect the way the world is, get their beauty from the Mind which formed them.

Design as Sense and Cognition

Several philosophers have pointed out that our ability to perceive and think about the world accurately is evidence that these abilities were designed by an intelligent being for such purposes. Two different notions of design and two different arguments can be distinguished.

First, Richard Taylor and A. C. Ewing have appealed to the existence of sensory and cognitive faculties themselves as evidence of design.[13] If our sensory and cognitive abilities were merely the results of irrational atoms in motion or brute, mindless physical laws, then there would be no reason

11. See A. C. Ewing, *Value and Reality* (London: George Allen and Unwin, 1973), pp. 175–76.

12. Stanley L. Jaki, *The Road of Science and the Ways to God* (Chicago: University of Chicago Press, 1978), pp. 188–90, and n. 65 on p. 410; see also Davies, *God and the New Physics*, pp. 220–22.

13. Taylor is cited in John H. Hick, ed., *Arguments for the Existence of God*, Philosophy of Religion series (New York: Herder, 1971), pp. 21–26; see also Ewing, *Value and Reality*, pp. 177–78. Noam Chomsky of MIT has argued that the mind has certain innate structures which serve as invariant preconditions for language acquisition and for knowledge in general. But how did the mind ever come to have such structures and what is the relationship between those structures and truth? How did it come about that these structures correspond to the world in such a way that knowledge is possible? Naturalism would seem to have to say that it is just a happy, brute given.

to trust that they accurately inform us of the external world. Suppose a person is riding in a train and sees these letters on a hillside: THE BRITISH RAILWAYS WELCOMES YOU TO WALES. He would feel that they were the result of a mind and were not arranged by chance, nonrational forces. If he did suppose that the letters were arranged by accident, then they would have no meaning nor would he be reasonable in trusting what they said. If our own sensory and cognitive faculties are the result of accidental, nonrational forces, why should we trust that they convey accurate information to us? We would trust them only if they were arranged by an intelligent mind for the purpose of *informing* us about the world.

Our capacities to accurately sense and think about the world cannot be explained by saying that they evolved over time because of their survival value. For one thing, it is not clear that the ability to know truth from falsity is necessary to survive. As long as an organism interacts consistently with its environment it need not interact accurately. For example, if an organism always saw blue things as though they were red and vice versa, or large things as small and vice versa, that organism and its offspring would adapt to its environment. It is hard to believe that an amoeba grasps the way the world is, but it does interact with the world consistently. It will react to heat in a consistent way regardless of whether or not it grasps the essence of heat.

Second, our capacities to sense and think accurately about the world go far beyond what is needed to survive. The mind grasps abstract truths which do not seem to have anything to do with the survival value they impart to the organism.

The second notion of design does not focus on our sensory or cognitive capacities, but on truths, concepts, and theories themselves. It would seem that truths, concepts, and theories are sometimes discovered and not invented. Such entities are nonphysical realities that are part of the furniture of the universe. When certain concepts or theories are discovered, and when it is seen that they describe the world accurately, then a puzzle arises. Why are two entirely different orders of being—the physical world on the one hand, and the world of logical relations, mathematical relations, concepts, theories, and propositions—such that they often correspond to each other?

It has often amazed scientists and mathematicians that a mathematical model which will accurately describe some aspect of the universe can be discovered. William Pollard puts it this way:

> We have discovered that systems spun out by the brain, for no other purpose than our sheer delight with their beauty, correspond precisely with the intricate design of the natural order which pre-dated man and his brain. That

surely is to make the discovery that man is amazingly like the designer of that order.[14]

Others have stated that the universe appears to have been designed by a mathematician. In sum, the correspondence between these two orders of being could not be an accident. It must be the result of design. Both orders of being were designed by the same mind such that one order is accurately about the other. When one discovers a true theory, one discovers an existent in one order which is truly about something in the physical universe.

Design as Information

Biologists Lane Lester and Raymond G. Bohlin have used a notion of design as information.[15] They distinguish two different kinds of design in nature. First, there is what they call design as order. Such design involves a simple structural unit which is repeated over and over again. An example would be the formation of a snowflake or a crystal. These structures contain high order but little information. They are like the following: ME ME ME ME ME ME ME. According to Lester and Bohlin, design in this sense can be derived from the internal properties of the component parts of the repeated units. For example, the order in an ice crystal is due to the properties of hydrogen, oxygen, and H_2O.

By contrast, DNA and protein formation must be described by making quite literal use of the linguistic terms *code, transcribe,* and *translate.* We speak of a genetic code, of DNA being transcribed into RNA, and RNA being translated into protein. The genetic code is composed of letters (nucleotides), words (codons or triplets), sentences (genes), paragraphs (operons), chapters (chromosomes), and books (living organisms). Such talk is not anthropomorphic, it is literal. Living organisms do not contain only order but information as well. By contrast to the simple repetition of ME, the genetic code is like the Encyclopaedia Britannica.

Whenever we are confronted with examples of language or information, two things are true. First, if the signs did not come from a rational agent then they have no meaning. For example, if one saw JOHN LOVES MARY in the sand and one knew that the letters got there by erosion, then there would be no real sentence with meaning. It would merely be a string of letters which resemble a meaningful sentence when such a sentence is

14. Cited in Horigan, *Chance or Design,* p. 117.

15. Lane Lester and Raymond G. Bohlin, *The Natural Limits to Biological Change* (Grand Rapids: Zondervan, Academie Books, 1984), pp. 153–57. See also Charles B. Thaxton, Walter L. Bradley, and Roger L. Olsen, *The Mystery of Life's Origin: Reassessing Current Theories* (New York: Philosophical Library, 1984), pp. 127–66.

written by a person. Second, the information exists outside of and prior to the arrangement of the parts of the sentence in the mind of the writer. In fact, the meaning is what determines which parts get in the sentence in what order. Meaning cannot be identified with the parts nor can it emerge from within those parts. The letters (parts) JONHVLOSERMAY do not have meaning. Rather, the meaning exists in the writer and he arranges letters (parts) in conventional ways to communicate his meaning.

Likewise, the information in the genetic code existed prior to and outside of the parts of that code and that information was imposed on those parts by a Mind.

Design and Cosmic Constants

The Data

In recent years some startling features of the universe, involving cosmic constants or singularities, have been discovered. A cosmic singularity is a basic physical constant (the weight of a proton or the rate of expansion of the big bang) which is a brute given. The numerical values of these constants could have been different and there appears to be no scientific reason why they are what they are. Furthermore, these constants obtain independently of each other; that is, the value of one constant is not a function of the value of another in most cases.

Any form of life even remotely like our own is remarkably sensitive to infinitesimal alterations in these constants. Had the values of these constants been slightly smaller or larger, then no life would have been possible. This has led some scientists to formulate what is called the anthropic principle. The anthropic principle has different formulations. Roughly, it means that the universe seems to have unfolded with life in mind; its conditions were such that observers would be formed. As theoretical physicist Paul Davies puts it: "It is hard to resist the impression that the present structure of the universe, apparently so sensitive to minor alterations in the numbers, has been rather carefully thought out . . . the seemingly miraculous concurrence of [these] numerical values must remain the most compelling evidence for cosmic design."[16]

Here is a small list of some of the cosmic constants given in the literature:[17]

1. Had the rate of expansion of the big bang been different, no life would have been possible. A reduction by one part in a million mil-

16. Davies, God and the New Physics, p. 189.
17. See Davies, God and the New Physics, pp. 177–89; The Accidental Universe (Cambridge: Cambridge University Press, 1982); John Wiester, The Genesis Connection (Nashville: Nelson, 1983), pp. 27–36, 47–50; John Leslie, "Anthropic Principle, World Ensemble, Design," American Philosophical Quarterly 19 (April 1982): 141–50.

lion would have led to collapse before the temperatures could fall below ten thousand degrees. An early increase by one part in a million would have prevented the growth of galaxies, stars, and planets.

2. The material of the observable universe is isotropic (evenly distributed) to an accuracy of 0.1 percent. Such an accuracy is antecedently improbable and slight variations would rule out life.

3. Had the values of the gravitational constant, the strong force constant (the force binding protons and neutrons in the nucleus), the weak force (the force responsible for many nuclear processes [e.g., the transmutation of neutrons into protons]), and the electromagnetic force been slightly greater or smaller, no life would have been possible.

4. In the formation of the universe, the balance of matter to antimatter had to be accurate to one part in ten billion for the universe to arise.

5. The random coalescing of several unrelated factors necessary for life someplace in the universe is highly improbable. This can be seen by examining the factors on earth necessary for life. The point is not, however, that it is amazing that these factors came together on earth instead of somewhere else. Rather, it is amazing that they came together anywhere, and earth is used to illustrate the factors necessary. Had the ratio of carbon to oxygen been slightly different, no life could have formed. If the mass of a proton were increased by 0.2 percent, hydrogen would be unstable and life would not have formed. For life to form, the temperature range is only 1–2 percent of the total temperature range, and earth obtains this range by being the correct distance from the sun, just the right size, with the right rotational speed, with a special atmosphere which protects earth and evens out temperature extremes. In addition, the planet which had these factors just happened to contain the proper amount of metals (especially iron), radioactive elements to provide the right heat source, and water-forming compounds. Perhaps the proper temperature range could be obtained in another way. But earth shows how delicate and multifaceted are the independent factors involved in maintaining the correct temperature for life.[18]

6. The chance formation of life from nonlife (abiogenesis) has been estimated at around $1 \times 10^{40,000}$. Thus, the probability of life forming anywhere in the cosmos is miniscule.[19] Furthermore, in the process of reacting in some prebiotic chemical soup, the reactants often need to

18. Wiester, *The Genesis Connection*, pp. 42–43, 47–50.

19. For examples of these estimates, see Thaxton, Bradley, and Olsen, *The Mystery of Life's Origin*, pp. 113–66, 218–19; Pierre Lecomte du Noüy, *Human Destiny* (New York: The New American Library of World Literature, 1949), pp. 30–39; Robert Shapiro, *Origins* (New York: Summit, 1986), pp. 117–31; Henry M. Morris, ed., *Scientific Creationism* (El Cajon, Calif.: Master, 1974), pp. 59–69.

be isolated from their environment at just the right time and reintro-
duced at just the right time for the reaction to continue. This is
achieved in the lab by investigator interference, but it is difficult to
conceive of a mechanism to do this in nature and to do it at just the
right time.

The Proper Use of the Data

At this point we should consider an objection which will help to clarify
how the data should be used in the design argument. From the time of
Hume to the present, opponents of the design argument have pointed out
that we should not be surprised at this data. If the world had been one in
which intelligent life could not evolve, then we should not be here to discuss the matter. These factors are necessary for people to be around to
puzzle over them.

To see what is wrong with this objection, consider the following sequence:

$$p—q—r—s—t—u—v—w—x$$

p = the mass of a proton

q = the balance of matter to antimatter

r = the rate of expansion of the big bang

s = the properties of carbon

t = factors necessary to maintain a certain temperature range

u = factors which promote organic reactions (enzymes, energy)

v = the simultaneous compresence of the right chemicals

w = the properties of H_2O

x = the existence of human knowers

Critics of the design argument are saying that theists argue in one of two
ways. Theists are supposedly saying: Isn't it amazing that life arose here
on earth and not somewhere else (i.e., that p through x occurred here and
not elsewhere)? This would be a poor argument, since "here" or "earth" is
just that place where p through x came together. If theists argued this way,
they would be saying, "Isn't it amazing that p through x came together in
just the place they came together!" It is hard to see where else p through x
could come together than that place where they coalesced.

Alternatively, theists might be saying: Isn't it amazing that the factors necessary for life preceded us instead of some other factors preceding us (e.g., that p through w came before x instead of a through h preceding x). This way of arguing would be wrong as well, since x can occur only given p through w. X could not occur given a through h.

But theists do not argue in either of these ways. They do not point out the amazement that p through x happened here and not elsewhere or that p through w and not a through h preceded x. They argue that it is amazing that the entire series of p through x came about at all. Another entire series of events could easily have happened. There is no reason why the factors of the cosmos are what they are and not something else. This is especially true when one considers that most of the members of p through w occur independently of one another. They are not causally connected to each other.

Consider an example. Suppose an alien from Mars woke up in a room here on earth without knowing how he got here or where he was. Suppose, further, that there was a television turned on in front of him, that this was the only television in existence, and that the Martian knew this to be the case. Now it would be pointless for the Martian to wonder why he was watching television in this room and not somewhere else, since this is the only place where a television exists. Further, it would be pointless for him to wonder how it could be that he was watching television in just that world where all the factors necessary for the production of a television had previously obtained. Had they not obtained, he could not watch television.

But suppose the Martian began to inspect the television and found that it is incredibly detailed and intricate. Suppose that he also wondered how he came to be in that room. It would be legitimate for him to be amazed that there was a television in existence at all and that he was there watching it. The whole sequence of events leading up to the production of the television and the Martian's location in just that room could have failed to obtain. Similarly, the whole sequence of events leading up to life—many of them independent of each other—could have failed to obtain. The accidental coalescing of these factors is immensely improbable, and just because we are here to puzzle over this fact does not remove this improbability. Even the atheist J. L. Mackie saw the flaw in the objection we are considering:

> There is only one actual universe, with a unique set of basic materials and physical constants, and it is therefore surprising that the elements of this unique set-up are just right for life when they might easily have been wrong. This is not made less surprising by the fact that if it had not been so, no one would have been here to be surprised. We can properly envisage and con-

sider alternative possibilities which do not include our being there to experience them.[20]

Different Forms of Design Arguments

We have seen that a variety of types of design has been appealed to in arguing for a Designer. This is important to keep in mind, because even if one type of design can be strongly criticized, other types of design remain untouched. For example, some critics of the design argument try to show that evolutionary theory has explained alleged examples of biological design in terms of blind forces. But even if this criticism is correct, and we will see later that it is not, other types of design remain untouched by evolutionary theory.

Just as different kinds of design are used to argue for a Designer, so different *forms* of the argument have been advanced. These different forms show how rich the design argument really is. And as was the case with kinds of design, the different forms of argument make the inference to God as Designer less vulnerable to criticism. Weaknesses in one form of argument are often irrelevant to other forms of the design argument. Three major kinds of design argument have been advanced.

The Synthetic A Priori Argument

Consider the following:

analytic	synthetic
a priori	a posteriori

An analytic statement is one which is true by virtue of the meaning of its terms alone. An example would be "all bachelors are unmarried males." To verify this, you do not do a survey to see how many bachelors are unmarried. The statement is true by definition.[21] A synthetic statement is one in which what is affirmed in the predicate adds something to the subject. Such a statement is verified by reference to the world. An example would be "all ravens are black." Something is known a posteriori if it is known on the basis of experience of the world. We know lemons are sour because we

20. J. L. Mackie, *The Miracle of Theism* (Oxford: Clarendon Press, 1982), p. 141. For further discussion, see John Leslie, "Modern Cosmology and the Creation of Life," in *Evolution and Creation*, ed. Ernan McMullin (Notre Dame: University of Notre Dame Press, 1985), pp. 94–107.

21. W. V. O. Quine has criticized the analytic/synthetic distinction, but most philosophers still take it to be a valuable one. For a helpful introduction to the analytic/synthetic and a posteriori/a priori distinctions, see William H. Halverson, *A Concise Introduction to Philosophy* (New York: Random House, 1967), pp. 28–63.

have tasted them. Something is known a priori if it can be known directly and immediately without being based on experience.

A synthetic a priori truth is one which is about the world; is known immediately by rational intuition, perhaps without being based on experience; is metaphysically necessary, expressing what must be the case in all examples which it covers.[22] When the design argument is presented as a synthetic a priori argument, then the argument begins with an alleged synthetic a priori truth. Here are examples of purported synthetic a priori truths:

Something cannot come from nothing.

There must be as much reality in a cause as in an effect.

A cause must resemble its effect.

Meaning or information must come from a mind.

Parts do not cooperate toward ends unless they were put together by a planner for that end.

The synthetic a priori form of the design argument is the strongest possible form that the argument can take. For example, if one accepts as a synthetic a priori truth the statement "meaning or information must come from a mind," then if DNA contains information, it follows that this information had to come from a mind. I will not discuss this form of the argument in detail, for it is the most controversial, and most theists do not use it. The major debate about this form of the design argument centers around whether there are any synthetic a priori truths, what they are, and how they are known. Opponents of the argument try to reduce synthetic a priori statements to analytic a priori or synthetic a posteriori statements. In the former case, statements like "meaning must come from a person" are true solely in virtue of the definition of "meaning" (e.g., "an utterance from a person according to conventional linguistic practices"). Critics go on to say that it begs the question to refer to certain DNA phenomena using the word *meaning,* for this entails the presence of a person by definition. In the latter case, the statements "meaning comes from a person" or "design implies a designer" are contingent, empirical generalizations that could be false. Whether or not a particular example of "meaning" or "design" implies a mind must be settled by the analogy form of the argument.

Suffice it to say that if there are synthetic a priori truths (I am inclined to believe there are) and if these truths can be known directly, then the theist

22. For a valuable discussion on the difference among the analytic/synthetic, a priori/a posteriori, and necessary/contingent distinctions, see Saul Kripke, *Naming and Necessity* (Cambridge: Harvard University Press, 1972).

can invite the nontheist to "look" at the principles to see if they appear true to them. Apart from this invitation, or something similar to it, the synthetic a priori form of the design argument appears to reach a stalemate.

The Argument from Analogy

The design argument in analogy form is empirical or a posteriori. It makes an appeal to evidence in the form of generalizations. This form of the argument runs something like this: living organisms are a lot like machines; in our experience machines are always designed by an intelligence with an end in view for the machine; therefore living organisms are most likely designed by a mind as well.

An argument by analogy is a form of argument by induction, where an inductive argument is one where the truth of the premises does not guarantee, but merely supports or makes likely, the truth of the conclusion.[23] The analogy form of the argument says that a has properties F, G, H, and I; b is like a in that b has F, G, and H; therefore, it is reasonable to hold that b also has I. Let a be an apple, F be redness, G be roundness, H be firmness, and I be sweetness. Apple a is red, round, firm, and sweet. A second object, b, is like a in that it too is red, round, and firm. Therefore, it is reasonable to hold that b is sweet as well.

In the design argument, a would be human artifacts or machines, F would be order, complexity, and simplicity, G would be mutual cooperation of parts toward an end, H would be having a beneficial end, and I would be being designed by an intelligent designer. The world or some facet of it would be represented by b. The argument holds that the world or some facet of it resembles human artifacts in order and movement toward an end, and since the latter are also designed by a mind, it is reasonable to see the former as designed by a mind as well.

The crucial questions for any argument by analogy are these: Are the two objects of comparison a great deal like each other, at least enough to offset the ways they are different? Are the two objects of comparison like each other in ways relevant to the analogy being used? Since objects are similar and dissimilar in many ways, both the quantity and quality of the respects of resemblance are relevant to the strength of an argument by analogy. Critics of the design argument try to weaken the analogy. Supporters of the argument try to strengthen it.

23. See Wesley C. Salmon, *Logic* (Englewood Cliffs, N.J.: Prentice-Hall, 1963), pp. 81–117, especially pp. 97–98; Ewing, *Value and Reality,* p. 166; Alvin Plantinga, *God and Other Minds: A Study of the Rational Justification of Belief in God,* Contemporary Philosophy series, (Ithaca, N.Y.: Cornell University Press, 1967), pp. 97–107; McPherson, *The Argument from Design,* pp. 43–61.

Probability Arguments

At least three different design arguments are appropriately called probability arguments. Each of the three has a different understanding of probability.[24]

The Possibility View

This is the classical view of probability and its fundamental principle is this: If an event can occur in h different ways out of a total number of n possible ways, all of which are equally likely, then the probability of the event is h/n. The outcomes must be equipossible. For example, when one flips a coin, it is equally possible to get heads or tails. The probability of getting heads is $1/2$ ($h=1$, $n=2$). The probability of getting a 2 on a roll of a die is $1/6$.

Two further points should be made. First, repeated experiences can cast doubt on the possibility theory by indicating that the outcomes may not be equally possible. For example, if one throws a die one thousand times and it always comes up on 2, then one should expect that the die is loaded. But in the absence of any good reason to suspect that one outcome is more likely than others, the possibility theory is justified.

Second, we are now in a position to state what is called the special conjunct rule—a rule which applies regardless of what view one takes about the meaning of probability. When a probability has been assigned to each of two events, A and B, and the occurrence of one has nothing to do with the occurrence of the other, then the rule states this:

$$P(A \text{ and } B) = P(A) \times P(B)$$

For example, the probability of getting two successive rolls of 2 on a single unloaded die are

$$P(A \text{ and } B) = 1/6 \times 1/6 = 1/36$$

The design argument uses the possibility view of probability in at least two different ways. First, when cosmic singularities are considered, there is no reason to say, for example, that the value of the rate of expansion of the big bang was antecedently favorable to some other value. Several values were equipossible. Furthermore, several cosmic singularities

---

24. For a helpful introduction to probability theory, see William H. Halverson, *A Concise Logic* (New York: Random House, 1984), pp. 260–307. For a more advanced treatment from a philosophical perspective which focuses on theories of confirmation, see Paul Horwich, *Probability and Evidence* (Cambridge: Cambridge University Press, 1982), pp. 16–50.

have nothing to do with each other, and thus the special conjunct rule applies to the probability of all of them obtaining.

Second, the equipossible theory is used to calculate the probabilities of the chance formation of life (DNA and so forth). Here, the word *chance* means accidental or indifferent.[25] One chain of events can intersect with another by chance. For example, I may bring about a certain chain of events consisting in my walking out of my house to my car. A second chain of events, consisting in a bird dropping a deposit while flying overhead, may come about. If the deposit hits my head the two chains intersect! But the second chain was not caused by the first. It was indifferent to the first chain and they intersected by chance.

When chemicals come together to form a complex molecule, the process occurs by chance in this sense. Later stages of development are not caused by former stages. Similarly, the intersection of an electric charge or energy source with a certain primordial soup is by chance. Energy sources could have discharged in a number of other places, and it seems that they were all equipossible.[26]

The Frequency View

According to this view, probability statements are essentially statistical summaries: they report the proportion of favorable occurrences to total occurrences in the past. If, after n repetitions of an experiment (where n is very large), an event is observed to occur in h of these, then the probability of the event is h/n. If we toss a coin 1000 times and it comes up heads 520, then the probability of getting a head is estimated at .52. As I mentioned earlier, a frequency test can refute an assumption of indifference. For example, one might assume that Fred, an adult male, is indifferent to becoming bald or keeping his hair. Both are equiprobable. But upon sampling thousands of males, one might discover that only 100/1000 are bald. The probability that Fred will be bald (in the absence of other factors) is .10.

The frequency view is not used very much in the design argument, unless one argues that 100 percent of the machines he has seen are designed by intelligent beings and therefore so is the human eye. But this is better construed as an analogy argument which may (or may not) use a frequency view of probability.

However, the frequency view does have one important use in the design argument when it comes to discussions of the origin of life. Twenty-five years of laboratory experiments have confirmed that a random distribution

25. For different senses of the word *chance*, see A. R. Peacocke, *Creation and the World of Science* (Oxford: Oxford University Press, 1979), pp. 90–97.

26. In addition to the sources listed in n. 20, another excellent treatment of the use of probability in calculations about the origin of life is Michael Denton, *Evolution: A Theory in Crisis* (London: Burnett Books, 1985), pp. 308–25.

of organic compounds will be formed in prebiotic soup experiments, in the absence of interference from the person conducting the experiment. For example, some have speculated that there may be some nonrandom factors involved in the polymerization of proteins (for instance, inherent self-ordering tendencies in matter or selective reaction preferences in amino acids [small organic building blocks of larger, more complex molecules necessary for life]). If this is true, then the formation of complex organic molecules from small amino acids would not be entirely random. Some chemicals would prefer to react with others, and at various steps in the chain, different alternatives would not be equiprobable. But Kok and Bradley have shown that laboratory formation of twenty-five important proteins shows a bond frequency distribution approaching that predicted by random statistics.[27] Reaction preferences were negligible. In other words, a frequency understanding of the probability of the formation of certain complex molecules necessary for the formation of life confirmed the possibility view of these probabilities.

The Evidential View

In this view, when one says that p is probable, one means that p is reasonable. This view focuses on how, and to what extent, evidence confirms a proposition. To say that p is probable is to say that, given the relevant evidence E, E confirms p to some degree x. Suppose one wants to know how much some body of evidence E supports some belief T. If E supports T, then Prob(T, E) is greater than Prob (T). That is, the probability of believing T, given evidence E, is greater than the probability of believing T without evidence E. E supports T. Suppose T is the belief that my wife, Hope, loves me. Suppose E is the fact that she often fixes what I like for dinner and that she shows kindness to me. Then the probability of believing T in the presence of E is greater than the probability of believing T without E.

Some try to put a numerical value on these probabilities. For example, in the case of my wife, $P(T)$ may be .7; that is, without the evidence E provides, I may have just over a two-thirds chance that my wife loves me (suppose I know that just over two-thirds of the wives in the U.S. love their husbands). But $P(T, E)$ may be .9; that is, given all that Hope does for me, I may have a very high degree of probability that she loves me. Others do not think that numerical values are appropriate in most cases, because it is hard to know how to assign them. So they settle for a rough, qualitative understanding of probability. Something is very probable if it is almost certain; for example, that I know my hand exists. Something is possible if I have only little reason to believe it (e.g., that I will bat for the Cleveland Indians before the year is over).

27. Thaxton, Bradley, and Olsen, *The Mystery of Life's Origin*, pp. 147–50.

Several theists use the evidential view of probability. In so doing, they mean that certain features of design in the world are more reasonable, given that God exists, than they are without God. Ewing is one person who has argued this way.[28] He points out that certain features of the world are highly unlikely (a qualitative understanding of probability) if they resulted without having some purpose behind them, but they become quite reasonable if one postulates a purpose behind them.

For example, if someone found a number of leaves arranged on the ground in a sentence, this state of affairs could have happened blindly, perhaps due to the wind. But if one postulates a person who arranged them this way, this arrangement no longer appears puzzling. Similarly, Ewing argues that it seems fantastically improbable that living bodies should show such extraordinary detailed adjustments to ends as they do unless some explanation of this can be given in terms of a plan behind the formation of bodies.

These three uses of probability have all been used in the design argument. We have surveyed the kinds of design used in the argument and the different forms that have been pressed into service.[29] It is time to consider some criticisms which have been raised against the design argument in its various manifestations.

Criticisms of the Argument(s)

Criticisms from David Hume

During the 1750s, Hume wrote his famous *Dialogues Concerning Natural Religion*. The work is a masterpiece in philosophy and is still one of the most important works ever written on the design argument. In this work, Hume raises a number of criticisms against the argument.[30]

28. Ewing, *Value and Reality,* pp. 166–82.

29. I have omitted two other ways that design enters into theistic belief. First, Plantinga takes experiences of design as conditions for forming the belief that God exists. But this seems to be some sort of argument in the area of religious experience. See Alvin Plantinga, "Reason and Belief in God," in *Faith and Rationality: Reason and Belief in God,* ed. Alvin Plantinga and Nicholas Wolterstorff (Notre Dame: University of Notre Dame Press, 1984), pp. 78–82. Second, some philosophers (John H. Hick and J. Wesley Robb) see examples of design as posing a question of mystery to us which we can answer by seeing the world as though it were designed. See Hick, *Arguments for the Existence of God,* pp. 33–36; J. Wesley Robb, *The Reverent Skeptic* (New York: Philosophical Library, 1979), pp. 173–86. Theism becomes a way of seeing the world and not a conclusion which can be rationally established by argument.

30. For helpful overviews of Hume's treatment of the design argument, see Mackie, *The Miracle of Theism,* pp. 133–45; Hick, *Arguments for the Existence of God,* pp. 7–14; Davies, *Introduction to the Philosophy of Religion,* pp. 52–61; Swinburne, "The Argument from Design," pp. 206–11; Leon Pearl, "Hume's Criticism of the Argument from Design," *The Monist* 54 (April 1979): 270–84. See also the exchange between Wesley C. Salmon and Nancy Cartwright over Hume's dialogues and probability considerations: Wesley C. Salmon, "Religion and Science: A New Look at Hume's *Dialogs,*" *Philosophical Studies* 33 (1978): 143–76; Nancy Cartwright, "Comments on Wesley Salmon's 'Science and Religion . . .'," *Philosophical Studies* 33 (1978): 177–83.

The Uniqueness of the Universe

Hume argues that we can infer a cause for some effect only if we see that the cause and effect go together whenever we experience the effect. But no one saw the universe originate. Further, one cannot reach conclusions regarding objects which are one of a kind. Analogies work when one experiences several objects of a kind repeatedly. For example, I have seen several watches originate, and each was designed. So when I see a new watch, I can infer that it was designed as well. But the universe is one of a kind and no one saw it originate.

Hume's objection seems to involve two distinct principles. First, he assumes that we can infer from an observed A to an observed B only when we frequently see As and Bs together, and we can infer to a B only when we have actually seen other Bs. Such an assumption is simply false. Scientists often infer theoretical entities (electrons or quarks) which have never been seen and which may not be possible to see (e.g., a magnetic field). When observed As have a relation R to Bs, it is often reasonable to postulate that observed A^*s similar to As have the same relation to observed and unobserved B^*s similar to Bs.[31] For example, the pressure of colorless gases varies with the temperature of those gases, and on this basis, one could infer that a change in pressure of a colored gaseous substance would likewise vary with the temperature regardless of the fact that he had never seen a substance of this sort.

Second, Hume seems to assume that the universe is unique and conclusions cannot be reached about unique objects by analogy. But this is false as well. Astronomers reach conclusions all the time about the origin of the universe and this is unique. Furthermore, all events are unique in some sense, but no one would want to say that arguments by analogy do not apply to any objects whatever. The fact that the universe or some other object is unique does not rule out the possibility that it has properties in common with some other object, including some of its parts. For example, there may be only one object which satisfies the description "the tallest man in Maryland," but one could still compare this object with other objects and make judgments about the origination of the object. If one accepted Hume's principle it would seem to rule out the possibility of discovering a new culture and inferring that an utterly new and unique object in that culture was designed. But such an inference seems to be quite possible.

The Problem of Infinite Regress

Hume also argues that one can ask who designed the designer. If one needs to postulate that design needs a designer, then so does the designer, and this leads to an infinite regress.

---

31. Swinburne, "The Argument from Design," pp. 207–8.

Three things can be said in response. First, as Hume himself noted, y can explain x even if y itself needs explanation. The properties of water can be explained by the properties of hydrogen and oxygen with or without an explanation of these latter properties. Second, explanation cannot keep going on forever. One has to stop somewhere with an explanatory ultimate.[32] And when it comes to examples of design as order or purpose, we normally accept an explanation in terms of a rational agent as a proper stopping point and do not so regard an explanation in terms of physical causes. For example, when one sees a complex machine and asks why it is there, one can explain the machine by appealing to the physical laws governing the working of its parts. But such an explanation is not complete. It is proper to go on and say that these particular parts were put into this particular machine so the machine would operate according to the plan of the maker of the machine. One does not need to go on and explain the design of the plan in the machine-maker's mind. Rational agents cause their own ideas to come together freely, and an appeal to a rational agent and his intentions can be a proper stopping place.[33]

Third, Hume seems to assume that if the parts of an object are ordered, the ideas in the mind of the object's designer must exhibit the same order. But it is not clear that ideas can be said to exhibit any order, at least not the kind of order that physical objects exhibit. Ideas do not stand in that sort of relation to one another. When we say that ideas are ordered we usually mean that they stand in logical relations to one another or that the objects which they are about exhibit order. And even if ideas are ordered in some sort of way (e.g., logically), it is not clear from experience that that order needs a designer, as does the order found in the parts of a machine. If the order between ideas does need to be accounted for, it seems that the free agency of the rational mind itself is all that is needed. Agents can freely bring their ideas together in a variety of ways which are spontaneous.[34]

The Kind of God Postulated

Hume argues that even if the design argument is correct, one does not get the full-blown Creator God of Christian theism out of the argument. When one sees a watch, one only postulates a finite watchmaker. In fact,

---

32. For a good treatment of infinite regresses and explanatory justification, see James Cornman, "Foundational versus Nonfoundational Theories of Empirical Justification," in *Essays on Knowledge and Justification,* ed. George Pappas and Marshall Swain (Ithaca, N.Y.: Cornell University Press, 1978), pp. 229–52.

33. See Swinburne for a defense of this point.

34. The parts of the mind are not at issue here. It is reasonable to hold that a composite mind would need to be designed as well. Most theists take God to be a simple entity and thus his intellect would not need to be designed. If God is not simple, the theist can still hold that explanation must stop somewhere and there is a general presumption for mind to be a better stopping place than matter.

there may have been several designers involved in the process. Further, one infers a watchmaker who is corporeal, and if the watch has imperfections, one does not infer a perfect watchmaker. Finally, the watchmaker is not seen as the creator of the watch, but only as its designer. The same points could be made about god(s) and the world.

Several things can be said in response. First, Hume does have a point here. The whole case for Christian theism does not rest on the design argument, but on the convergence of a host of arguments. If the kalam argument is reasonable, if the historicity of the New Testament can be established (especially the historicity of the resurrection of Jesus), and if other arguments for God are considered, then the cumulative effect of all the arguments goes into establishing the rationality of Christianity. The design argument alone is not sufficient. Second, even if one grants that the design argument gives us several, corporeal, finite gods, this would itself be a significant conclusion and would be enough to refute naturalism. Hume thought the design argument made theism more reasonable than naturalism, and he was right to argue that the argument by itself does not establish the existence of the Christian God.[35] But if one really felt that the design argument does refute naturalism, then one should passionately search for more evidence to see which religion most accurately depicts the way God is.

One God is a simpler explanation than the polytheistic one and it makes more intelligible the fact that we live in a *uni*verse and not a plurality of universes. Regarding the corporeality of God, two things can be said. First, such corporeality would itself exhibit the kind of harmony of parts which the argument is designed to explain. Second, when one explains the design in human machines by postulating a human designer, the *design* of the machine is explained by the intellect of the designer and not his corporeality. Corporeality is a constant concomitant of human intelligence, but it is present per accidens. In other words, when one postulates an explanatory entity, one should attribute to that entity only what is needed to explain, and not accidental features which may be present but are not necessary. All examples of human artifacts have the properties of coming from intelligence and coming from beings ninety-three million miles from the sun. However, if artifacts were discovered on another planet, the former would be relevant but not the latter. The design argument supports a rational, free, powerful designer and these properties are relevant to the argument. Human corporeality is not.

35. Hume states that *The Dialogues Concerning Natural Religion* really focuses on the nature of God and not on the existence of God (see the beginning of part 2). Hume concludes the dialogues with a statement that theism is more reasonable than naturalism, given the fact of design. The sincerity of this admission has been questioned, though I take it to reflect Hume's considered opinion on the matter.

Finally, the problem of evil and imperfection is beyond the scope of this chapter.[36] But two things can be said. First, disorder presupposes order. The presence of the latter does not eliminate the former, nor does it remove the need for an account of the presence of order. Second, when theists say that God is all-powerful, they do not mean that God can do anything whatever, but only that he can do anything that power can do. God cannot make a square circle and he cannot cease to exist, but these are not limitations on his power since power is not relevant to them. Many theists hold that God could not make free creatures who could not sin, for that would be to make free creatures who were not free. Evil is traceable to the free will of God's creatures. So evil is not evidence of a limit to God's power any more than his inability to make a square circle limits his power.

The Viability of Rival Hypotheses

Hume argues that the theistic hypothesis has rival theories which make it impossible to decide which one is best. For example, the universe could have come from several deities. Or it could be like a vegetable which has its own principle of generation and order within itself. Or order could have come about entirely by chance. We have already considered the hypothesis of several deities. We will consider objections from chance later, but for now, I want to note that Hume himself believed that one ought to proportion his beliefs to the amount of evidence available. Because something is possible, it does not follow it is reasonable.

The analogy of the vegetable is an attempt to break down the analogy between the world and human machines. According to Hume, a vegetable has its order within itself and this order arises and disappears as the vegetable grows and decays. Two things can be said against Hume's analogy. First, in the case of the design of a machine one is dealing with the radical origination of a thing where its parts are transformed from a nonorderly state into a highly orderly one. In the case of a vegetable, we have a process where organized bodies generate other organized bodies. Trees produce other trees. There is no radical generation of order here but merely transmission of order from one entity to another. Living organisms cannot be used to explain order, for they themselves presuppose and exemplify such order. Second, vegetables themselves conform to laws and formulas of scientific laws which are themselves examples of what Swinburne calls regularities of temporal succession. Such regularities can be explained by postulating a rational agent behind them—as in the case of the movements of a dancer or the movement of a song—and thus the behavior of vegeta-

---

36. For helpful treatments of the problem of evil, see Norman L. Geisler, *The Roots of Evil* (Grand Rapids: Zondervan, 1978); John H. Hick, *Evil and the God of Love*, rev. ed. (San Francisco: Harper and Row, 1977); Alvin Plantinga, *God, Freedom, and Evil* (New York: Harper and Row, 1974).

bles can be explained by intelligent design. So the analogy of the vegetable does not remove the need for a designer. At best, it merely shifts the kind of design appealed to from mere spatial compresence of inhomogeneous parts to regularities of temporal sequences. Machines exhibit both of these kinds of design and both kinds of design need a designer in machines. One could grant that the former does not need a designer in a vegetable (spatial compresence could be explained in terms of scientific laws) but the latter would still need a designer (since scientific laws are regularities of temporal sequences which can themselves be explained by an appeal to rational agency).

A Further Criticism of Analogy

B. C. Johnson, Wallace Matson, and George H. Smith have raised a further difficulty with the analogy form of the design argument.[37] Johnson, Matson, and Smith argue that the design argument begins with a criterion to identify clear examples of design (watches) and must use the same criterion to identify alleged examples of divine design. What is the theist's criterion for design? It is the presence of a curious arrangement of parts adapted toward an end. But this is not a good criterion. If another criterion can be shown to be the correct one, and if that criterion breaks down the analogy between human artifacts and aspects of the world, then the analogy argument will be weakened. How do we identify products designed by beings other than God? The proper criterion is *whether or not the object bears the marks of machinery or other artifacts and does not resemble normal objects found in nature.*

Cases are set up to show how this criterion works. Johnson invites us to imagine going to another planet and trying to learn that intelligent inhabitants exist just by examining objects there.[38] Suppose these beings constructed some objects resembling watches and others resembling cats. The former would tip us off to the existence of these beings, but the latter would not. Both objects have curious arrangements of parts but only the watches resemble our artifacts and do not resemble objects in nature. So this latter criterion is the proper one for identifying intelligent design, and since natural objects do not fall under this criterion, they cannot be identified as examples of intelligent design. Several things can be said in response.

37. B. C. Johnson, *The Atheist Debater's Handbook*, Skeptics Bookshelf series (Buffalo: Prometheus, 1981), pp. 37–47; Wallace Matson, "The Argument from Design," in *Critiques of God*, ed. Peter Angeles (Buffalo: Prometheus, 1976), pp. 81–89; George H. Smith, *Atheism: The Case Against God*, Skeptics Bookshelf series (Buffalo: Prometheus, 1979), pp. 262–69.

38. Johnson, *The Atheist Debator's Handbook*, pp. 38–39.

First, the criterion appears to be circular. How does one identify cases of intelligent design? By whether or not they resemble cases of intelligent design. This is like saying that one identifies red things by whether or not they are red, and then saying that red is what red things have in common. To escape the charge of circularity, one can understand Johnson and the others as merely recommending that we adopt this criterion as an appropriate definition of the term *intelligent design*. But this recommendation begs the question by ruling out natural objects by definition. Such objects are what are at issue. One could grant the criterion for the sake of argument in the case of intelligent design by creatures, terrestrial or otherwise, since their products are nonnatural by definition. But it is question-begging to apply this definition to natural objects.

Second, the criterion is too strong. It makes it *impossible* for God to be known by man. For man to do so, God must, according to this criterion, design something which is like a human artifact. But in that case, one could say that the object was made by some unknown alien or some ancient tribe. It would also make it impossible to recognize a product from an alien culture which was unique. Suppose people in a primitive culture had never seen a painting and had no developed mythology. Could not a person from that culture recognize that a painting of a dragon on a cave wall was so intricate that it came from intelligence? This criterion also makes it impossible to acknowledge the creation of life in a lab by a scientist. Since such life would resemble natural objects and not human artifacts, one would not be able to recognize it as having come from an intelligently directed experiment. One would have to say the scientist introduced the life into the experiment while no one was looking.

Third, one could grant the criterion and go on to argue that design as information still passes the test. DNA exhibits essential features of human language, and one could identify it as coming from an intelligent communicator in the same way that one could identify by radio detection a new language from outer space or a new language on a stone tablet. One does not need to be able to translate the language to recognize that it is a language. The same applies to the information in DNA. It resembles human products (meaningful sequences of symbols which transmit information), and thus it passes the test of the criterion.

Fourth, Johnson, Matson, and Smith misunderstand the nature of a criterion. Sometimes criteria are formulated because of their convenience but they do not necessarily mark off the essence of the things they pick out. For example, a criterion for water is its boiling point. But this criterion does not tell us what the nature of water is. The deep structure of water is what the scientist holds to be the essence of water, but it would be impractical to say that one cannot identify water except by knowing a detailed scientific statement of its structure. Suppose a scientist uses the boiling point of water to determine that he had water in a beaker. Suppose this allowed him to study the structure of water. Now suppose he finds a new liquid which boils at the same temperature as water but is not H_2O. The boiling-point criterion would be helpful in most cases, but inadequate in this case. A new, more deeply grounded criterion would need to be found. Gold could be determined by its color, but when fool's gold was found, the old criterion was adequate in some cases but not in others, so better criteria were needed. A criterion for knowing that one has some entity A is not necessarily the same thing as a factor which constitutes the nature of A.

The criterion of resembling human artifacts and not natural objects may be convenient in most cases, but it does not constitute the nature of objects of intelligent design. The presence of the different kinds of design constitutes the nature of objects of intelligent design.

An object's likeness to human artifacts may alert us to the presence of a nonnatural object (artifacts are nonnatural objects by definition). But it is the presence of different kinds of design in the objects which alerts us to the presence of *intelligence* behind the objects. The greater the intricacy of the object, the greater the intelligence one would infer from the object. If one discovered a primitive wooden or bone axe, or saliva or excrement in the forest, one would be alerted to the presence of a nonnatural object. But little or no intelligence (in the case of saliva or excrement) would be inferred. Why? Even though these objects resemble human artifacts or by-products, they bear a low degree of design.

One could use the criterion "resembles human artifacts and not natural objects" to initially pick out a class of designed entities, and go on to discover a better criterion (bearing traits of design) which is more deeply grounded in that which constitutes the essence of the class. This new criterion could then be used to rule out or minimize poor members of the class (excrement or the axe). It could also be used to admit new members which failed to pass the old criterion, but which pass the new one—natural objects displaying design. Such an advance in criteria occurs often in science (see the examples of water and gold). When this happens, an old criterion may be useful in many cases ("boils at one hundred degrees," "is a yellowish metal," "is like a human artifact and nonnatural"), but it does not constitute the essence of the relevant class.

So the criterion "boils at one hundred degrees" is like the criterion "resembling human artifacts and not natural objects." It is a convenient criterion which allows one to go on and discover what constitutes the nature of the class of objects picked out—H_2O in the former case and having beauty, information, and harmony of parts toward a beneficial end in the latter case. Natural objects do meet this criterion, so the analogy argument is not refuted.[39]

Evolutionary Criticism of the Design Argument

The theory of evolution has been used to criticize the design argument.[40] The theory allegedly shows that what appear to be examples of design—for instance, the adaptation of an organism to its environment—are only examples of apparent design. Neal Gillespie puts the point this way:

> It has been generally agreed (then and since) that Darwin's doctrine of natural selection effectively demolished William Paley's classical design argument for the existence of God. By showing how blind and gradual adaptation could counterfeit the apparently purposeful design that Paley, the Bridgewater writers, and others had seen in the contrivances of nature, Darwin deprived their argument of the analogical inference that the evident purpose to be seen in the contrivances by which means and ends were related in nature was necessarily a function of mind.[41]

Theists have adopted three general strategies to answer this objection. First, one can point out that evolution is a theory which applies only to biological examples of design—it is an equivocation on the term *evolution* to extend it to nonbiological examples of change—and several examples of design outside the biological realm are left untouched by evolution (beauty, cosmic singularities, natural laws). So one can go outside of evolution to find examples of design.[42]

Second, some theists have accepted and used evolution as a whole as an example of design.[43] F. R. Tennant argues that evolution as a whole is amazing. The fact that the world is such that organisms have the capacity to change and adapt is itself an example of intelligent design. Such abilities presuppose a complex set of abilities and nature itself reveals anticipatory order; that is, it seems to anticipate the needs of adaptable life in its physi-

39. See Johnson, Matson, and Smith for further criticisms. See Denton, *Evolution*, pp. 326–43, for a useful comparison between the artifact-like character of life and humanly designed machines. Denton argues persuasively that recent discoveries in the biochemistry of life have strengthened the analogy used in the design argument.

40. Biologists have not been able to escape talking about the apparent purposefulness of organisms. They do so by using the word *teleonomy* instead of *teleology*. The former does not contain any reference to a plan in the mind of a designer to explain this apparent purposefulness, whereas the latter does. See John Bowker, "Did God Create This Universe?" in *The Sciences and Theology in the Twentieth Century*, ed. A. R. Peacocke (Notre Dame: University of Notre Dame Press, 1981), pp. 99–119.

41. Neal Gillespie, *Charles Darwin and the Problem of Creation* (Chicago: University of Chicago Press, 1979), pp. 83–84.

42. See Horigan, *Chance or Design*, p. 43, for a good statement of this point.

43. See F. R. Tennant, *Philosophical Theology*, vol. 2, *The World, the Soul, and God* (Cambridge: Cambridge University Press, 1956), pp. 78–120.

cal constants. Such abilities show that a mind is behind the process of evolution itself. Final causes (the end or purpose for which a change takes place) and efficient causes (that by which change is wrought) are compatible. The fact that water is boiling can be explained by efficient causes (chemical theory) and by final causes (someone wants tea). Evolutionary theory focuses on the efficient causes for change, but the presence of these mechanisms is evidence of a purpose or final cause, and the latter argues for a designer.

Third, one can seek to argue against the general theory of evolution and thus try to show that it is not adequate to account for all the biological phenomena in the world. Some of the arguments in this debate will be touched on in chapter 7, but for now, two points need to be mentioned. First, critics of evolution mean to attack macroevolution (the large-scale, general theory that states that all life arose from one ancestor, or a very small number of ancestors, and this ancestor arose from inanimate matter) and not microevolution (that organisms change and adapt within species or some other low level of classification).[44] Microevolution is a fact, but macroevolution is not. Second, it is simply false to say that macroevolution is clearly true and without serious problems. A number of thinkers (regardless of their view of theism) have been criticizing the adequacy of the theory of macroevolution.[45]

Probability and the Design Argument

In this section, I want to consider two objections raised against the probability forms of the design argument. The first objection comes from Matson.[46] Matson argues that when theists point to the immense improbability that life arose from nonlife by chance, they employ the equipossible notion of probability; he contends that the relative-frequency notion of probability is the preferable one. The relative-frequency interpretation of probability is inapplicable to such things as cosmic constants (e.g., there is no reference class which contains a thousand different values discovered for the rate of expansion of the big bang from which the actual value in this universe can be calculated as 1/1000) and thus the design argument bases its force on an inappropriate interpretation of probability.

Three things can be said in response to Matson. First, his claim is simply false. As I have already shown, theists use all three notions of

44. L. Duane Thurman, *How to Think About Evolution*, 2d ed. (Downers Grove: Inter-Varsity, 1978), pp. 85–114.

45. In addition to the works by Denton, Thaxton, Bradley, and Olsen, Lester and Bohlin, Morris, Wiester, and Shapiro, see Pattle P. T. Pun, *Evolution: Nature and Scripture in Conflict?* (Grand Rapids: Zondervan, 1982); Gordon Rattray Taylor, *The Great Evolution Mystery* (New York: Harper and Row, 1983). Both contain helpful criticisms of the general theory of evolution.

46. See Matson, "The Argument from Design," pp. 71–76, especially pp. 73–74.

probability—including the relative-frequency definition—in their arguments. Second, I see no reason for preferring the relative-frequency view to the possibility view. If there is no reason to expect one outcome over another, then each should be taken as equally possible. Third, scientists themselves use an equipossible understanding of probability when thermodynamics is given a statistical interpretation.[47] When scientists estimate the probability of a certain organic molecule forming, and assign it an entropy value, they use the equation $S = k \ln \Omega$, where S is the entropy of the system, k is Boltzmann's constant, and Ω is the number of possible ways the system can be arranged.

A second objection has been raised by a number of critics of the probability form of the design argument, including Johnson, Matson, Smith, Francis Crick, and Philip Kitcher.[48] Johnson puts the objection this way:

> If the combination of atoms composing the eye is only one out of billions of possible combinations, then so is every other possible combination. Take whatever combination you wish; there are always billions of others that could have happened. Thus, if the chances are billions to one against the eye combination, then the same probability would hold for any other combination. And yet, even in a random shuffling of atoms, one combination would occur despite the chances against it. When it did occur it would be just as improbable as the eye.[49]

Consider any bridge hand one could be dealt. The odds for any hand are very small and a random hand has the same probability as a perfect bridge hand. Yet one gets some hand or other every time one deals, so the improbable happens all the time.

Something has gone wrong here. Surely there is warrant for one to be surprised at getting a perfect bridge hand and not to be surprised at getting a random hand. Similarly, if one were dealt a hand of thirteen cards and they were all spades, it would be reasonable for that person to question the deal in a way not appropriate if he is dealt a more mixed hand. In order to evaluate this objection, let us consider what is known as the lottery paradox.

Suppose there is a lottery with one million people competing for one prize. Each person has one chance out of a million to win. Take at random some person named Smith. One knows that Smith's chances of winning

47. See Thaxton, Bradley, and Olsen, *The Mystery of Life's Origin*, pp. 113–43, and the article entitled "Entropy" in *The Encyclopedia of Philosophy*.

48. Johnson, *The Atheist Debator's Handbook*, pp. 53–57; Matson, "The Argument from Design," pp. 70–76; Smith, *Atheism*, pp. 269–72; Francis Crick, *Life Itself: Its Origins and Nature* (New York: Simon and Schuster, 1981), pp. 89–93; Philip Kitcher, *Abusing Science: The Case Against Creationism* (Cambridge, Mass.: MIT Press, 1983), p. 86.

49. Johnson, *The Atheist Debator's Handbook*, p. 54.

are one in a million. The same is true of Jones, Johnson, and each of the other persons in the lottery. It seems that one would be justified in believing that Smith will not win. Similarly, one would be justified in believing that each of the others, considered in isolation, will not win either. But this leads to a paradox. It seems that one would be justified in believing that no one will win if one adds up all his individual beliefs. But surely someone or other must win, since the drawing is about to be held.

The lottery paradox points out that it is important how one characterizes exactly what it is one is attaching his probability of belief to. The belief that someone or other will win is not the same as the belief that Jones will win. The belief that the parts of the eye or the constitutents of DNA will be arranged in some random way or another is quite reasonable. But this is not the same belief as the one about some particular arrangement (e.g., the one which produces the eye or life) and its likelihood.

What is the difference in the two cases? Crick offers the following answer.[50] The chance that one person will be dealt all hearts, another all spades, another all diamonds, and another all clubs in the same hand is one in 5×10^{28}. Yet each time we get some hand or other it has the same probability. But this is wrong. In order for the calculation to apply, one must say in advance exactly what set of hands we are considering. We are not allowed to deal the cards and then pretend that the result was just what we were looking for.

Crick is on to something here. Clearly, some factor is at work which separates the cases, but he has identified the wrong factor. It does not seem to me that some particular hand needs to be specified antecedently from the deal, but rather independently from the mere fact that it was the one which turns up. Consider the following case. One is trying to decide whether a given hand is rigged. If the dealer gave himself a perfect bridge hand, this would constitute evidence for the hypothesis that the deal was rigged. If his hand was more mixed, this would constitute evidence that the deal was honest. This could be argued, even if no prediction had been made at all. Someone from another culture could, once he understood the rules, judge the two hypotheses even if his judgment was made after the deal.

This case shows that the situation where probability comes in is one which relates evidence to hypothesis and this relationship is not a temporal one. Evidence either does or does not support a hypothesis and which way the evidence falls is not dependent on the evidence being known before or after the hypothesis was formed.

In the card game, a perfect bridge hand can be judged to have special significance due to the rules of the game which were formed indepen-

---

50. Crick, *Life Itself*, pp. 90–91.

dently from the deal. But one need not know those rules prior to the deal or predict the deal to be surprised at the outcome. A perfect bridge hand raises suspicion in a way that another hand would not because it has special traits (determined by the rules of the game)—independent from the mere fact that it was the one someone happened to get—which make its occurrence surprising and improbable.[51]

Now this is what we have in explaining cosmic singularities or the formation of life. Two hypotheses are being judged: a theistic and a naturalistic account. The naturalistic account can provide no reason for expecting the arrangement which yielded life to come about, other than the fact that it was just the one that happened. The naturalist cannot simply assert that some arrangement or other had to occur, for this is an improper characterization of the situation. The theist is not asking what the chances are that some arrangement or other would occur. He is asking what the chances are that a particular "deal of the cards" would occur where this particular "deal" is made probable by an explanatory hypothesis. The concurrence of this particular "deal" with a state of affairs made special and probable by the hypothesis of theism vis-à-vis naturalism is the proper way to characterize the issue.

The theist uses several of the features of design (beauty, information) to independently characterize what, in fact, did come about in the universe. These features of design characterize aspects of the world in a way independent of the mere fact that they happened. Further, the theist has a hypothesis which provides a set of propositions which make the presence of life, beneficent order, and the like probable. In this regard, the theist is like the person deciding whether the perfect bridge hand was rigged or random. His hypothesis (theism) provides independent rules for marking off the special features of life, just as the rules of bridge mark off as special a perfect hand independently from the mere fact that it just happened to be the hand that was dealt. Further, the hypothesis that the deal was rigged explains the presence of a perfect hand better than does the hypothesis that the deal was random. It is improbable, though possible, that the dealer dealt himself a perfect hand. But if given a choice between the two hypotheses, one should prefer the hypothesis that the deal was rigged.

51. One could even grant Crick the point that probability considerations apply when one predicts something in advance. Before scientists discovered that the genetic code contains literal information as in a language, most would have predicted that the possibility of discovering meaningful information in the universe was very small and such a discovery would have been seen as pointing to intelligence (e.g., in radio scans of outer space for a message from extraterrestrial intelligence). For helpful expositions of the probability issues we are discussing, see Henry M. Morris, *Creation and the Modern Christian* (El Cajon, Calif.: Master, 1985), pp. 162–64; *King of Creation* (San Diego: C.L.P. Publishers, 1980), pp. 132–36. In his otherwise excellent discussion (especially in *King of Creation*) Morris makes the same mistake that Crick does. He says the outcome must be prespecified instead of independently specified. Another article which is quite helpful, though a bit technical, is Richard Campbell and Thomas Vinci, "Why Are Novel Predictions Important?" *Pacific Philosophical Quarterly* 63 (April 1982): 111–21.

Theism provides a way of marking off as special the various aspects of design in the cosmos (they are features which usually go with intelligence) and the theist has an explanatory hypothesis that makes such features probable. The naturalistic view can only mark off these examples by saying that the conditions which generated them are just there—they are simply the ones which occurred. And the naturalist faces the adoption of a hypothesis (accidental, random events) which is exceedingly unlikely.

We have considered the various kinds of design used in design arguments and the major forms that design arguments have taken. We have considered a number of objections raised against the design argument(s) and responded to those objections. It seems to me that the design argument still has considerable force, but I leave it to the reader to weigh the evidence for himself.

3

God and the Argument from Mind

At the beginning of his *Institutes of the Christian Religion*, John Calvin observes: "No man can survey himself without forthwith turning his thoughts towards the God in whom he lives and moves; because it is perfectly obvious, that the endowments which we possess cannot possibly be from ourselves. . . ."[1] A number of thinkers have made similar observations. How could consciousness have evolved from matter? Can matter think? If we are simply material beings, then determinism is

---

1. John Calvin, *Institutes of the Christian Religion* (1536; Grand Rapids: Associated Publishers and Authors, n.d.), 1.1.1.

true for all human processes. But if we are determined, why should we trust our own thought processes? These questions are associated with a family of arguments which have gone by different names—the anthropological argument, the argument from mind or consciousness, or the argument from rationality. In one way or another, these arguments point out that man as a rational agent implies God as the Ground or Cause of his rationality.[2]

The purpose of this chapter is to clarify and defend a case for God's existence from the existence of rational minds in human beings. First, mind/body dualism will be explained and defended by offering general arguments for dualism and by centering in on an argument which tries to show that physicalism—the view that reality in general, and humans in particular, are made up entirely of matter—is self-refuting. Second, we will explore the possibility that rational minds evolved from matter and try to show why this is not plausible. This will lend support to the view that our rational minds come from another rational Mind—God.

Arguments for Dualism

Dualism Defined

The mind/body problem focuses on two main issues. First, is a human being composed of just one ultimate component or two? Second, if the answer is two, how do these two relate to one another? Physicalism is one solution to the problem. As a general worldview, physicalism holds that the only thing which exists is matter (where matter is defined by an ideal, completed form of physics). Applied to the mind/body problem, physicalism asserts that a human being is just a physical system. There is no mind or soul, just a brain and central nervous system.[3] Dualism is the opponent of physicalism and it asserts that in addition to the body, a human being

2. See J. R. Lucas, *The Freedom of the Will* (Oxford: Clarendon Press, 1970), pp. 114–23; A. C. Ewing, *Value and Reality* (London: George Allen and Unwin, 1973), pp. 76–77, 176–78; Richard Purtill, *Reason to Believe* (Grand Rapids: Eerdmans, 1974), pp. 38–49; Stephen Clark, *From Athens to Jerusalem* (Oxford: Clarendon Press, 1984), pp. 96–157; C. S. Lewis, *Miracles: A Preliminary Study* (New York: Macmillan, 1947), pp. 2–39.

3. Helpful introductory works on the mind/body problem are Jerome A. Shaffer, *Philosophy of Mind*, Foundations of Philosophy series (Englewood Cliffs, N.J.: Prentice-Hall, 1968); Paul M. Churchland, *Matter and Consciousness: A Contemporary Introduction to the Philosophy of Mind* (Cambridge, Mass.: MIT Press, 1984); Keith Campbell, *Body and Mind*, Problems in Philosophy series (Garden City, N.Y.: Doubleday, Anchor Books, 1970). Shaffer's work is a bit dated and Churchland's is heavily biased toward physicalism, but both are still helpful. Campbell's book is fairly balanced. The three main varieties of modern physicalism are the identity thesis, functionalism, and eliminative materialism. These three are discussed in David Rosenthal, ed., *Materialism and the Mind-Body Problem*, Central Issues in Philosophy series (Englewood Cliffs, N.J.: Prentice-Hall, 1971).

also has a nonphysical component called a soul, mind, or self (words which will be used interchangeably for our purposes).

There are two main varieties of dualism—property dualism and substance dualism. In order to understand the difference, we must first spell out the distinction between a property and a substance. A property is an entity: redness, hardness, wisdom, triangularity, or painfulness. A property has at least four characteristics which distinguish it from a substance. First, a property is a universal, not a particular. It can be in more than one thing or at more than one place at the same time. Redness can be in my coat and your flag at the same time. Second, a property is immutable and does not contain opposites (hot and cold, red and green) within it. When a leaf goes from green to red, the *leaf* changes. Greenness does not become redness. Greenness leaves the leaf and redness replaces it. Greenness and redness remain the same. Third, properties can be had by something else. They can be in another thing which has them. Redness is in the apple. The apple *has* the redness. Fourth, properties do not have causal powers. They do not act as efficient causes. Properties are not agents which act on other agents in the world.

A substance is an entity like an apple, my dog Fido, a carbon atom, a leaf, or an angel. Substances contrast with properties in the four characteristics listed. First, substances are particulars. For example, my dog Fido cannot be in more than one place at the same time. Second, a substance can change and have opposites. A leaf can go from green to red or hot to cold by gaining or losing properties. During the process of change, the substance gains and loses properties, but it is still the same substance. The same leaf which was green is now red. Third, substances are basic, fundamental existents. They are not *in* other things or *had by* other things. Fido is not a property of some more basic entity. Rather, Fido *has* properties. Fido is a unity of properties (dogness, brownness, shape), parts (paws, teeth, ears), and dispositions or capacities (law-like tendencies to realize certain properties in the process of growth if certain conditions obtain; for instance, the capacity to grow teeth if the fetus is nourished). They are all united into the substance Fido and possessed by him. Finally, a substance has causal powers. It can act as a causal agent in the world. A carbon atom can act on another atom. A dog can bark or pick up a bone. A leaf can hit the ground.

Property dualists hold that the mind is a property of the body. As Richard Taylor puts it, "A person is a living physical body having mind, the mind consisting, however, of nothing but a more or less continuous series of conscious or unconscious states and events . . . which are the effects but never the causes of bodily activity."[4] This view is called *epiphenomenalism*.

---

4. Richard Taylor, *Metaphysics* (Englewood Cliffs, N.J.: Prentice-Hall, 1963), p. 28.

The mind is to the body as smoke is to fire. Smoke is different from fire, but smoke does not cause anything. Smoke is a byproduct of fire. Similarly, mind is a byproduct of the body which does not cause anything. It just "rides" on top of the events in the body. Body events cause mind as a byproduct. The mind is a property of the body which ceases to exist when the body ceases to function.

Though some theists have denied it recently, the historic Christian view has been substance dualism. The mind, distinct from the body, is a real substance which can cause things to happen by acting and which can exist when the body ceases to function.[5]

Dualism Defended

Problems with Physicalism as a General Worldview

Physicalism as a worldview holds that everything that exists is nothing but a single spatio-temporal system which can be completely described in terms of some ideal form of physics.[6] Matter/energy is all that exists. God, souls, and nonphysical abstract entities do not exist. If physicalism is true at the worldview level, then obviously, mind/body physicalism would follow. But is physicalism adequate as a worldview? Several factors indicate that it is not.

First, if theism is true, then physicalism as a worldview is false. God is not a physical being. Second, a number of people have argued that numbers exist and that they are abstract, nonphysical entities (e.g., sets, substances, or properties).[7] Several arguments can be offered for the existence of numbers, but two appear frequently. For one thing, mathematics claims to give us knowledge. But if this is so, there must be something that mathematics is about. Just as the biologist *discovers* biological truths about biological objects (organisms), so the mathematician often *discovers* mathematical truths (he does not invent them all the time) and these truths are about mathematical objects. If one denies the existence of numbers, then it is hard to rescue mathematics as a field which conveys knowledge about

---

5. Examples of Christian writers who have denied substance dualism are Richard Bube, *The Human Quest* (Waco: Word, 1971), pp. 29–37, 134–59; Donald M. MacKay, *Human Science and Human Dignity* (Downers Grove: Inter-Varsity, 1979); David Myers, *The Human Puzzle: Psychological Research and Christian Belief* (San Francisco: Harper and Row, 1978). My own view is that substance dualism is the biblical view, but this does not mean Descartes's version of dualism. More in line with the biblical data is the dualism of Aristotle or Aquinas. For a good treatment of the relationship between substance, soul, and mind in both Aristotle and Aquinas, see Thomas Ragusa, *The Substance Theory of Mind and Contemporary Functionalism* (Washington, D.C.: Catholic University of America, 1937). A good treatment of biblical anthropology is Robert Gundry, *Soma in Biblical Theology* (Cambridge: Cambridge University Press, 1976).

6. See D. M. Armstrong, *Nominalism and Scientific Realism*, 2 vols. (Cambridge: Cambridge University Press, 1978), 1:126–32.

7. A brief discussion of the issues involved in the existence of numbers and modern set theory can be found in Keith Campbell, *Metaphysics: An Introduction* (Encino, Calif.: Dickenson, 1976), pp. 200–205.

something. Without numbers, mathematics becomes merely an internally consistent game which is invented.

A second argument is often given for holding to the existence of numbers. Scientific laws and theories seem to assert their existence. For example, a calcium ion has a positive charge of two which is expressed in the formula Ca^{+2}. The number two here seems to be more than a mere formula for calculating relative amounts of compounds in laboratory reactions. Two expresses a property of the calcium ion itself. The property of twoness is just as much a real property of the charge of the calcium as the property of positiveness. If one denies that numbers exist, it is hard to continue to maintain that science gives us a real description of the world rather than a set of operations that work in the laboratory. In sum, without numbers, mathematical and scientific knowledge is hard to maintain. But if numbers exit, physicalism as a worldview is false because numbers are not physical entities.

Some have argued that values, in addition to God and numbers, exist and are not physical.[8] Certain objects (persons, animals) and certain events (helping a stranger, for example) have a nonphysical property of worth or goodness. Furthermore, moral laws are often held to be absolute, objective realities (e.g., one should not torture babies). But if certain objects possess goodness, and if certain moral laws are objective realities, then physicalism must be false, because the property of goodness and the nature of moral laws are not physical. For example, it makes no sense to ask how much goodness weighs, or to ask where a moral law exists. Such realities are not physical.

Fourth, if physicalism is true, it is hard to see what one should make of the existence and nature of theories, meanings, concepts, propositions, the laws of logic, and truth itself. It would seem that theories themselves exist and can be discovered. The laws of logic seem to be real laws that govern the relationships between propositions. Propositions seem to exist and be the content of thoughts which become associated with the physical scratchings of a given language called sentences. Sentences may be made of black ink, be on a page, and be four inches long. But it is hard to see how the *content* of the sentence (i.e., the proposition or thought expressed by the sentence) could be on the page. Such entities seem to be nonphysical entities which can be in the mind.[9] Truth appears to be a relation of corre-

8. For a good treatment of how different ethical systems view the ontological status of value, see C. D. Broad, *Five Types of Ethical Theory* (London: Routledge and Kegan Paul, 1930).

9. Physicalists attempt to do away with semantic notions like "truth," "denotation," and "proposition" by reducing them to sentences (strings of physical markings) and the like. For two examples of this strategy, see Hartry Field, "Tarski's Theory of Truth," *The Journal of Philosophy* 69 (July 1972): 347–75; W. V. O. Quine, *Philosophy of Logic* (Englewood Cliffs, N.J.: Prentice-Hall, 1970), pp. 1–14. For a critique of such physicalist strategies, see Dallas Willard, *Logic and the Objectivity of Knowledge: Studies in Husserl's Early Philosophy* (Athens, Ohio: Ohio University Press, 1984), pp. 205–18. Three good defenses of the existence

spondence between a thought and the world. If a thought really describes the world accurately, it is true. It stands to the world in a relation of correspondence. But whatever else one wants to say about the relation of correspondence, it does not seem to be a physical relation like cause and effect.

Finally, universals seem to exist and they are not material.[10] A universal is an entity that can be in more than one place at the same time. Some universals are properties (redness, hardness, triangularity); others are relations (larger than, to the left of). Whatever else one may use to characterize the nature of matter, it is clear that a clump of matter is a particular. A piece of matter cannot be in more than one place at the same time. Physicalists deny the existence of universals at the level of general worldview, because universals are not physical entities.

The entities listed have caused a lot of difficulty for physicalists. They have spent a good deal of time trying to do away with numbers, values, propositions, laws of logic, and universals by reducing them to notions compatible with physicalism. But these reductionist attempts have failed and physicalism as a worldview cannot adequately handle the existence of these entities. Theism can embrace them, however, by holding that God created these nonphysical entities and sustains them in existence. The falsity of physicalism as a worldview does not refute mind/body physicalism. One could hold to the existence of numbers and values but deny the existence of the soul. But much of the motivation for mind/body physicalism has been the desire to argue for physicalism at the worldview level. If physicalism at that level is false, then part of the reason for holding to mind/body physicalism is removed. For example, just because one cannot see the soul, weigh it, or say where it is, it does not follow that the soul does not exist. One cannot see, weigh, or locate numbers or values, but they still exist.[11]

---

of propositions are Alonzo Church, "The Need for Abstract Entities in Semantic Analysis," in *Contemporary Readings in Logical Theory,* ed. Irving M. Copi and James A. Gould (New York: Macmillan, 1967), pp. 194–203; George Bealer, *Quality and Concept* (Oxford: Clarendon Press, 1982); Dallas Willard, "The Paradox of Logical Psychologism: Husserl's Way Out," *American Philosophical Quarterly* 9 (January 1972): 94–100. The question arises as to what the basic entities are which are involved in the laws of logic. For a survey of different attempts to answer that question, see Dallas Willard, "Husserl's Critique of Extensionalist Logic: 'A Logic That Does Not Understand Itself,'" *Idealistic Studies* 9 (May 1979): 143–64. Alvin Plantinga used the existence of propositions and truth to argue for God's existence in his presidential address ("How to Be an Anti-Realist") to the American Philosophical Association on April 29, 1982.

10. See J. P. Moreland, *Universals, Qualities, and Quality-Instances: A Defense of Realism* (Lanham, Md.: University Press of America, 1985). See also Howard Robinson, *Matter and Sense* (Cambridge: Cambridge University Press, 1982), pp. 46–50.

11. Matter is a difficult notion to understand, since the concept of matter has played such different roles in the history of philosophy. For different understandings of what matter is, see Ernan McMullin, ed., *The Concept of Matter in Greek and Medieval Philosophy* (Notre Dame: University of Notre Dame Press, 1963); *The Concept of Matter in Modern Philosophy* (Notre Dame: University of Notre Dame Press, 1963); M. P. Crosland, ed., *The Science of Matter* (Middlesex, England: Penguin, 1971); John Yolton, *Thinking Matter: Materialism in Eighteenth-Century Britain* (Minneapolis: University of Minnesota Press, 1984). For a criticism of several notions of matter, see Robinson, *Matter and Sense,* pp. 108–23.

Problems with Mind/Body Physicalism

In order to facilitate an understanding of some of the arguments against mind/body physicalism, we must first examine the nature of identity. Suppose you know that someone named J. P. Moreland exists and that the author of this book exists. Assume further that you do not know that J. P. Moreland wrote this book. If someone asked you whether J. P. Moreland is identical to the author of this book, how would you decide? How would you determine that the "two" individuals are identical instead of being two different people? If you could find something true of J. P. Moreland which is not true of the author of this book or vice versa, then they would be different people. They could not be identical. For example, if J. P. Moreland is married to Hope Moreland but the author of this book is not, they would be different people. On the other hand, if everything true of one is true of the other, "they" would be one person.

In general, if "two" things are identical, then whatever is true of the one is true of the other, since in reality only one thing is being discussed. However, if something is true of the one which is not true of the other, then they are two things and not one. This is sometimes called the indiscernibility of identicals and is expressed as follows:

$$(x)\,(y)\,[(x=y) \rightarrow (P)\,(Px \leftrightarrow Py)]$$

For any entities x and y, if x and y are really the same thing, then for any property P, P is true of x if and only if P is true of y. If x is the mind and y is a part or state of the body (e.g., the brain), then if physicalism is true, x must be identical to y.[12] On the other hand, if something is true of the mind which is not true of some part or state of the body, then the mind is not identical to the body and physicalism is false. This would be true even if the mind and body are inseparable. The roundness of an apple cannot be separated from its redness. One does not find redness sitting on a table by itself and roundness sitting next to it. But the redness of an apple is not identical to the roundness of the apple. One is a color and one is a shape.

Every time something happens in the mind (someone has a thought of an ice cream cone), some event may be going on in the brain which could be described by a neurophysiologist. In general, brain events may always have mental events that correlate with them and vice versa. They may be inseparable in that one does not occur without the other in an embodied

---

12. Functionalism is somewhat illusive on this point, since it identifies a mental state with a functional state which receives certain input, gives certain output, and advances to another internal state. Thus mental states are likened to the software and not the hardware of simple computation machines (e.g., Turing machines). Nevertheless, functionalists who are materialists want to say that these states are ultimately physical in nature or are the behaviors of physical states. For an analysis and critique of various forms of functionalism, see Robinson, *Matter and Sense*.

person. But this does not mean that the mental thought is identical to the brain event. The redness and roundness of an apple, though inseparable, are not identical. The property of having three sides (trilaterality) and the property of having three angles (triangularity) always go together. They are inseparable. But they are not identical. Physicalists must not only show that mental and brain phenomena are inseparable to make their case. They must also show that they are identical. With this in mind let us turn to some arguments for dualism.

The Distinctiveness of Mental and Physical Properties   Mental events include thoughts, feelings of pain, the experience of being a person, or a sense image or picture of a ball in my mind. Physical events are events in the brain or central nervous system which can be described exhaustively using terms of chemistry, physics, and (for now) biology. The difficulty for physicalism is that mental events do not seem to have properties that hold for physical events. My thought of Kansas City is not ten centimeters long, it does not weigh anything, it is not located anywhere (it is not two inches from my left ear). Nor is it identical to any behavior or tendency to behave in a certain way (shouting "Kansas City" when I hear the name *George Brett*). But the brain event associated with this thought may be located inside my head, it may have a certain chemical composition and electrical current, and so forth. My afterimage of a ball (the impression of the ball present to my consciousness when I close my eyes after seeing the ball) may be pink, but nothing in my brain is pink. Mental events and properties have different attributes and therefore they are not identical.

Private Access and Incorrigibility   I seem to be in a position to know my own thoughts and mental processes in a way not available to anyone else. I am in a privileged position with regard to my own mental life. I have private access to my own thoughts in a way not open to anyone else. Furthermore, my mental states seem to be incorrigible, at least some of the time. That is, I cannot be mistaken about them.[13] Suppose I am experiencing what I take to be a green rug. It is possible that the rug is not there or that the light is poor and the rug is really gray. I could be mistaken about the rug itself. But it does not seem to be possible for me to be mistaken that I am experiencing what I take to be a green rug right now. That is, my mental state is directly present to me and I know my own mental states immediately.

It would be possible for a brain surgeon to know more about my brain than I do. He may be looking into my brain, seeing it better than I, and

---

13. See Roderick Chisholm, *The First Person: An Essay on Reference and Intentionality* (Minneapolis: University of Minnesota Press, 1981), pp. 75–91.

knowing its operations better than I. But he does not—indeed, he cannot—know my mental life as well as I. I have private, privileged access to that. Further, it seems that one could always be wrong about his knowledge of some physical state of affairs in the world. The brain surgeon could be wrong about what is happening in my brain. But I cannot be wrong about what is currently happening in my mind. It would seem then that I have privileged, private access to my mental states which is sometimes incorrigible. But neither I nor anyone else has private access to my brain states, and whatever access someone has is irreducibly third-person access (described from a standpoint outside of me) and is not incorrigible.[14]

The Experience of First-Person Subjectivity   The subjective character of experience is hard to capture in physicalist terms.[15] The simple fact of consciousness is a serious difficulty for physicalism. To see this consider the following. Suppose a deaf scientist became the world's leading expert on the neurology of hearing. It would be possible for him to know and describe everything there is to the physical processes involved in hearing. However, something would still be left out of such a description—the experience of what it is like to be a human who hears. As Howard Robinson puts it:

> The notion of *having something as an object of experience* is not, *prima facie*, a physical notion; it does not figure in any physical science. *Having something as an object of experience* is the same as the subjective feel or the *what it is like* of experience.[16]

14. See H. D. Lewis, *The Elusive Self* (Philadelphia: Westminster, 1982), pp. 20–32. On pp. 31–33 of *Matter and Consciousness*, Churchland criticizes the argument I am advancing as an example of the intensional fallacy in logic. In normal, truth-functional logic the connectives ("if, then," "if and only if," "or," "and," "not") are extensional. Equals can be substituted for equals and truth is preserved. Thus, if $P = Q$, then it is correct to say that if one has Q or S, $-S$, therefore Q, one can also have P or S, $-S$, therefore P. But in intensional contexts where one has words like "know," "believe," or "recognize," equals cannot be substituted for equals and preserve truth. I may know that Muhammad Ali was the world champion, but I may *not* know that Cassius Clay was the world champion (if I fail to know that Clay is identical to Ali). It is the intensional fallacy to assume that such substitutions can be made in intensional contexts. Similarly, I may know my mental states and not know my brain states, but the two may still be identical, says Churchland, if I fail to appreciate that such an identity holds. Two responses can be given to Churchland. First, my argument from private access does not turn on a supposed ignorance of an identity between mental and brain states, but on a difference in the relations I sustain with them. My mental states are directly present to me and my brain states are not, and this difference in relation is what makes the former have incorrigibility. If two entities stand in different relations with other things, they cannot be identical. Second, the very existence of irreducibly intensional contexts that defy extensional treatment is evidence for dualism. See George Bealer, "The Logical Status of Mind," in *Studies in the Philosophy of Mind*, ed. Peter A. French, Theodore Uehling, and Howard Wettstein, Midwest Studies in Philosophy, vol. 10 (Minneapolis: University of Minnesota Press, 1986), pp. 231–74.

15. Thomas Nagel, "What Is It Like to Be a Bat?" in his *Mortal Questions* (Cambridge: Cambridge University Press, 1979), pp. 165–80.

16. Robinson, *Matter and Sense*, p. 7.

Subjective states of experiences exist. My experience of what it is like to be me, to hear a bird or see a tree, exists, and I have a first-person subjectivity to it. Such first-person experiences of my own self or "I" which has experiences cannot be reduced to a third-person "he" or "it," because the latter do not describe the experience itself or its first-person standpoint. A physicalist, scientific description of the world leaves out this character of subjective awareness. Such a description characterizes the world in impersonal, third-person terms (e.g., "there exists an object with such and such properties and states") and leaves out the first-person, subjective experience itself (e.g., "I feel sad and food tastes sour to me").

Speaking of the character of subjective awareness, Thomas Nagel has this to say:

> If physicalism is to be defended, the phenomenological features [the sounds, colors, smells, tastes of experience that make the experience what it is] must themselves be given a physical account. But when we examine their subjective character it seems that such a result is impossible. The reason is that every subjective phenomenon is essentially connected with a single point of view, and it seems inevitable that an objective, physical theory will abandon that point of view.[17]

Secondary Qualities   Secondary qualities are qualities such as colors, tastes, sounds, smells, and textures. Physicalism seems to imply that such qualities do not exist in the external world. But we do sense such qualities, so where are they, if they are not in the external world? They must exist as sense data (mental objects or images) in the mind. Frank Jackson has put the point this way:

> It is a commonplace that there is an apparent clash between the picture Science gives of the world around us and the picture our senses give us. We *sense* the world as made up of coloured, materially continuous, macroscopic, stable objects; Science and, in particular, Physics, tells us that the material world is constituted of clouds of minute, colourless, highly-mobile particles. . . . Science forces us to acknowledge that physical or material things are not coloured. . . . This will enable us to conclude that sense-data are all mental, for they are coloured.[18]

17. Nagel, p. 167. See also Geoffrey Maddell, *The Identity of the Self* (Edinburgh: The University Press, 1981). The fact that first-person subjectivity cannot be reduced to a third-person point of view without making essential reference to a mental state can be seen by noting that philosophers who reduce an A-Series view of time to a B-Series still have to refer to conscious mental states in order to account for our experience of temporal becoming. For more on this, see Richard M. Gale, ed., *The Philosophy of Time* (New York: Humanities Press, 1968), pp. 65–85. Note especially pp. 73–74.

18. Frank Jackson, *Perception* (Cambridge: Cambridge University Press, 1977), p. 121. See also Colin McGinn, *The Subjective View* (Oxford: Clarendon Press, 1983).

In other words, science does away with secondary qualities, but since we know they do exist—we see them—they must exist in our minds as sense data. This shows that there must be minds, and sense data must be little images or pictures which exist as mental objects in minds.

I do not accept this understanding of secondary qualities, because it implies that I do not see the world when I use my senses. Rather, it implies that I see my sense images of the world.[19] But if this view is correct, then it would seem that some form of dualism is correct. If, on the other hand, one holds (as I do) that secondary qualities are real properties of objects in the world, physicalism as a worldview may still be in trouble. If macroscopic objects (regular-sized tables, apples, dogs) do have properties of color, odor, stability, continuous surfaces, and the like, then there must be more to them than what physics tells us. Physics tends to reduce objects to mere heaps of colorless, odorless, rapid-moving packets of matter/energy. But if objects have macroproperties which escape description in these terms, then these properties, call them metaphysical properties, are not physical. That does not mean that they are mental. But it does show that a full treatment of objects must appeal to metaphysical properties which deal with the objects as wholes. If physicalism reduces objects to the mere heaps of microphysics, then physicalism is incomplete as a worldview. On the other hand, if secondary qualities are in fact mental sense data, then physicalism is inadequate as a mind/body theory. Either way, physicalism as a general theory is in trouble.

Intentionality   Some have argued that the mark of the mental is intentionality. Intentionality is the mind's aboutness or ofness. Mental states point beyond themselves to other objects even if those objects do not exist. I have a thought *about* my wife, I hope *for* a new car, I dream *of* a unicorn. The mind has the ability to transcend itself and be of or about something else. This aboutness is not a property of anything physical.[20] Some physicalists have tried to reduce intentionality to the mere ability to receive input, give output, and advance to some other internal state. A computer receives input from a keyboard, gives output on a printer, and advances to a new internal state where it is ready to receive new input. But the com-

---

19. For a critique of this view of perception, see Dallas Willard, "A Crucial Error in Epistemology," *Mind* 76 (October 1967): 513–23.

20. John Searle tries to argue that intentionality is just a property of a physical system. But his view leads to a denial of real intentionality and leads Searle to adopt physical determinism, a position with which he is somewhat uncomfortable. See his *Minds, Brains, and Science* (Cambridge: Harvard University Press, 1985). In the same vein, Peter Smith and O. R. Jones argue that mental states can be treated as functional states which are mere physical happenings. But like Searle, they are forced to deny real human freedom and they settle for a reduced form of freedom compatible with determinism. See Peter Smith and O. R. Jones, *The Philosophy of Mind* (Cambridge: Cambridge University Press, 1986), pp. 252–68.

puter still has no awareness of or about anything.[21] It seems, then, that physical states do not have intentionality and thus the fact of intentionality is evidence that the self is not physical but mental.

Personal Identity   Imagine a wooden table which had all its parts removed one by one and replaced by metal parts. When the top and all the legs were replaced would it still be the same table? The answer would seem to be no. In fact, it would be possible to take all the original wooden parts and rearrange them into the original table. Even when the table had just one leg replaced, it would not literally be the same table. It would be a table similar to the original.

Losing old parts and gaining new ones changes the identity of the object in question. But now a question arises regarding persons. Am I literally the same self that I was a moment ago? Are my baby pictures really pictures of *me* or are they pictures of an ancestor of me who resembles me? I am constantly losing physical parts. I lose hair and fingernails; atoms are constantly being replaced, and every seven years my cells are almost entirely replaced. Do I maintain literal, absolute identity through change or not?

Substance dualists argue that persons do maintain absolute identity through change, because they have, in addition to their bodies, a soul that remains constant through change, and personal identity is constituted by sameness of soul, not sameness of body.[22]

Physicalists have no alternative but to hold that personal identity is not absolute. Usually they argue that persons are really ancestral chains of successive "selves" which are connected with one another in some way. At each moment a new self exists (since the self or physical organism is constantly in flux, losing and gaining parts) and this self resembles the self prior to and after it. The relation of resemblance between selves plus the fact that later selves have the same memories as earlier selves and the body of each self traces a continuous path through space when the whole chain of selves is put together, constitute a relative sense of personal identity.

So substance dualists hold to a literal, absolute sense of personal identity and physicalists hold to a loose, relative sense of personal identity which amounts to a stream of successive selves held together into "one" person by resemblance between each self (also called a person stage), sim-

21. See Hilary Putnam, *Reason, Truth, and History* (Cambridge: Cambridge University Press, 1981), pp. 8–12. Putnam asks us to imagine a case where two computers are connected in such a way that the input of one feeds into the output of the other and vice versa. In such a case, the two computers could "talk" to each other forever and "refer" to things in the world, even if the world disappeared! This example illustrates that intentionality cannot be identified with a functionalist analysis in terms of artificial intelligence.

22. This does not mean that the soul is inert and static. See David Wiggins, *Sameness and Substance* (Cambridge: Harvard University Press, 1980).

ilarity of memory, and spatial continuity. For the physicalist, a person becomes a space-time worm (i.e., a path traced through space and time). The
person is the entire path marked off at the time and place of his birth and
death. At any given moment and location where "I" happen to be, "I" am
not a person, just a person stage. The person is the whole path. So there is
no literal sameness through change.

But now certain problems arise for physicalism.[23] First, why should "I"
ever fear the future? When it gets here, "I" will not be present; rather, another self who looks like me will be there but "I" will have ceased to exist.
Second, why should anyone be punished? The self who did the crime in
the past is not literally the same self who is present at the time of punishment. Physicalism seems to require a radical readjustment of our
common-sense notions of future expectations and past actions because
both presuppose a literal identity of the same self present in past, present,
and future.

Third, physicalists not only have difficulty handling the unity of the self
through time, but also cannot explain the unity of the self at a given time.
As Harvard philosopher W. V. O. Quine puts it, according to physicalism
the self becomes a sum or heap of scattered physical parts. The unity of the
self is like the unity of an assembly of building blocks. If I have a pain in my
foot while I am thinking about baseball, each is a distinct experience involving different physical parts. There is no self which *has* each experience. The self is merely a bundle or heap of parts and experiences. It has no
real unity. The dualist says that the soul is diffused throughout the body
and it is present before each experience. The soul has each experience. The
unity of consciousness is due to the fact that the same soul is the possessor
of each and every experience of consciousness. But the physicalist must
say that each experience is possessed by different parts of the body and
there is no real unity. However, my own experience of the unity of my consciousness shows this unity to be genuine and not arbitrary. *I* have my experiences. They are all *mine*. Physicalism does not adequately explain this
fact.

Morality, Responsibility, and Punishment   As will be shown shortly,
physicalism seems to imply determinism. If I am just matter, then my
actions are not the result of free choice. They are determined by the laws of
chemistry and physics plus boundary conditions. For example, the position of a bullet can be calculated given Newton's laws plus the initial position and velocity of the bullet. But then it is hard to make sense of moral
obligation and responsibility. If I "ought" to do something, it seems to be

23. See Maddell, *Identity of the Self,* pp. 15–16; H. D. Lewis, *The Self and Immortality,* ed. John H. Hick,
Philosophy of Religion series (New York: Seabury, Crossroad Books, 1973), pp. 29–46.

necessary to suppose that I *can* do it. No one would say that I ought to jump to the top of a fifty-floor building to save a baby, since it is not possible for me to do that. But if physicalism is true, I do not have any genuine ability to choose my actions. It is safe to say that physicalism requires a radical revision of our common-sense notions of freedom, moral obligation, responsibility, and punishment.[24] If these common-sense notions are true, then physicalism is false.

This completes our survey of some of the major arguments for dualism. More could be said about each point, but perhaps enough has been offered to indicate the kinds of arguments relevant to a defense of dualism. There is, however, a major argument for dualism which may be the most important one. To this argument we now turn.

Mind/Body Physicalism Refuted

A number of philosophers have argued that physicalism must be false because it implies determinism and determinism is self-refuting.[25] Speaking of the determinist, J. R. Lucas says,

> If what he says is true, he says it merely as the result of his heredity and environment, and of nothing else. He does not hold his determinist views because they are true, but because he has such-and-such stimuli; that is, not because the *structure* of the universe is such-and-such but only because the configuration of only part of the universe, together with the structure of the determinist's brain, is such as to produce that result. . . . Determinism, therefore, cannot be true, because if it was, we should not take the determinists' arguments as being really arguments, but as being only conditioned reflexes. Their statements should not be regarded as really claiming to be true, but only as seeking to cause us to respond in some way desired by them.[26]

H. P. Owen states that

> determinism is self-stultifying. If my mental processes are totally determined, I am totally determined either to accept or to reject determinism. But if the sole reason for my believing or not believing X is that I am causally de-

---

24. See Bruce R. Reichenbach, *Is Man the Phoenix?* (Grand Rapids: Eerdmans, 1978), pp. 105–11.

25. I am not advancing a design argument to the effect that, if our minds were not designed, we would have no reason to trust their operations and deliverances. This sort of argument was advanced in chapter 2. Evolutionists point out, in response to this form of argument, that the mind's rational abilities aided the possessors of those abilities in the struggle for survival. But this is far from obvious. Some evolutionists point out that such rational activities require an increased information-processing capacity in the nervous system which is actually a reproductive liability prenatally (such a system requires a longer and more vulnerable gestation period) and postnatally (it takes longer to raise and teach the young). See John Barrow and Frank Tipler, *The Anthropic Cosmological Principle* (Oxford: Clarendon Press, 1986), pp. 129–33.

26. Lucas, *Freedom of the Will,* pp. 114–15.

termined to believe it I have no ground for holding that my judgment is true or false.[27]

Others have pointed out that property dualism (epiphenomenalism) suffers at the hands of this argument no less than does strict physicalism. A. C. Ewing holds that

if epiphenomenalism is true, it follows that nobody can be justified in believing it. On the epiphenomenalist view what causes a belief is always a change in the brain and never the apprehension of any reason for holding it. So if epiphenomenalism is true, neither it nor anything else can ever be believed for any good reason whatever.[28]

Hans Jonas echoes this sentiment by saying that the epiphenomenalist

passes judgment on himself by what his thesis says about the possible validity of any thesis whatsoever and, therefore, about the validity claim of his own. Every theory, even the most mistaken, is a tribute to the power of thought, to which in the very meaning of the theorizing act it is allowed that it can rise above the power of extramental determinations, that it can judge freely on what is given in the field of representations, that it is, first of all, capable of the *resolve* for truth, i.e., the resolve to follow the guidance of insight and not the drift of fancies. But epiphenomenalism contends the impotence of thinking and therewith its *own* inability to be independent theory. Indeed, even the extreme materialist must exempt himself *qua* thinker, so that extreme materialism as a doctrine be possible.[29]

In order to understand these statements, let us first examine the nature of self-refutation and then see why physicalism (and epiphenomenalism) is self-refuting.

What Is Self-Refutation?

A statement is about its subject matter. The statement "dogs are mammals" is about dogs. Some statements refer to themselves; that is, they are

---

27. H. P. Owen, *Christian Theism* (Edinburgh: T. and T. Clark, 1984), p. 118.

28. Ewing, *Value and Reality*, p. 77.

29. Hans Jonas, *On Faith, Reason, and Responsibility* (Claremont, Calif.: The Institute for Antiquity and Christianity, 1981), p. 43. For an application of this point to evolution, see Stanley L. Jaki, *Angels, Apes, and Men* (La Salle, Ill.: Sugden, 1982), pp. 51–60. C. S. Lewis used an argument of this sort to argue for God's existence in his book on miracles. G. E. M. Anscombe subsequently critiqued Lewis's argument, which led him to revise his view. For a favorable treatment of Lewis on this point, see Richard Purtill, *C. S. Lewis's Case for the Christian Faith* (San Francisco: Harper and Row, 1981), pp. 22–27. For a critique of Lewis, see John Beversluis, *C. S. Lewis and the Search for Rational Religion* (Grand Rapids: Eerdmans, 1985), pp. 58–83. Beversluis's critique is too detailed to examine here, but it should be pointed out that he grants that Lewis refutes a rather strict form of reductionist physicalism. However, Beversluis thinks that epiphenomenalism (he specifies his own view in terms of complementarity, not unlike Donald M. MacKay) is not refuted. But epiphenomenalism *is* refuted by Lewis's argument, for it is a compatiblist view of freedom which has no real agent theory of the self.

included in their own field of reference. The statement "all sentences of English are short" makes a statement about all English sentences, including itself. When a statement fails to satisfy itself (i.e., to conform to its own criteria of validity or acceptability), it is self-refuting.[30] Such statements are necessarily false. The facts which falsify them are unavoidably given with the statement when it is uttered.

Consider some examples. "I cannot say a word of English" is self-refuting when uttered in English. "I do not exist" is self-refuting, for one must exist to utter it. The claim "there are no truths" is self-refuting. If it is false, then it is false. But if it is true, then it is false as well, for in that case there would be no truths, including the statement itself.

On the other hand, the claim "there are no moral truths" is not self-refuting, for it is not necessarily a *moral* statement. The claim becomes self-refuting if it is combined with the claim that one *ought* (morally) to be a relativist. This second claim has a morally absolute sense of "ought" which the first claim rules out. The statement "there is no knowledge" is not self-refuting, since the one uttering the claim could merely believe the statement to be true without claiming to *know* it to be true. But if he claims to know this statement, then his claim is self-refuting, for he now claims to know there is no knowledge. In sum, if a statement is self-refuting, it refers to itself, it fails to satisfy its own criteria of acceptability, and it cannot be true.

Why Is Physicalism Self-Refuting?

Physicalism is self-refuting in much the same way that the example about knowledge is self-refuting. Assuming that theism is false and that a coherent notion of truth can be spelled out on physicalist assumptions (I have already argued against this latter assumption), physicalism could be true and the claim that it is true is not self-refuting. The world could have had nothing but matter in it. But if one claims to know that physicalism is true, or to embrace it for good reasons, if one claims that it is a rational position which should be chosen on the basis of evidence, then this claim is self-refuting. This is so because physicalism seems to deny the possibility of rationality. To see this, let us examine the necessary precon-

---

30. The following are good treatments of the nature of self-refutation: Michael Stack, "Self-Refuting Arguments," *Metaphilosophy* 14 (July/October 1983): 327–35; George Mavrodes, "Self-Referential Incoherence," *American Philosophical Quarterly* 22 (January 1985): 65–72; Carl Kordig, "Self-Reference and Philosophy," *American Philosophical Quarterly* 20 (April 1983): 207–16; Joseph Boyle, "Self-Referential Inconsistence, Inevitable Falsity, and Metaphysical Argumentation," *Metaphilosophy* 3 (January 1972): 25–42. In what follows I will not make a distinction among sentences, propositions, and statements. Such a distinction is important but too detailed for the level of discussion I am advancing. See the article by Boyle for more on this subject.

ditions which must hold if there is to be such a thing as rationality and show how physicalism denies these preconditions.

At least five factors must obtain if there are to be genuine rational agents who can accurately reflect on the world. First, minds must have intentionality; they must be capable of having thoughts *about* or *of* the world. Acts of inference are "insights into" or "knowings of" something other than themselves.

Second, reasons, propositions, thoughts, laws of logic and evidence, and truth must exist and be capable of being instanced in people's minds and influencing their thought processes. This fact is hard to reconcile with physicalism. To see this, consider the field of ethics. Morality prescribes what we ought to do; it does not merely describe what is in fact done. Objective morality makes sense if real moral laws or oughts exist and if normative, moral properties like rightness, goodness, worth, and dignity exist in acts (the act of honoring one's parents) and things (persons and animals *have* worth). If physicalism is true as a worldview, there are no moral properties or full-blooded oughts. Physical states just are, and one physical state causes or fails to cause another physical state. A physical state does not morally prescribe that another physical state ought to be. If physicalism is true, oughts are not real moral obligations telling us what one should do to be in conformity with the moral universe. Rather, "ought" serves as a mere guide for reaching a socially accepted or psychologically desired goal (e.g., "If one wants to have pleasure and avoid pain, then one 'ought' to tell the truth"). Moral imperatives become grounded in subjective preferences on the same level as a preference for Burger King over McDonald's.

In the area of rationality, there are rational oughts. Given certain forms of evidence, one ought to believe some things. Reasons and evidence imply or support certain conclusions, and if one is to be objectively rational, one "ought" to accept these conclusions. For example, if one accepts the propositions "all men are mortals" and "Socrates is a man," then one ought to believe "Socrates is a mortal." Failure to do so makes one irrational. But if physicalism is true, it is hard to see how one mental state (the state of believing the first two propositions) could stand to another mental state (the state of believing the last proposition) in an inferential relation which prescribes that one ought to have the last mental state. For these are now mere physical states in the brain. And one physical state does not logically imply another or prescribe that the other "ought" to occur logically. It either causes or fails to cause that second state. Physical states simply are; they are not things that "ought" to be. The connection between premises and conclusion is not a physical relation of cause and effect. It is a logical relation of inference.

Stephen Clark puts it this way:

> Any merely materialistic or naturalistic metaphysician must have consider-
> able difficulty in accommodating any rules of evidence. If what I think is the
> echo or epiphenomenon merely of material processes, so that my thought is
> what it is because my neural chemistry is what it is, it seems very difficult to
> see how that thought can be one that I ought to have or ought not to have. It
> might of course be better (because more accurate?) if I did, or if I did not, but I
> can be under no obligation to have it, whether because it is true or because it
> 'follows' from other thoughts of mine, any more than I have an obligation to
> cause my heart to beat. My thoughts 'follow' from other thoughts only in the
> sense that the causal processes which accompany them, or which (on the
> strictest materialist interpretation) we misdescribe as 'thoughts', take place
> in ways that can be duplicated in test-tubes, and partially understood. True
> and consistent materialists ought not to claim that their arguments are ones
> which anyone ought to accept, or which anyone has any reason to think are
> true-in-fact. Materialism generates pragmatic relativism, and this in turn
> renders the materialist hypothesis a mere fable.[31]

Third, it is not enough for there to be propositions or reasons which
stand in logical and evidential relations with one another. One must be
able to "see" or have rational insight into the flow of the argument and be
influenced by this act of perception in forming one's beliefs. William
Hasker puts it this way:

> It is clear, when we consider the matter, that rational thinking must be
> *guided by rational insight* in the light of principles of sound reasoning. That is
> to say, one must "see," rationally, that the conclusion is justified by the
> evidence—and one is helped to see this by principles of reasoning, such as
> the laws of inductive and deductive logic and the like.[32]

If physicalism is true, it is hard to make sense of this form of seeing.
What sort of property of matter could one hold to which would enable matter to see in the sense of rational insight? Whatever property the physicalist
comes up with, one suspects it would be an old-fashioned mental property
by another name. Further, if propositions and the laws of logic do not exist,
then there is nothing there to see. Most dualists hold to the existence of the
laws of logic and thoughts (propositions, concepts) which can be instanced in minds and, therefore, seen with rational insight which is a capacity of a mind.

Fourth, in order for one to rationally think through a chain of reasoning
such that one sees the inferential connections in the chain, one would have
to be the same self present at the beginning of the thought process as the

31. Clark, *From Athens to Jerusalem*, pp. 96–97.
32. William Hasker, *Metaphysics: Constructing a World View* (Downers Grove: Inter-Varsity, 1983), p. 47.

one present at the end. As Immanuel Kant argued long ago, the process of thought requires a genuine enduring "I." In the syllogism about Socrates, if there is one self who reflects on premise 1, a second self who reflects on premise 2, and a third self who reflects on the conclusion, there is literally no enduring self who thinks *through* the argument and *draws* the conclusion. Physicalism has difficulty maintaining the existence of an enduring "I" and thus it has difficulty accounting for the need for such an "I" in the process of rational reflection. Thinking is a rational experience, and as H. D. Lewis has noted, "one thing seems certain, namely that there must be someone or something at the centre of such experience to hold the terms and relations of it together in one stream of consciousness."[33]

Finally, the activity of rational thought seems to require an agent view of the self which, in turn, involves four theses:

1. I must be able to deliberate, to reflect about what I am going to do. I deliberate about my behavior and not that of others, future events and not past ones, courses of action which I have not already settled. These facts of deliberation make sense only if I assume that my actions are "up to me" to perform or not perform.
2. I must have free will; that is, given choices *a* and *b*, I can genuinely do both. If I do *a*, I could have done otherwise. I could have chosen *b*. The past and present do not physically determine only one future. The future is open and depends, to some extent, on my free choices.
3. I am an agent. My acts are often self-caused. I am the absolute origin of my acts. My prior mental or physical states are not sufficient to determine what I will do. *I* must act as an agent.
4. Free will is incompatible with physical determinism. They cannot both be true at the same time.

If one is to be rational, one must be free to choose his beliefs based on reasons. One cannot be determined to react to stimuli by nonrational physical factors. If a belief is caused by entirely nonrational factors, it is not a belief that is embraced *because* it is reasonable. For a belief to be a rational one, I must be able to deliberate about whether or not I accept it, I must be free to choose it, and I must enter into the process as a genuine agent.[34]

Physical determinism is the view that, given a physical description of the world at a given time, it would be possible in principle to predict later states of the world, for they are causally settled by the laws of chemistry

33. Lewis, *The Self and Immortality*, p. 34.
34. It is interesting to read discussions of ethics with an agent theory of the self in mind. See Thomas Mappes and Jane Zembaty, *Biomedical Ethics*, 2d ed. (New York: McGraw-Hill, 1980), pp. 26–29.

and physics coupled with the boundary conditions of earlier states.[35] Determinism is the thesis that, given the past and the laws of nature, there is only one possible future. There is no room for nonphysical factors like agents, evidence, reasons, or rational insight to affect the course of the world. Only causal, physical relations act. A person's output is *wholly* caused by physical factors.

In sum, it is self-refuting to *argue* that one *ought* to *choose* physicalism *because* he should *see* that the *evidence* is *good* for physicalism. Physicalism cannot be offered as a rational theory because physicalism does away with the necessary preconditions for there to be such a thing as rationality. Physicalism usually denies intentionality by reducing it to a physical relation of input/output, thereby denying that the mind is genuinely capable of having thoughts *about* the world. Physicalism denies the existence of propositions and nonphysical laws of logic and evidence which can be in minds and influence thinking. Physicalism denies the existence of a faculty capable of rational insight into these nonphysical laws and propositions, and it denies the existence of an enduring "I" which is present through the process of reflection. Finally, it denies the existence of a genuine agent who deliberates and chooses positions because they are rational, an act possible only if physical factors are not sufficient for determining future behavior.

A case has been presented for dualism, the belief that in addition to a body, a person has a soul or mind. Several general arguments have been offered in support of dualism and a case has been presented which seeks to show that physicalism is self-refuting. Some of the arguments presented can be used to establish either property dualism (epiphenomenalism) or substance dualism. However, some of them—in particular, the arguments which show that rationality requires a free agent—rule out epiphenomenalism and establish substance dualism.

The question now arises: From whence comes mind or soul? Could it evolve from matter or did it need to be created by God? To these issues we now turn.

The Origin of Mind

We have seen that there are good reasons for holding that strict physicalism is false. But most physicalists are recalcitrant. If they embrace dualism

---

35. See Lucas, *Freedom of the Will*, pp. 65–95; Peter van Inwagen, *An Essay on Free Will* (Oxford: Clarendon Press, 1983), pp. 58–65. The indeterminacy of quantum mechanics is not relevant here. First, it can be taken epistemologically, not ontologically. Second, if it is to be taken ontologically, then determinism still holds at the level of macro-objects. Third, indeterminacy of the self is not what is needed for rationality. Self-determination is what is required.

at all, they embrace epiphenomenalism because, as I will show later, it is more compatible with physicalism than is substance dualism. Mind is not matter, but it comes from matter through evolution when matter reaches a suitable structural arrangement for mind to emerge.

If mind emerged from matter without the direction of a superior Intelligence, two problems arise immediately. First, why should we trust the deliverances of the mind as being rational or true, especially in the mind's more theoretical activities? No one would trust the printout of a computer if he knew that it was programmed by random forces or by nonrational laws without a mind being behind it. Theoretical activity does not seem to contribute to survival value. And less theoretical activities (e.g., sensing the world) would not need to give true information about the world to aid an organism; such activities would need only to help the organism interact with the world consistently. An amoeba which consistently sensed a large object as small and vice versa would learn which ones to avoid without having true insights into the way the world is. Further, according to epiphenomenalism, mental activities do not cause anything anyway. So even if mind emerged, it is hard to see how it could come about by aiding an organism in its evolutionary struggle for survival.[36] And even if it did, it would not need to give true information to do so. So it is hard to see why the mind should be trusted, given that it is an epiphenomenon which emerged in the process of evolution.

Second, if thinking involves having abstract entities (propositions, laws of logic, and the like) instanced in one's mind, then it seems to be incredibly unlikely that a property which emerged from matter in a struggle for survival would be the sort of thing that could *have* thoughts in it in the first place. Why this emergent property would be such that it could contain abstract entities would be a mystery. But let us set these two arguments aside. They are forms of the design argument considered in chapter 2. There are still serious difficulties with epiphenomenalism. To see these we must first clarify what epiphenomenalism involves. The view is also called holism, and when mind is seen to emerge through the coming together of matter in a certain way (for instance, through the evolution of the central nervous system and brain) the position is called the emergent property view (EPV). Here are four main features of the EPV.

The Emergent Property View

Wholes and Parts

In nature, wholes are often greater than the sum of their parts. Nature exhibits a hierarchy of systems—subatomic particles, atoms, molecules,

---

36. See n. 25 regarding the survival value of rationality.

cells, organs, whole organisms. Each level has properties of the wholes at that level which are not properties of their constituent parts. For example, water has the property of being wet, but this property is not true of either hydrogen or oxygen. Similarly, the mind is a property of the brain.[37]

Levels of Explanation and Complementarity

Each level in a hierarchy can be explained by using concepts appropriate at that level. Further, all the levels are complementary. For example, an explanation of a person's behavior could be given at a psychological level which used the concepts *beliefs, desires,* or *fears.* The same behavior could be given an explanation at the neurophysiological level using the concepts *neurons, synapses,* and so forth. These two levels of explanation are not in competition; they complement one another by offering descriptions of the same behavior at different levels.

Causation Between Levels

Lower levels in the hierarchy cause things to happen at higher levels but not vice versa. When it comes to persons, events at the physical level can be characterized in terms of physical laws which make no reference to the causal efficaciousness of future events (e.g., the purposes of the agent) or higher levels of organization. The events at the physical level obey deterministic physical laws and mental events are mere byproducts.[38]

Resultant View of the Self

The self is not some mental substance added to the brain from the "outside" when the brain reaches a certain level of complexity. It is an emergent property which supervenes upon the brain.[39] The self becomes a discontinuous series of mental events when mental properties are instanced in different brain events. The self is a series of events which "ride" on top of the brain. Consider the following diagram:

$$M_1 \quad M_2 \quad M_3 \quad M_4$$
$$\diagup \quad \diagup \quad \diagup \quad \diagup$$
$$B_1 \rightarrow B_2 \rightarrow B_3 \rightarrow B_4$$

Suppose M_1 is the mental state of seeing an apple from a distance of five feet. It is a *mental* state since it involves the conscious awareness of seeing

37. See MacKay, *Human Science and Human Dignity,* pp. 26–34; David Hull, *Philosophy of Biological Science* (Englewood Cliffs, N.J.: Prentice-Hall, 1974), pp. 125–41; Terence Horgan, "Supervenience and Microphysics," *Pacific Philosophical Quarterly* 63 (1982): 39.

38. See Searle, *Minds, Brains, and Science,* p. 93.

39. Emergence is roughly synonymous with supervenience, except the former is used diachronically and the latter synchronically.

the apple, and conscious awareness is something true of minds and not matter. Now suppose M_2 is the mental state of seeing the apple from one foot, M_3 the state of feeling a pain on the toe, and M_4 the state of hearing a plane fly overhead. B_1 through B_4 are brain states which are associated with each mental state.

Three things stand out immediately. First, B_1 through B_4 stand in rigid physical, causal relations with one another. B_1 causes B_2 and so on. There is no room for a rational agent to intervene in this causal sequence. Mental agents do not act here. The physical level determines all the action. Mental states are mere byproducts of their physical states as smoke is a byproduct of fire.

Second, there is no unified, enduring self at the mental level. According to substance dualism, the self is not identical to its states; it *has* its states. The mind *has* its thoughts and experiences and the same mind can have two experiences at the same time (hearing a plane and seeing an apple) or it can have one experience followed by another. The *self* is present at both experiences and underlies the change of experiences.

When a leaf goes from green to red, green does not become red. Rather, green leaves and is replaced by red *in* the leaf. The leaf is the same substance present at both ends of the process. When a substance gains or loses properties, *it* remains the same while the properties come and go. They are replaced. Red replaces green. The EPV says that M_1 through M_4 are properties of the body. There is no enduring mental substance which has them. There is just one mental property at one time which leaves and is replaced by another mental property at another time. The "self" is a series of mental events where mental properties are had by physical states.

Third, it is hard to see what sense can be given to intentionality. How is it that M_1 is of or about an apple? M_1 is just a dummy, a free rider on B_1. At best, B_1 would just be a state caused by light waves from the apple but it is hard to see how this would cause M_1 to be really a state *about* that apple. Even if it were, what difference would it make? Any further body states (the act of touching the apple or eating it) would be caused totally by brain states and make no reference to mental states at all.[40]

It should now be clear why epiphenomenalism was ruled out as an inadequate account of the necessary features of rationality. It cannot account for the existence of intentionality, it leaves no room for genuine rational agency to freely choose mental beliefs, and there is no enduring "I" to be present through the process of thought.[41]

40. I have said nothing about the relations which obtain among M_1 through M_4. Insofar as these mental states contain propositions and concepts, they must bear logical or epistemic relations with one another which the agent himself brings together and recognizes. It is hard to see where there is room for such relations at this level or to see where there is room for an agent to intervene at the lower level.

41. This has led several philosophers to radically revise our common-sense intuitions about the self in order to preserve physicalism. But in this case, as Robinson points out, the proper order between philoso-

The Origin of Mind as an Emergent Property

But let us waive these problems for the moment. Where would the mind as an emergent property come from? How can mind, the capacity to know truth, and so forth, emerge from mindless, nonrational matter?[42] Remember, mind here is not identical to the brain's structure. If it were, then the view would be some form of crude materialism or, perhaps, some unclear intermediate view between dualism and physicalism. But in either case, the position would be worse than epiphenomenalism, for it would suffer from the same deficiencies as the latter, as well as those raised earlier against physicalism in its pure form.

The EPV holds that mind is a genuine mental property (or series of properties) which supervenes on top of matter. Consider water again. Wetness emerges when hydrogen and oxygen come together into a structure known as H_2O. Wetness is not identical to that structure. Wetness is a simple quality; the structure is a set of relationships which can be quantified (spatial relations, relations of force, which can be given numerical values). So the structure is not the same thing as the wetness. Similarly, the mind is not the same thing as the brain's structure; it supervenes over that structure in the EPV view. So it is a genuinely new entity which must come into being somehow or other.

It does not seem that it could come into being from nothing. For one thing, that would violate a generally accepted principle that something does not come from nothing. Some have disputed this principle, but it still seems reasonable, especially at the macroscopic level and not the level of the microparticles of physics (though I believe it to hold at that level as well). And it is the macroscopic level that is involved when mind emerges, since it emerges over an object the size of a structured brain.

One could respond that the mind is not itself a macroscopic entity—perhaps by saying that the macro/micro distinction does not hold for minds. But if the EPV view means that mind emerges over a structured brain out of nothing and that this fact is not anchored to the nature of that brain, then it is hard to see why mind emerges time and again over just this type of structured matter and not over a nickel or a bowling pin. The de-

phy and science has been reversed. Philosophy is conceptually prior to science in a number of ways. See *Matter and Sense*, p. 109. Along these same lines, Bealer has argued that the distinction between mind and matter is logical and knowable a priori. Thus, it is a mistake to look to empirical means in the natural sciences to solve the mind/body problem. See "The Logical Status of Mind," pp. 231–74. For a brief, general treatment on the conceptual priority of philosophy over science, see John Kekes, *The Nature of Philosophy* (Totowa, N.J.: Rowman and Littlefield, 1980), pp. 147–63.

42. These are the problems that Max Delbruck proposes to answer in *Mind from Matter: An Essay on Evolutionary Epistemology*, ed. Gunther Stent and David Presti (Palto Alto, Calif.: Blackwell Scientific Publications, 1985), p. 22. After 280 pages of discussing the problem, he says: "To the question of how the mental capacity for such transcendence can have arisen in the course of biological evolution I have no satisfactory answer."

fender of the EPV cannot appeal to the causal efficacy of the mind itself and argue that the mind of a child comes from the mind of its parents, for this allows minds to cause something, and this is not allowed according to the EPV.

At the level of normal-sized macroscopic objects (objects visible to normal sight) things just do not pop in and out of existence. Even if mind is not such an object, its emergence seems to be tied to the brain. And the brain is such an object. So it is not very promising to account for the emergence of mind by saying it comes from nothing.

There is, however, a more promising view. Aristotle taught us long ago that when something new emerges, it does not come from nothing but from potentiality. When a leaf turns from green to red, the red does not simply come into existence; it was already in the leaf potentially. When an apple seed produces apples, the apples were in the seed potentially. In general, when a property emerges in a substance, it comes to actuality from potentiality, not from pure nonbeing. The property was in the substance potentially and when it emerges, it becomes actual.

Mind must somehow be in matter potentially such that when matter reaches a certain stage of development, mind becomes actual. This is a more plausible version of the EPV, but it still has serious difficulties.

First, it is hard to see how this is compatible with the doctrines and motives of physicalism. Physicalism is embraced in part out of a desire to promote science as the ultimate, perhaps only, kind of knowledge. So physicalists often assert that the world is a network of physical causes wherein only physical causality does anything. Further, the world for a physicalist is in principle describable in strictly physical laws. But if mind is potential in matter, then physicalism seems to become some form of panpsychism, the view that mind is ultimate. Matter no longer is describable in terms of familiar physical properties and laws alone. Now it contains elusive mental potentialities.

After wrestling with this problem, Nobel Prize-winning scientist Max Delbruck argued that "our ideas about the objective character of the physical world, and hence of the nature of truth have been revised. In other words, mind looks less psychic and matter looks less materialistic. . . ."[43] So if one admits that mind is potential in matter, then one can no longer hold that reality is exhausted by the spatio-temporal physical universe.

Second, one could no longer hold that physical laws could exhaustively describe the causal processes of the universe. Richard Swinburne discusses this problem in some detail and argues that science will never be able to explain where mental properties come from or why they emerge when they do. He says,

43. Ibid., p. 279.

What of mental properties? Take the simplest such property—sensations. There can be a physico-chemical explanation of how an animal's genes cause his nervous system to have a certain structure, and how a mutation in a gene can cause the nervous system of his offspring to have a different structure. It can explain how an animal comes to have organs differentially sensitive to light of this and that range of wavelengths, sensitive to temperature or bodily damage; sensitive to these things in the sense that it responds differently to light of this wavelength from the way it responds to light of that wavelength and so on. But what physics and chemistry could not possibly explain is why the brain-events to which the impinging light gives rise, in turn give rise to sensations of blueness (as opposed to redness), a high noise rather than a low noise, this sort of smell rather than that sort of smell—why sodium chloride tastes salty, and roses look pink. And the reason why physics and chemistry could not explain these things is that pink looks, high noises, and salty tastes are not the sort of thing physics and chemistry deal in. These sciences deal in the physical (i.e. public) properties of small physical objects, and of the large physical objects which they come to form—in mass and charge, volume and spin. Yet mental properties are different from physical properties. . . .[44]

Third, this emergent property view could not rule out the future existence of God. If mind can emerge from matter when a high-level system reaches a certain point of complexity, why is it not possible for a large-scale Mind to emerge at a later period in evolutionary development? In other words, the EPV cannot rule out Hegelianism, the view that mind emerges from matter all the way up to the emergence of God himself. This may sound far-fetched. But the point is that the EPV cannot rule it out, for the emergence of mind over brains is a startling fact which could hardly have been predicted from the properties of matter alone. So why should one think the process of emergence should stop with finite, human minds? Why could not some form of deity emerge, since mind is in some sense a basic constituent of the universe? Christian philosopher Richard Purtill has called this the God-not-yet view. And it should come as no comfort to an atheist, who is trying to save some form of minimal physicalism, to be told that his view seems to imply some form of emergent theism. At the very least, emergent theism cannot be ruled out.

Finally, Clark points out that it is hard to specify just what these potential mental properties are.[45] Are these potential properties conscious? If so, then why do we have no memory from them when they emerge to form our own minds? Does it really make sense to say that my mind is composed of several particles of mind dust (i.e., little selves which came together to form my own mental life)? If these potential properties are not

44. Richard Swinburne, *The Evolution of the Soul* (Oxford: Clarendon Press, 1986), p. 186.
45. Clark, *From Athens to Jerusalem*, pp. 143–46.

conscious, how are they still mental? These questions may have an answer, but they are certainly puzzling and the EPV seems to commit one to the existence of rather odd potential mental properties, odd at least from the standpoint of one who wants to maintain some form of respectable physicalism.[46]

The simple fact is that the existence of mind has always been a problem for the physicalist. As physicalist Paul M. Churchland argues,

> The important point about the standard evolutionary story is that the human species and all of its features are the wholly physical outcome of a purely physical process. . . . If this is the correct account of our origins, then there seems neither need, nor room, to fit any nonphysical substances or properties into our theoretical account of ourselves. We are creatures of matter.[47]

Physicalist D. M. Armstrong agrees:

> It is not a particularly difficult notion that, when the nervous system reaches a certain level of complexity, it should develop new properties. Nor would there be anything particularly difficult in the notion that when the nervous system reaches a certain level of complexity it should affect something that was already in existence in a new way. But it is a quite different matter to hold that the nervous system should have the power to create something else, of a quite different nature from itself, and create it out of no materials.[48]

Physicalism is false because it fails to adequately handle several general arguments raised against it. And it is self-refuting, for it undercuts the very prerequisites of rational thought itself. Once one grants the existence of mind, then the question arises as to where it came from. The emergent property view is one answer to this question. But it fails as an adequate theory of mind itself, and it postulates either the origin of mind from nothing or its emergence from potentiality in matter. Both options are problematic. Mind appears to be a basic feature of the cosmos and its origin at a finite level of persons is best explained by postulating a fundamental Mind who gave finite minds being and design. As Calvin put it, the endowments which we possess cannot possibly be from ourselves. They point to the ultimate Mind and ground of rationality himself.

---

46. For a novel attempt to integrate emergentism with a scientific worldview without embracing substance dualism, see Roger Sperry, "Changed Concepts of Brain and Consciousness: Some Value Implications," *Zygon* 20 (March 1985): 41–57.

47. Churchland, *Matter and Consciousness*, p. 21.

48. D. M. Armstrong, *A Materialist Theory of the Mind* (London: Routledge and Kegan Paul, 1968), p. 30.

4

God and the Meaning of Life

Rumor has it that Woody Allen was engaged in a philosophical discussion one evening at a dinner party when he was asked his opinion about the meaning of life. His response was equal to the occasion: "You ask me about the meaning of life? Good Lord, I don't even know my way around Chinatown!" Questions about the meaning of life can appear to be so difficult that some people think they are unanswerable.[1] On

---

1. Some philosophers (e.g., Paul Edwards) deny that there is any point in asking the question, often on the grounds that the question itself is cognitively meaningless or that it would be impossible to know what an answer to the question would look like. See E. D. Klemke, ed., *The Meaning of Life* (New York: Oxford University Press, 1981), pp. 175–261; David R. Chaney and Steven Sanders, eds., *The Meaning of Life: Questions, Answers and Analysis* (Englewood Cliffs, N.J.: Prentice-Hall, 1980). Two brief responses are in order. First, such a claim often rests on an inadequate criterion of cognitive meaning or of what an answer must look like—it must be empirically verifiable, testable by science, and so forth. Usually such a

the other hand, questions about the meaning of life will not go away. Everyone, at one time or another, wonders whether or not life has any real meaning or significance. In *The Myth of Sisyphus*, Albert Camus expresses the urgency of this question:

> There is but one truly serious philosophical problem, and that is suicide. Judging whether life is or is not worth living amounts to answering the fundamental question of philosophy. All the rest—whether the world has three dimensions, whether the mind has nine categories or twelve categories—come afterward. These are games; one must first answer. . . .
>
> If I ask myself how to judge that this question is more urgent than that, I reply that one judges by the actions it entails. I have never seen anyone die for the ontological argument [for the existence of a god]. Galileo, who held a scientific truth of great importance, abjured it with the greatest of ease as soon as it endangered his life. In a certain sense he did right. That truth was not worth the stake. Whether the earth or the sun revolved around the other is a matter of profound indifference. To tell the truth, it is a futile question. On the other hand, I see many people die because they judge that life is not worth living. I see others paradoxically getting killed for the ideas or illusions that give them a reason for living (what is called a reason for living is also an excellent reason for dying). I therefore conclude that the meaning of life is the most urgent of questions.[2]

But what does the question itself mean? What are we getting at when we ask for an answer to our questions about the meaning of life?[3] The question is not asking whether or not people find life subjectively satisfying and of personal significance. Meaning in this sense would be involved in the statements "I get a lot of meaning (satisfaction) out of golf" or "the county fair means a lot to me (I find that it matters to me)." As interesting as this sense of meaning may be, it is not the one intended when most people raise the question of the meaning of life. Two distinctions may help us clarify the question.

First, the question of the meaning of life can be raised with different scopes in mind. For example, one can ask:

---

criterion is self-refuting. Second, it is antecedently incredible that a question which has occupied the minds of most human beings down through history, including some of the finest minds who have ever lived, would be a meaningless question. It is one thing to say no positive answer exists to the question. It is quite another thing to deny the question itself.

2. Cited in Klemke, *The Meaning of Life*, p. 4. For a Christian analysis of existentialism, see C. Stephen Evans, *Existentialism: The Philosophy of Despair and the Quest for Hope* (Grand Rapids: Zondervan, Academie Books, 1984).

3. In addition to the volumes by Klemke and Chaney and Sanders, see Robert Nozick, *Philosophical Explanations* (Cambridge: Harvard University Press, Belknap Press, 1981), pp. 571–647; Karl Britton, *Philosophy and the Meaning of Life* (Cambridge: Cambridge University Press, 1969); W. D. Joske, "Philosophy and the Meaning of Life," *Australasian Journal of Philosophy* 52 (August 1974): 93–104; Jeffrey Gordon, "Is the Existence of God Relevant to the Meaning of Life?" *The Modern Schoolman* 60 (May 1983): 227–46.

1. Why does the universe exist? Why is there something rather than nothing?
2. Why do human beings in general exist?
3. Why do I exist?

Although these are different questions, one's answer to one of these questions can affect his answer to the others. It would be possible to hold that the universe as a whole is without meaning, but that objective human values exist as a brute fact and the meaning of my life consists in my relationship to those values. On the other hand, one could hold that the cosmos as a whole has meaning; for example, that it is evolving into God, but that humans are of no significance to that meaning. So these questions can be treated separately and in an unrelated way. On the other hand, it is possible (and I think reasonable) to hold that one's answer to the first question will have a bearing on one's answers to the second and third questions. For example, nihilists hold that there is no purpose in the cosmos and, therefore, there is no purpose for humans in general or my life in particular. Christians hold that God has a purpose for the cosmos and this purpose informs the purpose of human life in general and each individual life in particular.

Second, the question of the meaning of life involves the notions of value and purpose. Do values exist objectively and if so, what is the nature of those values? How does one know what values are the right ones? Is there any point to life (i.e., is there any end or goal which is objectively and intrinsically valuable and toward which life should move)?

With these distinctions in mind, the question of the meaning of life as we will use it in this chapter is this: Are there any objective values which provide significance for the universe as a whole, human life in general, or my life in particular, and which provide a goal or purpose for the universe, human life, or my life?

In what follows, I will examine four different answers to the question of the meaning of life and argue that Christian theism is the best answer to the question. The four answers we will examine are nihilism and naturalism, temporal purpose and optimistic humanism, immanent purpose and transcendentalism, and cosmic purpose and Christian theism.[4] However, before we can analyze these positions, two preliminary issues regarding moral values should be discussed. Questions about the meaning of life involve questions about the existence and nature of values. Two questions will help us focus on problems of value: What is the meaning of moral

---

4. The terminology is William H. Halverson's, except I designate optimistic humanism what he calls humanism. See William H. Halverson, *A Concise Introduction to Philosophy* (New York: Random House, 1967), pp. 413–76.

statements?[5] What is the meaning of the question "why should I be moral?"

Metaethics and the Meaning of Moral Statements

In order to understand what a view means by asserting that life is or is not meaningful, it is important to understand what that view means when it makes certain moral statements of value. Metaethics is that branch of philosophy which analyzes the meaning of certain moral terms (right, wrong, good, bad, ought, worth, and so forth). Certain moral statements make reference to persons or actions. With regard to persons, one might affirm the moral statement "persons ought to be treated as ends in themselves" or "persons have intrinsic value and dignity." With regard to actions, one might affirm that "the act of loving your neighbor is morally right" or "murder is wrong." In general, many moral statements are of this form: X is right (or wrong). X has value (or fails to have value).

Different metaethical views have been offered which analyze statements like these differently. The major options in metaethics can be summarized as follows:

I. Noncognitivist Theories
   A. Emotivism
   B. Imperativalism
II. Cognitivist Theories
   A. Subjectivist Theories
      1. Private Subjectivism
      2. Cultural Relativism
   B. Objectivist Theories
      1. Ethical Naturalism
      2. Ethical Nonnaturalism

Noncognitivist Theories

Noncognitivist theories of moral statements deny that moral statements (e.g., "x is right") are indicative statements which can be either true or false. Consider the statement "the apple is red." This is an indicative state-

---

5. In addition to moral values, there are also epistemic values and aesthetic values. I have chosen to focus on the former because they seem to be closer to the heart of the question of the meaning of life than the latter two, though all three kinds of values are relevant (Gordon tries to argue that life is meaningful in light of aesthetic values). Furthermore, the same kind of classification could be given to meta-axiological theories in epistemology and aesthetics as is given in metaethics, since the same issues arise in all three.

ment. It asserts an alleged fact which has ontological implications. It asserts that there is an apple which exists and has an existent property, redness, in it. So indicative statements have ontological implications. Further, they can be either true or false. In this case, if the apple really is red, the statement is true. If the apple were green, it would be false. So indicative statements are cognitive in the sense that they can be either true or false and they have ontological implications because they assert that some state of affairs obtains in the world.

Noncognitivist theories deny that moral statements are either true or false and that moral statements have ontological implications. Emotivists hold that the meaning of moral statements consists in the *expression* of emotions. "X is right" really means "hurrah for *x*!" Statements like "*x* is wrong" really mean "ugh! *x*!" For example, when someone says that murder is wrong, emotivists hold that the person is merely expressing the feeling "ugh! I hate murder!"

Imperativalists agree with emotivists that moral statements are not indicative statements of fact. But they do not think that moral statements are expressions of feeling. Rather, they hold that moral statements are merely moral commands. "X is right" is merely the command "do *x*!"

Noncognitivist theories of moral statements fail to do justice to the nature of morality. At least three objections can be raised against both views. First, moral judgments can occur in the absence of feelings or in the absence of commands and some expressions of feelings or some commands are not moral judgments. For example, one can form the judgment "killing rats is wrong" without feeling or commanding anything. But if a moral judgment just *is* an expression of a feeling or the issuing of a command, then it would be impossible to have a moral judgment without feeling or without commanding. Feelings and commands may be a part of a general theory of morality, but they do not exhaust the nature of morality. Similarly, someone can express a feeling when he stubs his toe on a table (ugh! I hate tables!), but this expression is not a moral judgment. So moral judgments can occur without feelings or commands and vice versa. Thus, they cannot be identical.

Second, emotivism and imperativalism imply that there is no such thing as *moral* education (since there is no cognitive information to learn) and there is no such thing as a moral disagreement. Consider two people who appear to be having a moral disagreement about abortion. Person *A* says "abortion is right" and person *B* says "abortion is wrong." Emotivism analyzes these statements such that *A* is saying "hurrah! I (*A*) love abortion!" and *B* is saying "ugh! I (*B*) hate abortion!" According to emotivist (and imperativalist) translations of the statements, there is no disagreement occurring, since neither person is making a factual claim which could be true or false. Disagreements occur when one person asserts that some claim is true and another asserts that it is false. So emotivism (and imperativalism) implies the impossibility of moral disagreement. But any view which implies such an implausible assertion as this is inadequate as a general theory of moral meaning.

Finally, some moral statements seem to stand in logical relations with other moral statements. For example, the statement "I have a duty to do x" seems to logically imply the statement "I have a right to do x." But emotional utterances or mere imperatives do not stand to other emotional utterances or mere imperatives in logical relationships. Only indicative statements can stand in logical relationships to one another. So emotivism and imperativalism fail to account for this feature of morality.

Cognitivist Theories

Cognitivist theories of the meaning of moral statements agree in holding that moral statements make truth claims because they are indicative statements which convey descriptive factual information. The statement "x is right" can be either true or false. Cognitivist theories differ, however, over what the object is which ethical statements describe.

Subjectivist Theories

Subjectivist theories hold that moral statements convey information about the speaker of the moral statement. According to private subjectivism, "x is right" states the psychological fact that "I dislike x." This differs from emotivism. Emotivism holds that moral statements merely *express* feelings. Private subjectivism holds that moral statements do not *express* feelings but describe the psychological state of the speaker. An expression of feeling cannot be false. But if person A says "I dislike x," then this can be false if he really likes x but does not want to admit it. Cultural relativism is the view that statements like "x is right" state the sociological fact that "we in our culture dislike x."

Cultural relativism and private subjectivism are very much alike and they will be criticized more fully in chapter 8. But for now, it should be pointed out that few philosophers hold that these metaethical theories are adequate treatments of morality. The main reason is that they make moral statements into nonmoral statements. The statement "x is right" appears to be a *moral* statement which makes a normative claim about right and wrong and it carries with it a statement about what one *ought* to do. But the psychological and sociological translations of this statement—"I like x" and "we in our culture like x"—make no normative claims whatever. They merely assert what people happen to like. So they do not translate moral statements; they transform them inappropriately into nonmoral statements. Thus, private subjectivism and cultural relativism cannot be adequate understandings of moral meaning.

Objectivist Theories

Objectivist theories agree with subjectivist theories of moral meaning in holding that moral statements assert true or false statements of fact. However, they do not think that moral statements are stating facts about the speakers of moral statements but about the acts of morality themselves or the objects which are said to have value.

The statement "the apple is red" says something about the apple. The statements "persons have value" and "murder is wrong" say something about persons and acts of murder. Just as "the apple is red" asserts that the apple has a property (redness) so moral statements assert that persons or moral acts have certain properties. In short, objectivist theories hold that moral statements convey information about persons or moral acts by describing properties of those persons or acts.

It is here that agreement ends. The two major versions of objectivism—ethical naturalism and ethical nonnaturalism—disagree over the nature of the moral properties that moral judgments ascribe to persons or acts. The debate between them is over the issue of moral reductionism (i.e., over whether or not moral properties can be reduced to and identified with nonmoral properties). Ethical naturalists say that such a reduction is correct and ethical nonnaturalists say that moral properties are unique and cannot be reduced to nonmoral properties.

Ethical naturalism is a reductionist view which holds that ethical terms ("goodness," "worth," and "right") can be defined by or reduced to natural, scientific properties which are biological, psychological, sociological, or physical in nature. For example, according to ethical naturalism the term *right* in "*x* is right" means one of the following: "what is approved by most people," "what most people desire," "what is approved by an impartial, ideal observer," "what maximizes desire or interest," "what furthers human survival," and so on. The important point here is that these moral terms and moral properties are not irreducibly moral in nature. Moral properties (e.g., worth, goodness, or rightness) turn out to be properties which are biological or psychological. These properties can, in turn, be measured by science by giving them operational definitions.

Consider an example. Suppose "*x* is right" means "*x* is what most people desire" and one goes on to argue that the presence of pleasure and the absence of pain is what most people desire. A scientist could measure the presence of pleasure and the absence of pain by defining such a state in physiological terms—the presence of a certain heart rate, the absence of certain impulses in the nervous system, slight coloration of the skin. Rightness means what is desired by most people, what is desired by most people is the presence of pleasure and the absence of pain, and pleasure and pain can be defined by certain physical traits of the body. Thus, the moral property of rightness has been reduced to a natural property which can be measured.

Two major objections can be raised against ethical naturalism. First, it confuses an "is" with an "ought" by reducing the latter to the former. Moral properties are normative properties. They carry a moral ought with them. If some act has the property of rightness, then one ought to do that act. But natural properties like the ones listed do not carry normativeness. They just are. Second, every attempted reduction of a moral property to a natural one has failed because there are cases where an act is right even if it does not have the natural property, and an act can have the natural property and not be right. For example, suppose one reduces the moral property of rightness in "x is right" to "x is what is approved by most people." This reduction is inadequate. For one thing, the majority can be wrong. What most people approve of can be morally wrong. If most people approved of torturing babies, then according to this version of ethical naturalism, this act would be right. But even though it was approved by most people, it would still be wrong. On the other hand, some acts can be right even if they are not approved of (or even thought of, for that matter) by most people.

Ethical nonnaturalism is the only view we have considered which holds that irreducible moral facts and properties really exist as part of the furniture of the universe. In addition to natural properties (redness and so forth), there are moral properties (rightness, goodness, worth) which persons and acts have and which moral statements ascribe to persons and acts. "X is good" ascribes an unanalyzable, irreducible moral property to x just as "the apple is red" ascribes the natural property redness to the apple. Most Christian theists have been some form of ethical nonnaturalists since they hold that God himself has moral properties (goodness, holiness, and so forth), persons made in his image have worth and dignity (as he does), and some acts have the property of moral rightness.

Critics of nonnaturalism often use what J. L. Mackie has called the argument from queerness, which has both a metaphysical and an epistemological component. Mackie argues:

> If there were objective values, then they would be entities or qualities or relations of a very strange sort, utterly different from anything else in the universe. Correspondingly, if we were aware of them, it would have to be by

some special faculty of moral perception or intuition, utterly different from our ordinary ways of knowing everything else.[6]

Mackie is arguing—asserting might be a better word, for this is not much of an argument as it stands—that moral values are so odd that their existence would be strange and our ability to know them would be odd. But why should anyone agree with Mackie about this? If morals do exist, why would anyone expect them to be like other kinds of things? Mackie appears to be faulting moral values for not behaving like physical objects. But this is an absurd example of fault-finding. If moral values are not physical objects, then why should we expect them to be like physical objects? If Mackie is correct in his view, then a host of entities—numbers, persons, laws of logic, universals, sets, and any other nonphysical entity—go by the boards because they are "queer." Mackie's objection is a mere assertion of bias in favor of naturalism.

In sum, these are the major options in metaethics. Different views about the meaning of life will entail different views about the meaning of moral statements and the existence and nature of moral values.

Reasons for Being Moral

A position about the meaning of life will also include an answer to the question of why one should be moral. But the question—why should I be moral?—needs clarification. Three points should help to clarify the question.[7]

First, one can distinguish specific moral acts (an act of kindness, an act of self-sacrifice) from what philosophers call the moral point of view. The question "why should I be moral?" is really asking "why should I adopt the moral point of view?" so it is important to understand what the moral point of view is. If one adopts the moral point of view, then one does the following: he subscribes to normative judgments about actions, things (persons, the environment), and motives; he is willing to universalize his judgments; he seeks to form his moral views in a free, unbiased, enlightened way; he seeks to promote the good. In other words, if one adopts the moral point of view, one submits to and seeks to promote the dictates of

6. J. L. Mackie, *Ethics: Inventing Right and Wrong* (New York: Penguin, 1977), p. 38. Basil Mitchel shows the subtle danger in denying the existence of real, irreducible values and redefining them in the operational terms of science in *Morality: Secular and Religious* (Oxford: Clarendon Press, 1980), pp. 1–29.

7. See William Frankena, *Ethics* (Englewood Cliffs, N.J.: Prentice-Hall, 1963), pp. 113–16; Ronald M. Green, *Religious Reason: The Rational and Moral Basis of Religious Belief* (New York: Oxford University Press, 1978), pp. 13–79; and the articles by John Hospers and Kai Nielsen in Wilfrid Sellars and John Hospers, eds., *Readings in Ethical Theory* (Englewood Cliffs, N.J.: Prentice-Hall, 1970).

normative, universalizable morality in a mature, unbiased, impartial way. One embraces the dictates of morality and seeks to live in light of the moral point of view. Such a viewpoint governs his life and priorities. So understood, the question "why should I be moral?" becomes the question "why should I adopt the moral point of view as a guiding force over my life?"

Second, one can distinguish between motives and reasons for adopting the moral point of view. Regarding the former, the question is asking what motivates one to adopt the moral point of view. Motives do not need to be rational factors. For example, one could say that he was motivated to adopt the moral point of view because it gave him approval with his parents and with society. Regarding reasons, the question is asking what rational justification can be given for adopting the moral point of view. The question is usually framed in terms of reasons, but both reasons and motives are relevant to a full discussion of why one adopts the moral point of view.

Third, it is not clear what kind of justification the question is seeking. What kind of "should" is involved in "why should I be moral?" If it is a moral "should," then the question is asking for a moral justification for adopting the moral point of view. If a moral "should" is used in the question, then some philosophers think that the question involves a pointless self-contradiction. For one is then asking for a moral reason for accepting moral reasons. In other words, if one is using a moral "should" in the question, then one is already reasoning from *within* the moral point of view, since one is already willing to acknowledge a moral answer to a moral question. But if one has already adopted the moral point of view, then there is not much point in asking for a moral reason for doing so. About the only answer one could give to the question would be that it is just morally right to adopt the moral point of view. But if one is willing to adopt the moral point of view because such an act is morally right, then one has already adopted the moral point of view without knowing it. So the question "why should I be moral?" is not really using a moral sense of "should," and if it is, the only answer is that such an act is just the morally right thing to do.

But there is a different notion of "should" which is better suited as a part of the question. This is a rational sense of "should." According to this sense of "should," one is not asking the question "why should I be moral?" from within the moral point of view, but outside the moral point of view altogether. In other words, one is asking the question "what rational justification can be given to me as to why it would be reasonable for me to adopt the moral point of view rather than some other point of view (say, an egoistic self-interested point of view where I govern my life for my own best interests without regard for the moral point of view at all)." As I seek to formulate a rational life plan for myself, a well thought-out, reasonable approach to the way I will live my life so as to be a rational person, why should the moral point of view be a part of that rational life plan?

In sum, the question "why should I be moral?" is asking for the motives, but more importantly, the reasons why someone should adopt the moral point of view as a part of a rational plan of life. It is now time to consider four major options for the question of the meaning of life.

Four Views of the Meaning of Life

Nihilism and Naturalism

Nihilism is the view that human existence is totally and irremediably meaningless and that nothing is of real value.[8] Nihilism is a pessimistic philosophy of life and has been held by philosophers Friedrich Nietzsche and Camus. According to nihilism, life is absurd. There is no reason why the universe rather than nothing exists, there is no purpose toward which the cosmos is moving, and human history has no goal or end. Human beings are not the favored creation of a loving God, but are modified monkeys. Humans are the chance product of random mutations, natural selection, and the struggle for survival. There is no life after death. There is no objective reason why suicide is not a more rational option than the desire to continue living.

Nihilists deny the existence of values. The theory of metaethics most consistent with nihilism would be private subjectivism. Values are mere expressions of individual likes and dislikes. According to nihilism, one is free to adopt a set of likes which bring personal satisfaction, such as the desire to be free and open to the present moment, and to obtain pleasure and satisfaction in life. Cultural relativism and noncognitivism would also be options for a nihilist.

Why should a nihilist be moral? The answer is that there is no rational justification for adopting the moral point of view. Private egoism (the view that I will do right if and only if it is in my own interests to do so) is the only motivation for being moral. If I find a moral life satisfying or if doing what society says is moral will help me enjoy the moment, then I will be motivated to be moral on that occasion. But if the demands of morality go against my own personal interests, then morality has no rationally justified demand on me.

Nihilism and the Death of God

Two main reasons are often given for adopting nihilism. First, some nihilists argue that since God is dead (i.e., since the concept of God can no

8. See Halverson, *Concise Introduction to Philosophy,* pp. 457–62, for a simple overview of nihilism.

longer be believed and no longer holds sway for modern men), then life is absurd and values do not exist. If God is dead, do whatever you please.

Two things can be said against this argument. First, as a matter of factual observation, the concept of God is not vanishing from Western culture. In fact, it seems that the view which asserts that God is dead is itself dying. Christian theism has experienced a small revival in the last few decades in culture in general and in the academic community in particular. This does not mean that God exists, but it does show that the assertion that modern men do not find the concept of God to be relevant any longer is false.

Second, it is false that values do not exist. I know with a high degree of certainty that torturing babies is wrong, that what the Nazis did to the Jews was wrong, and that one ought to treat persons with respect and dignity. These values exist and they can be used in an argument for the existence of God.

A nihilist could respond by saying that I have begged the question by simply asserting that values exist. I have not proved they exist, for I have given no criteria for knowing that they are real or for knowing what values are true and what values are false. Underlying this nihilist objection seems to be the assumption that in order to know that p, where p is some statement like "values exist" or "torturing babies is wrong," I must have a criterion for how it is that I know that p. I must always be able to answer the question "what criterion can you offer for asserting that you know that p?" Nihilists assert that this question cannot be sufficiently answered, so when one asserts the truth of p, one has begged the question.

But do I have to always have a criterion for p before I am within my epistemic rights in asserting that I know that p? No, I do not. Roderick Chisholm has pointed out that there are many things one can know without having a criterion for knowing them.[9] If this were not the case (that is, if there were not cases where I could simply know something without having a criterion for my knowledge), then every time I make a knowledge claim, I would have to supply criteria for that claim. But then I would be asserting that I know these criteria are true ones and before I could make *that* claim, I would need criteria for my first criteria, and so on to infinity. This would lead to a vicious infinite regress such that I could never know anything. But I *do* know some things (e.g., that I exist, that I had breakfast this morning, that there is an external world, that other persons exist, and that values exist).

9. See Roderick Chisholm, *The Problem of the Criterion* (Milwaukee: Marquette University Press, 1973). For a critique of Chisholm, see Jonathan Dancy, *Introduction to Contemporary Epistemology* (Oxford: Basil Blackwell, 1985), pp. 227-39.

To illustrate the point further, consider a puzzle from the ancient Greeks known as the sorites problem.[10] Given a small heap of wheat, can I get a large heap by adding one grain? It seems not, for how could one go from a small to a large heap by merely adding one grain? But then it seems that one could add grains of wheat one at a time to a small heap and *never* reach a large heap, which is absurd.

Consider another puzzle. If one gradually changes a color from red to orange, can he tell when the color changes from red to orange? Probably not. But in the absence of such a criterion, how can I know when I see red and not orange?

The problem with both puzzles is this. They assume that in the absence of criteria for borderline cases, one cannot have knowledge of clear cases. Without being able to judge when the heap becomes large—in the absence of a general criterion of knowledge in this case—I can never know that it *is* large. Without being able to state a criterion for how I know when the color changes from red to orange, I can never know that it *is* orange. But the fact is that I can know a large heap and an orange color even if I have no criteria for all cases.

I am not dismissing the value of criteria altogether. Indeed, they are crucial for an overall theory of knowledge. But I do not need criteria in all cases to know something. In general, criteria are not needed in clear cases of different areas of knowledge claims, but they are needed in borderline cases. And the criteria I use to judge the borderline cases are ones I surface after I know the clear ones. I extend the criteria to the borderline cases.

Some different areas of knowledge claims are these: knowledge of the external world, knowledge of other minds, knowledge of my past through memory, and knowledge of values. In each area, I *start* by knowing some things without criteria, even though some borderline cases may require criteria. For example, I do not need to supply the skeptic with criteria for how I know the external world exists *before* I am rationally justified in claiming to know that a table is before me. I do not need to supply the skeptic with criteria for how I know my memory is reliable in general *before* I am rationally justified in claiming to know that I had breakfast this morning. There may be specific cases—mirages or lapses of memory—where criteria may be needed before I can make a claim to know something. But before I am justified in taking an alleged case as a possible mirage or lapse of memory, I must have some reason to think I am seeing a mirage or being forgetful, and the reason will rest on some other knowledge claim in that area (someone else does not see the tree, or someone else was at the time meeting with me and does not think I remember it correctly).

10. See Max Black, "Reasoning with Loose Concepts," *Dialogue* 2 (1963): 1–12.

In the area of values, I just know some values are true directly. I do not need general criteria for this knowledge *before* I can assert this fact, even though in some difficult moral cases (e.g., in bioethics), I may need criteria. If the nihilist tells me that the Nazis were not really wrong or that torturing babies is not really a violation of a true moral value, then he is simply mistaken. It is proper to save resources for future generations even though they do not yet exist, and if nihilism cannot justify that value it is a false theory. So it is rational to assert that values do exist in spite of what nihilism says.[11]

Nihilism and Science

A second reason for nihilism is the view that science has shown that life is meaningless.[12] Science allegedly shows that the cosmos is just a brute given, that final causes or movements toward goals are not a part of the natural world, that man is the product of blind evolutionary forces, that he is a biochemical animal who does not survive the grave and who must struggle for survival during his brief stay on a small planet in a spatially and temporally immense universe which is silent and uncaring.[13]

In chapter 7, we will examine science and try to show how it relates to theological questions and issues. But for now, three brief responses are in order. First, questions of meaning and value are outside the limits of science. They are not scientific questions at all, though admittedly science can make a contribution to a discussion of broad questions of worldview. But the point is that science is just one voice in that discussion and not the only voice. Second, it is a self-refuting claim to assert that philosophical questions are meaningless or false and only scientific claims are true and rational. For this is itself a philosophical claim *about* science, not a claim *of* science. For example, science is itself committed to epistemic values (one should prefer simple theories over less simple ones) and moral values (one should conduct and report experiments honestly). So if values do not exist, how can science itself be justified?[14]

Third, some moral values can be known with more certainty than some

11. For more on begging the question, see Oliver Johnson, *Skepticism and Cognitivism: A Study in the Foundations of Knowledge* (Berkeley: University of California Press, 1979), pp. 226–39.

12. For examples of (inadequate) attempts to wrestle with the problem of values within the constraints of science, see Francis Crick, *Life Itself: Its Origins and Nature* (New York: Simon and Schuster, 1981), pp. 161-66; Michael Ruse, "Evolutionary Ethics: A Phoenix Arisen," *Zygon* 21 (March 1986): 95-111; Jeffrie G. Murphy, *Evolution, Morality and the Meaning of Life*, Philosophy and Society series (Totowa, N.J.: Rowman and Littlefield, 1982).

13. See A. R. Peacocke, *Creation and the World of Science* (Oxford: Oxford University Press, 1979), pp. 147-54. Donald M. MacKay rightly points out that questions of meaning are outside the bounds of science in *Science and the Quest for Meaning* (Grand Rapids: Eerdmans, 1982).

14. This is argued by Hilary Putnam in *Reason, Truth, and History* (Cambridge: Cambridge University Press, 1981), pp. 201-16. However, rather than adding a nonnaturalist view of values to scientific realism,

scientific theories. I know more certainly that torturing babies is wrong than I know that carbon atoms exist, at least as they are currently construed by chemistry and physics. The former has been known by the great majority of people throughout history. The latter concept could be given up in fifty years. Given the fact that in the history of science, theories frequently replace earlier ones and make them obsolete (instead of merely refining them and making them more accurate), can anyone say with certainty that the chemistry and physics of fifty years from now will conceive of carbon atoms in a way that is close enough to current concepts to warrant the claim that the future picture will merely be a refinement of current conceptions? It is not unreasonable to say that future theories will replace current ones altogether. But could the same be said for the moral value of torturing babies?[15]

Two Final Objections to Nihilism

Two further objections can be raised against nihilism before we move on to the next view. First, a nihilist cannot rationally recommend that others have a moral responsibility to be nihilists. At best, he can only say that if you find nihilism to be in your own best interests, then you may like to try nihilism. But a nihilist may not even wish to do this, for it may not be in *his* own best interests for everyone to adopt nihilism.[16] A nihilist may have a more satisfying life if society in general adopts the moral point of view, since in that case others may continue to treat *him* with respect when it is not in *their* own best interests. A nihilist may be happiest if others do not adopt nihilism.

Second, nihilism is unlivable. A person's real views are often seen in his spontaneous reactions to life rather than in his stated views. If someone were to steal a nihilist's car, would he really react on the spot by saying nothing was wrong with that act? I am not raising a mere ad hominem argument here. I am arguing that one test for truth is whether a view can be consistently lived out. It does not seem that nihilism can. And in the absence of convincing arguments for nihilism—surely the case for nihilism is

---

Putnam adopts a neo-Kantian view of the world in general wherein both facts and values are part of the way knowing subjects constitutes the world. Putnam's own view reduces to a form of conceptual relativism not unlike that of Thomas Kuhn, though Putnam denies that this is the case.

15. Some argue that it is a virtue of science that it is tentative and refinable whereas philosophy and ethics are not. But it may be that the latter are not refinable because they deal with questions at a very general level where there are only a small number of options, these options have been known for a long time, and one of them may be true. On the other hand, the revisability of science may indicate that it often fails to have even approximate truth, especially when one notes how the history of science is often a history of successive replacement and not refinement of theories.

16. A similar argument is sometimes raised against various forms of utilitarianism, especially act utilitarianism. It may be the case that more utility is produced if people do not believe utilitarianism, an odd result for a moral theory if there ever was one.

not overwhelming—why should one rush to embrace it when it is such a pessimistic, unlivable view?

Temporal Purpose and Optimistic Humanism

The View

Optimistic humanism holds much in common with nihilism: there is no reason why something rather than nothing exists, there is no purpose toward which the cosmos or human history is moving, humans are modified monkeys which have resulted from a blind process of chance mutations, and real, irreducible moral values do not exist.

But it is here that optimistic humanists say they part company with nihilists. They do not draw the pessimistic conclusion that life has no meaning and that we should bemoan that fact. Suicide is not an option, says the optimist humanist. Nihilism is essentially a life-denying enterprise whereas optimistic humanism is a life-affirming enterprise. How does life have meaning? Because we create our own values and give life whatever meaning we choose to give it. A. J. Ayer puts the point this way:

> But without the help of such a myth [religion] can life be seen as having any meaning? The simple answer is that it can have just as much meaning as one is able to put into it. There is, indeed, no ground for thinking that human life in general serves any ulterior purpose but this is no bar to a man's finding satisfaction in many of the activities which make up his life, or to his attaching value to the ends which he pursues, including some that he himself will not live to see realized.[17]

Philosopher Paul Kurtz, one of the leading humanists in North America, says this:

> The humanist maintains as his first principle that life is worth living, at least that it can be found to have worth. . . . The universe is neutral, indifferent to man's existential yearnings. But we instinctively discover life, experience its throb, its excitement, its attraction. Life is here to be lived, enjoyed, suffered, and endured.[18]

Later, Kurtz makes this point:

> Again—one cannot "prove" this normative principle to everyone's satisfaction. Living beings tend instinctively to maintain themselves and to re-

17. A. J. Ayer, *The Central Questions of Philosophy* (New York: Holt, Rinehart, and Winston, 1973), p. 235.
18. Paul Kurtz, *In Defense of Secular Humanism* (Buffalo: Prometheus, 1983), pp. 156–57.

produce their own kind. This is the primordial fact of life; it is precognitive and prerational and it is beyond ultimate justification. It is a brute fact of our contingent natures; it is an instinctive desire to live.[19]

When optimistic humanists say that life has meaning they do not mean that objective values or an objective point to life exists. Rather, they mean that life can be subjectively satisfying if we create values and live life for them. Why should I be moral? Because it will give me personal satisfaction to be moral.

It is not clear what it means to "create" values. What metaethical theory is involved here? Perhaps the optimistic humanist means that we should act *as if* real, irreducible values exist. But this would merely be to live one's life in a self-induced delusion on the humanist's own views, so if this is what he means, then satisfaction comes from living a lie. Life would be a placebo effect.

It seems that the metaethical theory of optimistic humanism is either imperativalism for Kurtz or private subjectivism or emotivism for Ayer, though an optimistic humanist could adopt cultural relativism or ethical naturalism (provided that one merely chose the relevant reduction term for a moral term—what people desire, what promotes survival—and did not argue that any particular reduction was the right one). Kurtz holds that values do not describe the world or offer truth, but are mere regulational guides for life. They command by offering us imperatives. Ayer holds that morals either express our desires (emotivism) or describe our desires (private subjectivism).

Three Objections to Optimistic Humanism

Three things can be said against optimistic humanism. First, there is no rational justification for choosing it over nihilism. As far as rationality is concerned, it has nothing to offer over nihilism. Therefore, optimistic humanism suffers from some of the same objections we raised against nihilism. Kurtz himself admits that the ultimate values of humanism are incapable of rational justification. Second, a specific area where optimistic humanism is especially vulnerable is in its metaethical views. We need not rehearse our objections to emotivism, private subjectivism, or imperativalism here, except to note one point. When Kurtz tells us that we simply must choose guidelines in keeping with our natural instincts (which find satisfaction in the throb and excitement of life), and when Ayer tells us that we can find satisfaction by attaching values to ends we desire to pursue, then it would seem that neither of them can offer a *rational* objection to Nazi treatment of the Jews in World War II. After all, many of the Nazis found a

19. Ibid., p. 159.

lot of excitement in killing other humans, and this activity was obviously one to which they attached value. If an optimistic humanist responds by saying that we ought not to do this, then he is inconsistent. For now he is using an absolutist sense of ought. It even seems he uses an absolutist sense of ought if he tells us we have a moral obligation to be optimistic humanists. So optimistic humanism either fails to provide the rationale for a moral objection to obviously immoral behavior, or if it does provide such a rationale, it becomes inconsistent.

Third, optimistic humanism really answers the question of the meaning of life in the negative, just as nihilism does. For the optimistic humanist, life has no objective value or purpose; it offers only subjective satisfaction. One should think long and hard before embracing such a horrible view. If there is a decent case that life has objective value and purpose, then such a case should be given as good a hearing as possible. The next two views offer such a case.

Immanent Purpose and Transcendentalism

The View

This view is like the first two in some respects. The immanent purpose view holds that there is no reason why something rather than nothing exists, that there is no purpose for human history, that there is no life after death, and that humans are the result of a blind process of evolution. But while there may be no reason to believe that there is any objective meaning or purpose outside human life which gives it meaning, this does not mean that life is not objectively meaningful. Life has objective meaning because objective values can be found within life.

According to the philosophy of immanent purpose, objective values exist and are part of the furniture of the universe. Values are there as brute givens. They are like Platonic forms (according to one reading of Plato)—they are ultimate entities which do not need to come from anywhere, including God, to exist. This could be understood along the lines of ethical naturalism. But it is more reasonable to see in this view of values a statement of ethical nonnaturalism. Values exist as irreducible, moral entities, and they attach to various things within life—the pursuit of truth, the intrinsic value of persons, and so on. As Karl Britton says, "The relationships between persons matter in themselves and many are of value in themselves."[20]

Why should I be moral? My motives may be varied, but some of them can be the desire to love persons, to do what is right, and to be a virtuous person. It is simply morally right to be moral. It is rational to adopt the

20. Britton, *Philosophy and the Meaning of Life*, p. 189.

moral point of view in my life plan because that point of view allows my life to have objective meaning. Life becomes objectively meaningful, as opposed to merely subjectively satisfying, when I pursue the realization of objective values which exist. When I seek to promote the good, moral values are realized within my life and my life becomes virtuous. This provides meaning in life, but this meaning does not come from God or some overarching meaning to the cosmos. Rather it comes from objective values which are immanently realized in life itself.

In sum, the immanent purpose view seeks to give real, objective meaning to life, not mere subjective satisfaction, and it does so by postulating the existence of objective moral values. But the meaningfulness of life does not depend on the existence of God or of some external purpose outside human life. Values realized within human life can give it real meaning. This view is an improvement over the first two views, for it recognizes the existence of objective, irreducible moral values. It also recognizes that a major contributor to an objectively meaningful life is that one has a duty to live according to the dictates of the moral point of view. But in spite of its advantages, several objections can be raised against the immanent purpose view. Taken together, these objections make it inadequate as an answer to the meaning of life.

Objections to the Immanent Purpose View

For one thing, the immanent purpose view cannot account for at least three features of moral life as we really experience it. First, moral responsibility seems to imply free will. It makes no sense to say one "ought" to do something if someone has no ability whatever to do it. But we argued in chapter 3 that free will makes sense on the assumption of substance dualism, and substance dualism makes more sense if theism is true. So the immanent purpose view must either deny free will (which undercuts the possibility of morality) or postulate substance dualism as an unexplained fact about the world.

Another feature of the moral life is the feeling of moral guilt or shame at moral failure. H. P. Owen argues that it is often rational to have guilt feelings in the face of moral failure even when no human is present toward whom one feels shame, or even if someone is present, the sense of shame goes beyond what would be appropriate if only another human were involved.[21] Owen goes on to argue that guilt *feelings* do not make sense if abstract moral principles are all there is to moral failure. Guilt feelings make sense if one feels shame in the presence of a Person. So if the depth and presence of guilt feelings is to be rational, there must be a Person toward whom one feels moral shame.

21. H. P. Owen, *The Moral Argument for Christian Theism* (London: Allen and Unwin, 1965), pp. 49–50.

A third feature of the moral life is the fact that we often believe in retributive punishment, that is, punishment of a crime which is not merely for the purpose of rehabilitation, protection of society, or deterrence. We sometimes feel that we should pay back evil for evil. As Joel Feinberg, H. L. A. Hart, and others point out, retributive punishment makes sense only if we think that in such cases we are balancing the moral universe (i.e., setting the moral record straight by balancing the good and evil in the universe by paying the moral universe back for the evil). But if such talk is to make sense when no clear victim of the crime is present, then there must be some being that we have in mind when we "pay the moral universe back." Such talk makes sense if God exists, for he is always a victim of crime, and thus his justice deserves to be paid back in the presence of evil. But without God, there is often no victim to pay back, and in such cases it is hard to make sense of retribution. These three features of the moral life—free will, guilt feelings, and retribution without a human victim—do not have an adequate explanation in the immanent purpose view, but they do in light of Christian theism.

Second, the existence of moral values as an ultimate, brute given in an impersonal universe is counterintuitive and puzzling.[22] We usually think of a command involving a Commander. Propositions or principles usually come from or exist in minds, so absolute moral propositions—ones which existed before humans evolved (as they would in the immanent purpose view)—would seem to come from or exist in an objective Mind. So either we take moral claims to be self-evident modes of impersonal existence or we explain them in terms of an ultimate Person. The latter makes their existence less puzzling than the former.

This point can be strengthened by the following consideration. Suppose I claim to see a table in front of me. I am prima facie justified in making this claim in the absence of defeaters of that claim.[23] In other words, I am entitled to my knowledge claim unless there is some reason to suspect that I am wrong. One source of defeaters, one source of information for suspecting my knowledge claim, is background information about the way the world is in general. For example, suppose I have background knowledge that when people think they see water on a highway when it is hot outside, they are really seeing heat waves. The experience is a mirage. If I saw water in front of my car while driving in the desert, I would not be justified in believing that water was really there.

    22. See Dom Illtyd Trethowan, *Absolute Value* (London: George Allen and Unwin, 1970), pp. 80–107; Robert Adams, "Moral Arguments for Theistic Belief," in *Rationality and Religious Belief,* ed. C. F. Delaney (Notre Dame: University of Notre Dame Press, 1979), pp. 116–40.
    23. John L. Pollock, *Knowledge and Justification* (Princeton: Princeton University Press, 1975), pp. 23–49.

Now consider the claim of the immanent purpose advocate who says that he knows moral values exist. If one also accepts current evolutionary theory (and denies the existence of God), then this would constitute background information that goes against the claim that moral values exist and can be known. According to that theory, the entire cosmos came from a blind explosion and life arose by random mutation and struggle for survival. Morality is merely the result of this struggle, for men discovered that life was safer when they banded together in communities.[24] Moral rules are not reflections of an objectively existing moral universe. They are social conventions grounded in the human instinct to survive. They have evolutionary origin and promote survival.

One could argue that the evolutionary account of morality commits the genetic fallacy—it confuses how morality came about with what morality is and what justifies it. There is a point in this rejoinder. Taken by itself, the evolutionary account of morality *is* an example of the genetic fallacy. But there are some cases where the genetic fallacy is not really inappropriate. These are cases where the causal account of the origin of an idea serves to discredit that idea in some way. In a trial, if the testimony of a witness comes from someone with bad motives, then one can rule out his testimony because of where it came from. His testimony could still be true, but it is unlikely. In the case of the mirage, one can rule out the veridicality of this experience by citing what caused it (hot air waves), even though it *could* still be an accurate experience.

If evolutionary theory is all there is to the development of the cosmos from the big bang to man, then any view which postulates the brute existence of morals would seem to do so in an ad hoc way. The general background theory would count against the veridicality of the claim to know that morals exist, even though it would still be logically possible for them to exist. If theism is true, one's background theory explains the existence of human morality. But if one denies God and accepts evolution, then it would seem more reasonable to accept an evolutionary, subjectivist view of morality. The existence of objective values would still be possible, but it would be unlikely and ad hoc, given this background theory. The claim to intuitively perceive such values would have such a background theory as a defeater. The background theory of theism supports such claims and makes them prima facie justified because it removes the background theory (atheistic evolution as the only account for human life and morality) which is the defeater. So objective morality is puzzling in the immanent purpose view.

Third, even if we grant that moral values are part of the ultimate furni-

24. See Ruse, "Evolutionary Ethics," and Murphy, *Evolution*.

ture of the universe, it is hard to see why they would have anything whatever to do with human beings. Given that moral values are brute entities
which simply exist, why would those entities refer to a small, short-lived
species on a little planet circling around a moderate star called the sun?
What would cause the moral universe to overlap with the physical universe at the point where human life exists? Scientists John Barrow and
Frank Tipler have argued that humans are just one stage in evolutionary
development, which is moving toward higher and higher forms.[25] All intermediate stages from amoebas to humans have only instrumental value
insofar as they contribute to later stages. Earlier stages do *not* have intrinsic
value. In fact, Barrow and Tipler argue that humans do not have intrinsic
value, but the DNA program *in* humans is what has value. We exist in order to perfect that program for life that will exist in the future.

It is easy to see why humans would have value if Christian theism is
true, but it is hard to see in the immanent purpose view how morality ever
came to be related to human beings at all. It was just a happy coincidence.
In fact, evolution itself could be used to argue that the coincidence never
occurred. We have only instrumental value, not intrinsic value.

Fourth, it would seem inconsistent to allow that moral values can exist
and be known and not allow that God exists and can be known. According
to the immanent purpose view, some of the reasons for atheism count
against their own moral views as well. They cut both ways. For example, it
is sometimes said that science has explained features of the world and
made God unnecessary, but the same could be said about evolutionary
ethics. Sometimes it is claimed that God, heaven, and the soul are unclear,
odd concepts which seem out of place in a scientific world where scientific
concepts (allegedly) are clear, can be quantified, and so forth. But the same
can be said about the existence and nature of moral values. Sometimes it is
said that religious experience is not good evidence for God because the notion of spiritual intuition by which God is directly experienced or perceived is problematic. But spiritual intuition is similar to moral intuition.
Most thinkers who hold to the immanent purpose view are intuitionists
when it comes to moral values. They believe that a faculty of the self exists
which enables one to be aware of moral values. I agree with this view, but
the point is that ethical experience is very similar to religious experience,
and one cannot have it both ways.

Fifth, even if one grants that there is some sort of natural law or objective
morality which can be known by intuition—a view which seems to me to
be true—one still cannot know much about morality from such cases of
intuition, except broad, general ethical knowledge: "pursue the good,"

"treat humans with dignity," "truth has value," and so forth.[26] This is fine as far as it goes, but it does not go very far. The immanent purpose view cannot offer much help in trying to decide what specific values are true and worthwhile. This epistemological problem is solved in Christian theism by supplementing natural law or general revelation—broad ethical principles which exist and can be known by all men—with special revelation in the Bible. This is not to deny the reality of natural law. It is merely to point out its epistemological inadequacy if it is unsupplemented by special revelation. Speaking of the problem of defining human rights—a task that the immanent purpose view sees as important—John Warwick Montgomery points out that natural law is not adequate by itself: "This is not in any sense to deny the reality of natural rights: it is only to say that their content is left epistemologically ill-defined by natural law thinking, and it is precisely their content that is essential to solve the human rights dilemma."[27]

Finally, the immanent purpose view does not really have an adequate answer for why I should be moral when doing so goes against my own interest. Consider the problem of what are called supererogatory acts. These are acts of heroism which are not morally obligatory—no one would be immoral for failing to do them—but are morally praiseworthy if they are done. For example, the act of throwing one's body on a bomb in order to save others in the room would be a supererogatory act. It is not morally obligatory but it is praiseworthy if done.

Are such acts rational? Why is it ever rational to do such acts or why is it ever rational to do a morally obligatory act (e.g., turning myself in for murder) if it is not in my own best interests to do so? The answer cannot be merely that such acts are right. The question is why I would be rational in such cases to do what is right. The only answer the immanent purpose view can give is that such acts give objective purpose to life. This may be a sufficient answer, but if such acts cause me to lose my life, it is hard to see how I can be rational in paying this price for a short period of objective meaning.

According to Christian theism, God works all things together for those who love him. He guarantees the summum bonum, the harmony of happiness and the moral right. God has created human nature such that doing the right will bring happiness in the long run, and as Immanuel Kant argued, the presence of an afterlife and the omniscience and omnipotence of God provide a rational justification for acts which appear to pit happiness

26. On the subject of natural law, see Josef Fuchs, *Natural Law* (New York: Sheed and Ward, 1965); A. R. d'Entreves, *Natural Law* (London: Hutchinson, 1970). For a discussion of natural law and the Bible, see Alan Johnson, "Is There a Biblical Warrant for Natural-Law Theories?" *Journal of the Evangelical Theological Society* 25 (June 1982): 185–99.

27. John Warwick Montgomery, *Human Rights and Human Dignity* (Grand Rapids: Zondervan, 1986), p. 128.

against duty. God wants us to do our duty in part because it is right. But such acts are not futile or irrational, because he will harmonize happiness and duty. The immanent purpose view has no such guarantee and is less satisfying because of it. And the immanent purpose view has difficulty justifying the rationality of acts where my own interests, even my own life, are in conflict with the dictates of duty. Christianity says that such cases are moral duties, and they can be rationally performed in part because God will reward us for them.

These are some of the reasons why the immanent purpose view is an inadequate answer to the question of the meaning of life. Let us now turn to the fourth view.

Cosmic Purpose and Christian Theism

The View

According to Christian theism, the cosmos exists to glorify God and to promote the good of God's creatures, especially man. Human history has a purpose and can be seen as a struggle between good and evil, the king-dom of God and the kingdom of darkness, which moves toward the vindi-cation of God, justice, righteousness, and the reward of those who have trusted Christ and lived in accord with the dictates of morality (which come from God). Humans are creations of God, they have value in that they bear his image, they are objects of God's love and affection, and there is life after death. Values exist, they come from God, they can be known through intuition in the natural law and through inspection of Holy Scrip-ture. My motive for being moral should be because I love God, I recognize him as my creator, I want to do what is right for its own sake, and I desire my own welfare in this life and the life to come. I am rationally justified in adopting the moral point of view because it is morally right to do so and because God guarantees that he will reward and honor me if I obey him.

To be frank, it is hard to see how anything could be more exciting than Christian theism. It provides an answer to all the aspects of the question of the meaning of life and it does so in such a way that it succeeds where the other views fail and provides more meaning than the others even when they succeed. As an example of this last point, one can grant that the im-manent purpose view gives some sort of answer to the question of how life can be objectively meaningful by postulating the existence of values. But Christian theism does this as well, and it explains why those values exist and relate to man, it provides more reasons for pursuing them (e.g., it is rational to obey a kind Being [God]), and it offers more satisfaction (in this life and the life to come).

Objections to the Cosmic Purpose View

We need not offer a list of positive arguments for the Christian theistic answer to the meaning of life. These arguments have already been given in the criticisms of the first three views. What remains is to consider objections raised against the answer of Christian theism.

The first objection is that God does not solve the problem of values; he only complicates the problem. As Plato pointed out in the *Euthyphro,* either something is moral because God commands it or God commands it because it is moral. In the former case, God's commands are entirely arbitrary, his authority (the right to command compliance) reduces to his power (the ability to command compliance), and God becomes a bare willer of morality. His nature has nothing to do with the moral law; morality comes from a fiat act of his will alone, and obeying God makes no more sense than obeying a cosmic Hitler. In the latter case, God's commands are based on some reason outside God for why some things are right, and one ought to be moral for those reasons and not because God commanded them.

Most theists respond by splitting the horns of the dilemma. Morality does not come from an arbitrary act of God's will or from some reason or property outside of God. Morality is grounded in God's nature. Some things are right because a *good, loving* God commands them. So God's laws are not arbitrary or based on something outside himself. Rather, they are based on something inside his own being, namely, his own moral attributes.[28]

The second objection is that the presence of God undercuts the meaning of life, for God dictates to man what will and will not count as meaningful and man cannot choose this for himself. Further, man becomes a mere tool in God's own plan to promote *his* ends.

This objection is a caricature of the biblical view. For one thing, God has given man freedom to choose what he will do with his life. Second, God's establishment of moral values is not "dictated" to man in any inappropriate way. The existence of such values is a necessary precondition of the very possibility of meaning. Further, the nature of moral values is not arbitrary; rather, they are grounded in human nature as a reflection of the divine nature itself. And God has made us such that these values are not mere duties, but they also come from a kind, good God who has made us in such a way that we are protected, satisfied, and fulfilled best by doing what is right. Finally, man is not a mere tool in God's eyes. Man is a valuable end, according to the biblical view, and he is the object of a God who cares for him. True, God does wish to glorify himself, but the wisdom of

28. This is argued, for example, by Adams, "Moral Arguments for Theistic Belief."

God implies that he uses means appropriate to his ends and he chooses appropriate ends to begin with. So he will not use men as mere instruments (unless they freely reject his love, and even then, they are not *mere* instruments), and he also has created man to enter the joy of God for man's own good. So this objection may count against some conceptions of God, but it is a misrepresentation of the Christian view.[29]

The third objection is that the existence of God and an afterlife does not give meaning to life.[30] Bestowing eternity on an empty life does not make it meaningful. It may yield only an eternity of emptiness. It is also possible to conceive of the existence of God in such a way that life is still meaningless even if God exists. If life is not meaningful and valuable in itself, then even God cannot bestow meaning on it in a nonarbitrary way.

Two things can be said against this objection. First, at best it shows only that God and an afterlife are not sufficient conditions of a meaningful life. It is possible to imagine an afterlife and a type of deity which do not give life meaning. But this does not show that God and an afterlife are not necessary conditions for an objectively meaningful life. Christian theism does not assert that any kind of God or any kind of afterlife gives meaning. Christian theism asserts that the *Christian* God and the biblical worldview give meaning to life.

Second, this objection is a form of the Euthyphro dilemma. It assumes that either God confers meaning and value on life arbitrarily or else he does so because it already has meaning and value independently of him. But Christian theism holds that human life has value and purpose because humans reflect God's very nature and that the purpose of human life and history also reflects God's nature. So the value and purpose of life are neither arbitrary nor grounded in something outside God. They are grounded in God's nature.

The last objection is that the Christian answer to why one should be moral collapses into personal egoism. One should be moral because it is in one's own selfish interests to do so. One will get a payoff in the sky. But egoism is against the very nature of duty, which demands that we do what is right merely because it is right, and not because it is in our interests to do so.

Two things can be said in response to this. First, personal rewards are not the only motive or rational justification for being moral according to Christian theism. Other motives or reasons are given as well: because I love God, because I think it is rational to obey a kind, benevolent Being who created me and knows what is right and what is best for me, because I

29. The argument is raised against theism by Kurt Baier, "The Meaning of Life," in *The Meaning of Life: Questions, Answers and Analysis,* ed. David Chaney and Steven Sanders (Englewood Cliffs, N.J.: Prentice-Hall, 1980), pp. 47–63.

30. See Thomas Nagel, *Mortal Questions* (Cambridge: Cambridge University Press, 1979), pp. 11–23.

think it is simply right to do one's moral duty. There is no reason to suppose that Christian theism cannot embrace all of these, and more, at the same time.

Second, the desire for rewards is not grounded in a selfish, egoistic self-interest. According to Christian theism, I must recognize that I am a creature of value; I am an end in myself. Thus, I promote my own good, not in a selfish, greedy way where I attend to myself as a bundle of prudential desires I want to have satisfied. Rather I attend to myself as an image-bearer. Just as the Christian view is against suicide (such acts fail to treat the subject himself as an end, but as a mere means to some other end, perhaps relief from pain), so the Christian view is against any act by which I dehumanize or trivialize my own existence, including acts where I choose to live for satisfactions which hurt me or minimize my humanness. But rewards from God are recognitions of my dignity. So I am justified in seeking them because in obtaining them, I affirm that I am a creature of value who is worthy of such rewards.

Given my nature as a human being, some desires are appropriate and some are inappropriate. The former are natural desires grounded in my nature as a human being who reflects the image of God. The latter are grounded in my sinful tendencies to violate my humanness or the dictates of morality. The desire to be rewarded and recognized before a Being who is holy, kind, and good is not an inappropriate egoism. It is an appropriate expression of a need which God himself made me to have, and that need is grounded in my human nature which itself has value as it reflects God's image.[31]

We have investigated the different nuances involved in the question of the meaning of life and we have explored four answers to the question. The first two deny that life is objectively valuable and purposeful, and opt for a view of life which is personally satisfying. Nihilism takes a pessimistic attitude toward life; optimistic humanism takes a more life-affirming attitude. The last two views affirm the existence of objective values and purpose, but Christian theism was judged to be superior to the immanent purpose view. The former explains the existence and nature of meaning in life better than the latter, and Christian theism offers more meaning than does the immanent purpose view. Objections against Christian theism's solution to the meaning of life are not successful.

In light of the options discussed in this chapter, it would seem reasonable to end with a brief statement of a version of what is called Pascal's

---

31. Meeting these natural needs can result in achieving other satisfactions as a byproduct. For example, Warren T. Brookes argues that economic prosperity and well-being are byproducts of a culture that seeks moral righteousness and justice. See *The Economy in Mind* (New York: Universe Books, 1982), pp. 203–26.

wager.[32] If one chooses Christian theism, he has lost very little if he is wrong. In fact, it could even be argued that he gains more happiness in this life if he adopts the Christian worldview.[33] If he is right, and Christian theism is true, he gains a great deal.

On the other hand, if he chooses to deny Christian theism, then there is a great deal to lose. If Christianity is true, one can lose his real meaning in life and suffer the fate of hell in the next life. If Christianity is false, then he has not really lost that much anyway. For Christianity offers virtually everything the other views offer and more. Assuming that Christianity is false, the only loser would be someone who adopted a version of the good life so out of step with the basic moral structure of Christianity that adopting that structure would be a painful adjustment. In that case it would be a factual question as to whether such a change would produce more satisfaction in this life than would the discarded version of the good life.

In sum, it is both rational and prudent to wager that Christian theism is the best answer to questions about the meaning of life.

32. For a good treatment of Pascal's wager, see Nicholas Rescher, *Pascal's Wager: A Study of Practical Reasoning in Philosophical Theology* (Notre Dame: University of Notre Dame Press, 1985). It is sometimes argued against Pascal's wager that, for all we know, whatever God there is may not like us to wager with our lives and may, in fact, reward a sincere atheist over a wagering believer. But just because this is a logical possibility, that does not by itself constitute a serious objection to the way I am using Pascal's wager. In this book, I am presenting good evidence for believing that the Christian God exists. Unless someone can give good evidence for belief in a god who rewards sincere atheists over wagering believers in the Christian gospel, the mere logical possibility of the existence of such a god counts for very little. If I see what looks like the mailman coming up to the door, the mere logical possibility that he may be a dangerous Vulcan in disguise does not provide rational warrant for preventing me from wagering that he is really the mailman. I should open the door and receive the package he has for me and I am rational in doing so. Similarly, I should open my heart and receive the gift the Christian God has for me because there is evidence that the Christian conception of God is true and very little evidence for the existence of a god who rewards sincere atheists who will not wager.

33. This fact suggests an empirical test for Christianity. The church should be able to produce people who are moral and spiritual saints who experience full, satisfying lives to a greater extent than they would if they were not Christians and to a greater extent than a random sampling of the population in general. Thus, the closer one gets to living according to mature, New Testament Christianity, the closer one should be toward the goal of uniting in one's self the traits of a morally and spiritually virtuous life and the joy of a satisfying form of living. Authentic Christianity should produce people who exemplify the summmum bonum—the harmony of the right and the happy—in their lives.

5

The Historicity
of the New Testament

One of the central claims of Christianity is that Jesus of Nazareth was the incarnate Son of God who died on the cross to atone for the sins of humanity and rose bodily from the dead. Our acceptance of these claims depends on whether or not the New Testament documents are reliable historical sources about Jesus. It is the purpose of this chapter to argue that it is reasonable to accept the substantial historicity of the New Testament.[1]

---

1. For a defense of the full inerrancy of Holy Scripture, see J. P. Moreland, "The Rationality of Belief in Inerrancy," *Trinity Journal* 7 (Spring 1986): 75–86.

Detailed works have been written on this topic, but such detail is not possible here. Rather, this chapter will discuss the main features of five arguments bearing on New Testament historicity. Sources for further study will be offered in the notes. I will not discuss the archaeological confirmation of the New Testament or the extrabiblical evidence for the historicity of Jesus. These important facts have been nicely summarized elsewhere.[2]

For our purposes, let us assume that the New Testament is a collection of twenty-seven separate historical sources which, in turn, may have written or oral sources behind them. We will make no assumption which takes the New Testament as a divinely inspired document, although I believe such a position can be defended.[3]

General Tests for Historicity

Historiography is a branch of study which focuses on the logical, conceptual, and epistemological aspects of what historians do. Critical historiography studies, among other things, the different tests which should be applied to a document to determine whether or not it is historically reliable.[4] When many of these tests are applied to the New Testament documents, they show themselves to be as reliable as, or superior to, most other ancient documents.

For example, apologists have often appealed to three general tests for historicity: the bibliographical test, the internal test, and the external test. The internal test asks whether the document itself claims to be actual history written by eyewitnesses. More will be said about eyewitness testimony later. The external test asks whether material external to the document (in this case, archaeology or the writings of the early church

2. For a summary of archaeology and the New Testament, see Edwin M. Yamauchi, "Archaeology and the New Testament," in *Introductory Articles*, vol. 1 of *The Expositor's Bible Commentary*, ed. Frank E. Gaebelein (Grand Rapids: Zondervan, 1979), pp. 645–69. Two of the best summaries of extrabiblical evidence for Jesus are Gary R. Habermas, *Ancient Evidence for the Life of Jesus: Historical Records of His Death and Resurrection* (Nashville: Nelson, 1985); F. F. Bruce, *Jesus and Christian Origins Outside the New Testament* (Grand Rapids: Eerdmans, 1974).

3. It is sometimes said that Christians use circular arguments to prove the reliability of the Bible. For an analysis and refutation of this claim, see R. C. Sproul, "The Case for Inerrancy: A Methodological Analysis," in *God's Inerrant Word: An International Symposium on the Trustworthiness of Scripture*, ed. John Warwick Montgomery (Minneapolis: Bethany Fellowship, 1974), pp. 242–61. For a helpful study of circular arguments in general, especially their relationship to begging the question, see Oliver Johnson, *Skepticism and Cognitivism: A Study in the Foundations of Knowledge* (Berkeley: University of California Press, 1979), pp. 226–39.

4. A brief, helpful survey of various issues in historiography can be found in Norman L. Geisler, *Christian Apologetics* (Grand Rapids: Baker, 1976), pp. 285–304. More detailed discussions can be found in William H. Dray, *Philosophy of History* (Englewood Cliffs, N.J.: Prentice-Hall, 1964); Hans Meyerhoff, ed., *The Philosophy of History in Our Time* (Garden City, N.Y.: Doubleday, Anchor Books, 1959); John Warwick Montgomery, *Where Is History Going?* (reprint ed.; Minneapolis: Bethany Fellowship, 1972); Sidney Hook, ed., *Philosophy and History: A Symposium* (New York: New York University Press, 1963).

fathers) confirms the reliability of the document. It is beyond the scope of this chapter to delve into the external test. But it should be pointed out that the New Testament has been remarkably confirmed time and again by external evidence. This is not to say there are no problems; but to the unbiased observer, little doubt can be cast on the statement that archaeology has confirmed the historical reliability of the New Testament.[5]

The bibliographical test seeks to determine how many manuscript copies we have of the document and how far removed they are in time from the originals (see table 1).

Table 1

Author	When Written	Earliest Copy	Time Span	No. of Copies
Caesar	100–44 B.C.	900 A.D.	1,000 yrs.	10
Livy	59 B.C.–A.D. 17			20
Plato (Tetralogies)	427–347 B.C.	900 A.D.	1,200 yrs.	7
Tacitus (Annals)	100 A.D.	1,100 A.D.	1,000 yrs.	20 (-)
also minor works	100 A.D.	1,000 A.D.	900 yrs.	1
Pliny the Younger				
(History)	61–113 A.D.	850 A.D.	750 yrs.	7
Thucydides (History)	460–400 B.C.	900 A.D.	1,300 yrs.	8
Suetonius				
(De Vita Caesarum)	75–160 A.D.	950 A.D.	800 yrs.	8
Herodotus (History)	480–425 B.C.	900 A.D.	1,300 yrs.	8
Horace			900 yrs.	
Sophocles	496–406 B.C.	1,000 A.D.	1,400 yrs.	100
Lucretius	Died 55 or 53 B.C.		1,100 yrs.	2
Catullus	54 B.C.	1,550 A.D.	1,600 yrs.	3
Euripedes	480–406 B.C.	1,100 A.D.	1,500 yrs.	9
Demosthenes	383–322 B.C.	1,100 A.D.	1,300 yrs.	200*
Aristotle	384–322 B.C.	1,100 A.D.	1,400 yrs.	5†
Aristophanes	450–385 B.C.	900 A.D.	1,200 yrs.	10

*All from one copy.
†Of any one work.

From Josh McDowell, *Evidence That Demands a Verdict*, rev. ed. (San Bernardino, Calif.: Here's Life, 1979), p. 42.

A brief perusal of the table indicates that for a representative sample of ancient historical works, we possess only a handful of manuscripts which are, on the average, one thousand years removed from their originals.

In contrast to this, the New Testament documents have a staggering quantity of manuscript attestation.[6] Approximately 5,000 Greek manuscripts, containing all or part of the New Testament, exist. There are 8,000 manuscript copies of the Vulgate (a Latin translation of the Bible done by

5. In addition to Yamauchi, "Archaeology of the New Testament," see Habermas, *Ancient Evidence*, pp. 152–63.
6. See Norman L. Geisler and William E. Nix, *A General Introduction to the Bible* (Chicago: Moody, 1968); Bruce M. Metzger, *The Text of the New Testament: Its Transmission, Corruption, and Restoration* (New

Jerome from 382–405) and more than 350 copies of Syriac (Christian Aramaic) versions of the New Testament (these originated from 150–250; most of the copies are from the 400s). Besides this, virtually the entire New Testament could be reproduced from citations contained in the works of the early church fathers. There are some thirty-two thousand citations in the writings of the Fathers prior to the Council of Nicea (325).

The dates of the manuscript copies range from early in the second century to the time of the Reformation. Many of the manuscripts are early—for example, the John Rylands manuscript (about 120; it was found in Egypt and contains a few verses from the Gospel of John), the Chester Beatty Papyri (200; it contains major portions of the New Testament), Codex Sinaiticus (350; it contains virtually all of the New Testament), and Codex Vaticanus (325–50; it contains almost the entire Bible).

Too much can be made of this evidence, which alone does not establish the trustworthiness of the New Testament. All it shows is that the text we currently possess is an accurate representation of the original New Testament documents. Most historians accept the textual accuracy of other ancient works on far less adequate manuscript grounds than is available for the New Testament.

In this regard, the following statement about the New Testament by R. Joseph Hoffmann is naive: "What we possess are copies of copies, so far removed from anything that might be called a 'primary' account that it is useless to speculate about what an original version of the gospel would have included."[7]

As I have shown, the copies of the New Testament are not far removed from the originals. Furthermore, Hoffmann is using the wrong sense of the term *original* as it is employed in historical investigation. As Louis Gottschalk points out, "[A primary source] does not, however, need to be original in the legal sense of the word original—that is, the very document (usually the first written draft) whose contents are the subject of discussion—for quite often a later copy or a printed edition will do just as well; and in the case of the Greek and Roman classics seldom are any but later copies available."[8]

Other tests for historicity have been formulated, some of which are these: a document has a high probability of reliability if it is a personal let-

York: Oxford University Press, 1964). For a briefer treatment of the text of the New Testament, see Gordon D. Fee, "The Textual Criticism of the New Testament," in *Introductory Articles*, vol. 1 of *The Expositor's Bible Commentary*, ed. Frank E. Gaebelein (Grand Rapids: Zondervan, 1979), pp. 419–33.

7. R. Joseph Hoffmann, "The Origins of Christianity: A Guide to Answering Fundamentalists," *Free Inquiry* 5 (Spring 1985): 50.

8. Louis Gottschalk, *Understanding History: A Primer of Historical Method*, 2d ed. (New York: Alfred A. Knopf, 1969), pp. 53–54. For a good discussion of the concept of an original autograph in terms of the distinction between types and tokens, see Greg L. Bahnsen, "The Inerrancy of the Autographs," in *Inerrancy*, ed. Norman L. Geisler (Grand Rapids: Zondervan, 1980), pp. 151–93.

ter, is intended for small audiences, is written in unpolished style, and contains trivia and lists of details.[9] The absence of these features does not necessarily mean the document is unreliable; but their presence makes the prima facie acceptance of the document stronger. Much of the New Testament, especially the apostolic letters and some of the sources behind the Gospels, is made up of personal letters originally intended for individuals and small groups. In addition, much of the New Testament is in unpolished style, and there are several examples of inconsequential detail in the Gospels (see Mark 14:51–52; John 21:2, 11). Further, in 2 Corinthians 12:11–12, Paul writes to a church which is questioning his apostolic authority. To defend himself, he reminds the believers that while he had been with them (approximately four years earlier) he had performed miracles and wonders. If this had not been the case, then Paul would have been a fool to use what everyone knew was a lie to defend himself.

These considerations show that when general tests for historicity are applied to the New Testament documents, they pass them quite well.

The Presence of Eyewitnesses

Prima facie it would seem that a strong case could be made for the fact that much of the New Testament, including the Gospels and the sources behind them, was written by eyewitnesses. This is mentioned explicitly in a number of places (Luke 1:1–4; Gal. 1; 2 Peter 1:16). Further, apostolic position in the early church was widely known to include the qualification of being an eyewitness (Acts 1:21–22; Heb. 2:3), a qualification which shows that the early church valued the testimony of eyewitnesses and believed she had eyewitnesses leading her. The early speeches in Acts refer to the knowledge of unbelieving audiences (e.g., Acts 2:22), and no historian I know of doubts that Christianity started in Jerusalem just a few weeks after the death of Jesus in the presence of friendly and hostile eyewitnesses. Finally, there is indirect testimony to eyewitness evidence in the Gospels.[10] For example, if a number of pronouns in Mark (see 1:21, 29) are changed from the third-person plural *they* to the first-person plural *we*, they can easily be seen as eyewitness reminiscences of Peter, who gave Mark much of the material for his Gospel.

Arguments Supporting Eyewitness Influence

Several reasons can be offered for trusting these claims. First, as Gottschalk reminds us, a document should be assumed trustworthy unless, un-

---

9. Gottschalk, *Understanding History*, pp. 41–171.
10. Donald Guthrie, *New Testament Introduction* (Downers Grove: Inter-Varsity, 1970), p. 142.

der burden of proof, it is shown to be unreliable.[11] As Immanuel Kant showed long ago, a general presumption of lying is self-refuting, since if such a presumption is universalized (one always assumes someone is lying) lying becomes pointless (lying is impossible without a general presumption of truthtelling).[12]

Second, such a presumption of truthtelling is especially strong if the eyewitness passes these tests: he is able to tell the truth, he is willing to do so, he is accurately reported, and there is external corroboration of his testimony.[13] I have already shown that the New Testament eyewitnesses are accurately reported in the manuscript tradition, and I have alluded to external confirmation of the New Testament. What about the first two tests?

It seems clear that the New Testament writers were able and willing to tell the truth. They had very little to gain and much to lose for their efforts. For one thing, they were mostly Jewish theists. To change the religion of Israel with its observance of the Mosaic law, Sabbath keeping, sacrifices, and clear-cut non-Trinitarian monotheism would be to risk the damnation of their own souls to hell. A modern atheist may not worry about such a thing, but members of the early church surely did. For another thing, the apostles lived lives of great hardship, stress, and affliction (see 2 Cor. 11:23–29) and died martyrs' deaths for their convictions. There is no adequate motive for their labors other than a sincere desire to proclaim what they believed to be the truth.

Third, the presence of adverse eyewitnesses would have hampered the spread of Christianity. Christianity began, and remained for some time, in the same area where Jesus had ministered. If the early portrait of him was untrue, how could the apostles have succeeded there? Why would they have begun there in the first place?

Fourth, if the New Testament picture of Jesus was not based on the testimony of eyewitnesses, how could a consistent tradition about him ever have been formed and written? Assume that no eyewitnesses controlled the tradition about Jesus prior to the time the Gospels were written. Assume further that the scattered early believing communities were so caught up with the living "presence" of the resurrected Christ speaking to them through prophetic utterances in the church assemblies that they lost

11. Gottschalk, *Understanding History,* p. 89.

12. Thus, Van A. Harvey surely errs when he says that it is required of a modern historian that he adopt a standpoint of methodological skepticism. See *The Historian and the Believer* (New York: Macmillan, 1966), pp. 102–26. For a general theory of evidence based on a prima facie burden of proof for skepticism, see Roderick Chisholm, "A Version of Foundationalism," in *Studies in Epistemology,* ed. Peter A. French et al., Midwest Studies in Philosophy, vol. 5 (Minneapolis: University of Minnesota Press, 1980), pp. 543–64. For an excellent treatment of the legal aspects of testing the trustworthiness of witnesses and the application of this testing to the New Testament, see John Warwick Montgomery, *Human Rights and Human Dignity* (Grand Rapids: Zondervan, 1986), pp. 139–50.

13. Gottschalk, *Understanding History,* p. 150.

almost all interest in the historical Jesus as he really was. Then there would have been almost as many Christologies or portraits of Jesus and his significance as there were believing communities. Further, why would the churches tie themselves to four written sources if they could hear Christ "speak" afresh to them in their assemblies and if they felt free to make up sayings and stories about Jesus to meet the needs of their life setting? Eyewitness apostolic control over the tradition is the best explanation for the emergence of a consistent, written portrait of Jesus.

Three Objections to Eyewitness Influence

Certain objections have been raised against the eyewitness nature of the New Testament record of Jesus, however. Three of them are especially important. First, it has been argued that after the experience of the "Easter event"—a powerful, subjective feeling of the presence of the Christ after Jesus' death—the church lost interest in the biographical details of the historical Jesus who really lived. Rather, believers were interested in the ongoing experience of the Christ who was continually with them. In the early assemblies, prophets uttered sayings of the risen Christ as he spoke to his people through them. The church so identified the Christ who was speaking (the post-Easter experiences of "the Christ") with the Jesus who had spoken (the historical Jesus) that they lost interest in the latter. In fact, they freely made up episodes about Jesus which met their current needs. The Gospels are theological, kerygmatic, propagandistic works, not objective, historical biographies of Jesus. Thus, eyewitness testimony is irrelevant, given the nature of the Gospels.

Several things can be said against this objection. For one thing, David Hill has shown that there is no evidence that there ever were prophets in the early church who uttered "sayings of Jesus" which were attributed to the pre-Easter historical Jesus.[14] Those supporting such a view do so for two main reasons. First, a statement in Odes of Solomon 42:6 says, "For I have risen and stand by them, and speak through their mouth." However, this document dates from 110–150 and shows heavy influence from a post-Christian heresy, Gnosticism. Thus, it forms no basis for interpreting how the early church understood utterances in their assemblies. These sayings were understood as utterances of the Holy Spirit (or on a few occasions, of the resurrected and glorified Christ) and not of the historical Jesus.

A second argument for the existence of these prophets points to utterances of Christ in the Book of Revelation (see Rev. 1:17–20). But Revelation

---

14. See David Hill, "On the Evidence for the Creative Role of Christian Prophets," *New Testament Studies* 20 (April 1974): 262–74; *New Testament Prophecy* (Atlanta: John Knox, 1980); see also David E. Aune, *Prophecy in Early Christianity and the Ancient Mediterranean World* (Grand Rapids: Eerdmans, 1983).

was written later than the Gospels and differs from them in its literary genre—Revelation is apocalyptic literature, not theological history. Further, utterances in Revelation are acknowledged as sayings of the risen Lord. They are *not* attributed to the pre-Easter Jesus. In point of fact, the New Testament writers distinguish their inspired words from those of the historical Jesus (see 1 Cor. 7:25).

There is also good evidence that the Gospels *are* biographical. As G. N. Stanton has shown, the major examples of preaching in early Christianity come from Acts, and the sermons of Acts have, as an integral part, biographical details of Jesus' life.[15] C. H. Dodd has argued that the chronological order of Jesus' ministry as it is given in the sermons parallels nicely the order given in Mark.[16] This shows the Gospel writers were interested in historical detail. Furthermore, Paul himself showed interest in biographical details of Jesus' life (Rom. 15:3, 8; 2 Cor. 8:9; Phil. 2:6–11). These details form the basis of moral exhortation.

It is antecedently incredible that converts to and inquirers about Christianity in its early years would not want to know a good bit about the person they loved. This is especially true in light of the embarrassment of the crucifixion. People would want to know what sort of person Jesus really was. Why had he been crucified? Was he a troublemaker? The passion narratives of Jesus' last hours on earth were formed and circulated early in the missionary and teaching ministries of the church. These narratives would lead converts to expect more details about Jesus, and such details are what the Gospels attempt to provide.

When the Gospels are compared with ancient biographies, they can be seen to be biographical as well.[17] Biographies were often written to instruct and exhort and were not mere chronicles of information. But this does not mean biographers did not attend to historical facts. It is a false dichotomy to say something has to be either history or a document which promotes a message. The fact that the Gospels are kerygmatic does not rule out their historical dimension, especially when they emphasize the inseparability of the historical and the theological in understanding the incarnation.

A second objection to the eyewitness nature of the New Testament record of Jesus argues that ancient people were less interested in facts than we are today and thus ancient historians were not concerned or able to distinguish fact from fiction. So the presence or absence of eyewitnesses is not that important, since the value placed on factual reporting was not that great.

15. G. N. Stanton, *Jesus of Nazareth in New Testament Preaching* (Cambridge: Cambridge University Press, 1974), pp. 70–77.

16. C. H. Dodd, *New Testament Studies* (Manchester: Manchester University Press, 1953), pp. 1–11.

17. In addition to Stanton, *Jesus of Nazareth*, see Charles H. Talbert, *What Is a Gospel? The Genre of the Canonical Gospels* (Philadelphia: Fortress, 1977).

This objection does not accurately represent the nature of historical writing in the ancient world.[18] Many ancient Greek historians saw the importance of accurate reporting. Herodotus emphasized the role of eyewitnesses and the evaluation of sources. Thucydides attempted to evaluate the accuracy of reports coming to him, and when he invented a speech, he did so to represent, as well as possible, the views of the speaker. He did not feel free to invent narrative. Polybius held exacting standards. He advocated examining sources and evaluating eyewitnesses. Lucian stated that the historian's sole task is to tell the tale as it happened.

Roman historians were strongly influenced by the Greeks. Cicero affirmed that the historian must tell nothing but the truth. Livy was less critical and wrote to emphasize the greatness of Rome, but he did not feel free to invent stories. Tacitus attempted to test and evaluate his sources and did not wish to deliberately distort his information.

I will address the nature of Jewish oral tradition shortly. Suffice it to say here that it was concerned with accuracy. Furthermore, Josephus stated his commitment to truth and accuracy, and he tried to correct his sources when they were wrong.

Ancient historians were not as critical or precise as their modern counterparts. But the question "did it really happen?" made sense to them. The New Testament writers show a concern to preserve historical facts accurately (Luke 1:1-4; John 21:24; Heb. 2:3-4; 2 Peter 1:16). This does not prove they wrote history, but it clearly shows that they understood the difference between fact and fiction and that they were interested in the former.

A third objection against the eyewitness nature of the New Testament record of Jesus comes from D. E. Nineham.[19] Nineham argues that the Gospel materials present themselves in classifiable forms which met needs in the early church; thus, they are the result of a great deal of shaping at the hands of the early Christian community. But Nineham's objection fails. There is no reason to assume that Jesus did not teach in consistent forms which could be easily memorized. Further, when the church orally circulated its information about Jesus this material may have been put into forms that could be memorized and passed on easily. But this does not mean believers fabricated the stories. It is a false move from

18. See A. W. Mosley, "Historical Reporting in the Ancient World," *New Testament Studies* 12 (October 1965): 10-26. See also the bibliography on page 7 of C. F. D. Moule, *The Birth of the New Testament*, 3d ed., rev. (San Francisco: Harper and Row, 1981). It is sometimes objected that people in Jesus' day were gullible about miracles and miracle workers. It is alleged that miracle workers were plentiful in the ancient world, and that Jesus' miracles were fabricated to fit with the works of pagan or other Jewish miracle workers. For a good critique of this objection, see A. E. Harvey, *Jesus and the Constraints of History* (Philadelphia: Westminster, 1982), pp. 98-119.

19. D. E. Nineham, "Eyewitness Testimony and the Gospel Tradition, I, II, III," *Journal of Theological Studies* 9 (April 1958): 13-25; 9 (October 1958): 223-52; 11 (October 1960): 253-64.

the form of a narrative to its historical accuracy.[20] The forms of the Gospel material have more to do with preservation of the material than with creation of the material.

The Gospels and Jewish Oral Tradition

Over the last several years, trends in New Testament studies have been toward understanding the Gospels as Jewish documents with a Jewish influence shaping them. The Hellenistic influence on the genre and content of the Gospels has been seen as less significant.[21] This change is due in part to the influence of a school of New Testament studies known as the Scandinavian or Uppsala school founded by Harald Riesenfeld and Birger Gerhardsson.[22]

The classical form- and redaction-critical approach to the formation of the Gospels is roughly this. In light of their experience of the "risen Christ" and their expectation of his immediate return, persons in the early

20. See T. W. Manson, *Studies in the Gospels and Epistles*, ed. Matthew Black (Philadelphia: Westminster, 1962), p. 5; Pierre Benoit, *Jesus and the Gospel*, 2 vols. (New York: Seabury, Crossroad Books, 1973), 1:28.

21. The most helpful survey of Hellenistic influence on the New Testament is Ronald H. Nash, *Christianity and the Hellenistic World* (Grand Rapids: Zondervan, 1984). For a treatment of Aretalogies, divine men, and the Gospels, see Howard C. Kee, "Aretalogy and the Gospel," *Journal of Biblical Literature* 92 (September 1973): 402–22; "Huios," by W. V. Martitz, in *Theological Dictionary of the New Testament*, ed. Gerhard Kittel and Gerhard Friedrich, trans. Geoffrey W. Bromiley, 10 vols. (Grand Rapids: Eerdmans, 1964–76), 8:338–40; Michael Green, ed., *The Truth of God Incarnate* (Grand Rapids: Eerdmans, 1977), pp. 36–42; John W. Drane, "The Religious Background," in *New Testament Interpretation: Essays on Principles and Methods*, ed. I. Howard Marshall (Grand Rapids: Eerdmans, 1978), pp. 117–25.

22. See Harald Riesenfeld, *The Gospel Tradition and Its Beginnings* (London: A. W. Mowbray and Company, 1961); Birger Gerhardsson, *Memory and Manuscript: Oral Tradition and Written Transmission in Rabbinic Judaism and Early Christianity* (Uppsala: Gleerup, 1961); for brief summaries of this position, see I. Howard Marshall, *I Believe in the Historical Jesus*, I Believe series (Grand Rapids: Eerdmans, 1977), pp. 195–96; Peter H. Davids, "The Gospels and Jewish Tradition: Twenty Years After Gerhardsson," in *Gospel Perspectives I* (Sheffield: JSOT Press, 1980), pp. 75–99. Gerhardsson has responded to criticisms from Morton Smith and Jacob Neusner and has summarized and updated his position in *The Origins of the Gospel Traditions*, trans. Gene J. Lund (Philadelphia: Fortress, 1979). In *The Charismatic Leader and His Followers* (New York: Seabury, Crossroad Books, 1981), Martin Hengel has criticized Gerhardsson and has tried to show that there is no precise parallel between Jesus and Jewish rabbis. Three things can be said in response to Hengel. First, Gerhardsson argues in *Origins of the Gospel Traditions* that the fundamental point of comparison between Jesus and rabbis is memorization of the leader's teaching. But this feature was widespread in the ancient world and is the most likely parallel to hold between Jesus and the rabbis. Second, Hengel seems to prove only that Jesus was *more* than a rabbi, not less than one, and the addresses to Jesus as rabbi in the Gospels seem to go beyond a mere form of address equivalent to "sir." Third, Moule points out *(Birth of the New Testament*, pp. 231–34) that the language in the New Testament indicates that the message of Jesus was a deposit to be guarded and protected from error. Thus, Hengel's remark that there was an emphasis on obedience instead of accuracy of learning and knowledge seems to be an overstatement. R. T. France has pointed out that even if one does not see a close parallel between Jesus and first-century rabbis, there is still enough evidence about first-century educational practice in general to indicate that memorization was a major means of education and thus Jesus' teaching would have been accurately passed on to others. See R. T. France, *The Evidence for Jesus* (Downers Grove: Inter-Varsity, 1986), pp. 106–11.

church were not interested in the historical Jesus per se, but created stories about Jesus to meet their current needs. These stories were then attributed to the pre-Easter Jesus. Thus, during the time before the Gospels were written, the Jesus tradition (the material about Jesus) was altered and expanded freely into various forms of material which were finally put into writing. The process of selection and shaping was marked heavily by the interests and theology of the Gospel writers themselves.

In contrast, the Uppsala school holds that the Jesus tradition was shaped consciously by the same principles that governed the shaping of Jewish oral tradition in general. According to this view, Jesus was an authoritative teacher or rabbi who trained his disciples to be his apprentices. In keeping with the practices of their orally oriented culture, they were capable of accurately memorizing massive amounts of material. The disciples of Jesus took great care to memorize his teachings and deeds (they may have written down some of the material as well), and saw their responsibility as guardians of the tradition. Their role was to pass on the tradition faithfully and substantially unaltered. The Gospels, therefore, are in large measure the written results of a process of handling the tradition which preserved its accuracy.

Several arguments can be advanced to support this view. For one thing, Jesus' relation to his disciples was similar to that of Jewish rabbis to their pupils.[23] Second, the Gospels arose primarily in a Jewish milieu where there was respect for holy tradition and oral transmission. Third, this view explains the role of an apostle and his authority as it is presented in the New Testament, namely, as an authoritative, eyewitness guardian of the tradition. Fourth, it explains the way the New Testament writers themselves refer to their own view of the way they handled the tradition about Jesus (see 1 Cor. 15:3–8; Gal. 2:1–10; Col. 2:7; 1 Thess. 2:13). When they refer to the way they handled the material about Jesus, they say that they "delivered over" to others exactly what they "received." These terms are the ones used in Jewish oral tradition to describe the way such tradition was passed on.

It seems, then, that the early disciples of Jesus wrote down some of Jesus' sayings and deeds, memorized a great deal of his teaching (they were capable of this in that culture), and passed it on with accuracy. Two major objections have been raised against the Uppsala view.[24] The first is that the Uppsala school bases its view on rabbinic practices and traditions that were late (A.D. 200); it is, however, unwarranted to parallel that tradition with practices current in A.D. 70. This objection is far too radical in its

23. For practical implications of this point, see Cleon Rogers, "The Great Commission," *Bibliotheca Sacra* 130 (July 1973): 258–67; John Lozano, *Discipleship: Towards an Understanding of Religious Life* (Chicago: Claret Center for Resources in Spirituality, 1980), pp. 1–38.

24. See Marshall, *I Believe*, pp. 195–96.

skepticism. Rabbinic practices in 200 were surely influenced by earlier practices. And the New Testament practices themselves give evidence that the accurate handing over of received tradition was a cultural and religious practice in New Testament times. Furthermore, when one compares the synoptic Gospels with one another, one finds that there is greater word-for-word agreement in the words of Jesus than in the incidental details of the surrounding historical narrative. This is what one would expect if the material was handled as holy tradition.[25]

The second objection, that one cannot draw parallels between rabbinic and Christian tradition, is clearly overstated. There may be differences between Jewish and Christian tradition, but there are many similiarities, since Jewish culture provided the womb from which Christianity was born.

Marks of Historicity in the Gospel Materials

Several features of the Gospels attest to their substantial historicity. Some of these features are made more vivid when placed against the backdrop of a form- and redaction-critical approach. By way of review, this view holds that the Gospels were written between 70 and 95. Prior to this, there was a period during which material was freely created and modified in light of the community's experience of the "risen Christ." This material was intended to meet needs in the community, and it was transmitted orally. For example, after several years Jesus' return seemed to be delayed, and believers began to die. To comfort the bereaved, some community created a story of Jesus raising a widow's son (Luke 7:11–17). Eventually this story found its way into the Gospels. So, much of the Gospels reflects the needs and issues in the life setting of the early church (50–75) or in the life setting of the redactors of the Gospels at the time they were put into writing. With this scenario in mind, the following is a list of six general marks of historicity in the Gospels.

The Form of Jesus' Sayings

Many of Jesus' sayings are in poetic or otherwise easily memorizable form. These forms are largely confined to the sayings in the tradition, as opposed to the narratives.[26] There is no good reason to attribute this to some early catechesis (a list of teaching materials formulated by a school in

25. See R. T. France, "The Authenticity of the Sayings of Jesus," in *History, Criticism, and Faith,* ed. Colin Brown (Downers Grove: Inter-Varsity, 1976), pp. 101–43.

26. France, "Authenticity of the Sayings of Jesus," p. 123.

the early church) and not to Jesus himself, because the sayings present an internal unity and intentionality which evidences a single mind behind them. Further, it was common for a single rabbi to teach in forms that were easily memorizable, so it is not unreasonable to attribute the same practice to Jesus himself.

Other Distinctive Features of Jesus' Sayings

Other recognizable characteristics and terms are found in Jesus' words and hardly anywhere else. Jesus' use of the words *amen* and *abba* is unique.[27] There are sixty-four instances of threefold sayings (e.g., ask, seek, knock) in Jesus' words, and his use of questions is unique.[28] Jesus' use of the passive in contexts where he refers to God (e.g., "All things have been delivered to me by my Father" [Matt. 11:27]) and his employment of the phrases *how much more, which of you,* and *disciple* is not duplicated by Paul, Peter, or other writers.[29] Aramaisms (phrases transliterated, rather than translated, into Greek from Aramaic) have sometimes been retained; even when they are not, there is often parallelism, assonance, and alliteration when the Greek is put back into Aramaic.[30] This makes sense if these sayings reflect the actual words of Jesus (he taught in Aramaic as well as Greek), but the church from 50 on was predominantly Greek-speaking. Finally, Jesus' use of parables is unique.[31]

The Presence of Irrelevant Material

Some of the material in the Gospels is irrelevant to the issues facing the early church (50–90). So it is hard to attribute the creation of this material to the church. It must have been preserved, in spite of its lack of immediate relevance, because it came from Jesus himself. Especially noteworthy is Jesus' attitude of favor to Israel.[32] To this could be added Jesus' use of the phrases *the kingdom of God* and *the son of man.*[33] Jesus' controversies with the Pharisees (e.g., about keeping the Sabbath) and his comments on Corban practices were not relevant at the time the Gospels were written.[34] Fi-

---

27. C. F. D. Moule, *The Phenomenon of the New Testament* (London: SCM, 1967), pp. 47–55.

28. C. Leslie Mitton, *Jesus: The Fact Behind the Faith* (Grand Rapids: Eerdmans, 1974), pp. 136–39.

29. H. E. W. Turner, *Historicity and the Gospels* (London: A. R. Mowbray and Company, 1963), pp. 76–78.

30. Mitton, *Jesus,* pp. 135–36.

31. Joachim Jeremias, *The Parables of Jesus* (1954; New York: Charles Scribner's Sons, 1963), pp. 11–12.

32. Moule, *Phenomenon of the New Testament,* pp. 66–67.

33. France, "Authenticity of the Sayings of Jesus," p. 113.

34. Everett H. Harrison, "Gemeindetheologie: The Bane of Gospel Criticism," in *Jesus of Nazareth: Savior and Lord,* ed. Carl F. H. Henry (Grand Rapids: Eerdmans, 1966), pp. 157–73.

nally, the Eucharist narrative does not seem to have played an especially prominent role in the early churches' celebration of the Lord's Supper.[35]

The Lack of Relevant Material

The church failed to put into the Synoptic tradition material that would have helped the church a great deal during the period when the tradition was passed on orally. This is surprising if the Gospels were shaped to meet these needs. So the failure to create sayings of Jesus to meet these pressing needs shows restraint in handling the Gospel materials. No saying of Jesus is to be found on several issues because no saying of Jesus was given on those issues.

Some examples are circumcision, charismatic gifts, baptism, food laws, Gentile missions (Paul could not appeal to a saying of the historical Jesus to justify his Gentile mission), several ministries of the Holy Spirit, rules governing assembly meetings, and church-state relations.[36] Perhaps the most significant omission, however, is the omission of Pauline statements. T. W. Manson has said it well:

> The Pauline letters abound in utterances which could easily be transferred to Jesus and presented to the world as oracles of the Lord. How many are? None. It seems a little odd that, if the story of Jesus was the creation of the Christian community, no use should have been made of the admirable materials offered by one of the most able, active, and influential members of the community.[37]

Counterproductive Features

If a document contains features which are embarrassing or counterproductive to the purpose for which it was written, then it has a high probability of being historical.[38] There would be no sufficient reason other than their facticity for including such features.

Instances of this occur frequently in the Gospels. Jesus' denial of being good is an example.[39] Jesus' attitudes toward legalism, fasting, divorce, sinners, and women were radical and somewhat embarrassing. Several features of Jesus' character were stumbling blocks, including his displays of anger, his baptism, his death on a cross, and the fact that he was a car-

---

35. R. P. C. Hanson, "The Enterprise of Emancipating Christian Belief from History," in *Vindications*, ed. Anthony Hanson (New York: Morehouse-Barlow, 1966), p. 56.

36. Moule, *Phenomenon of the New Testament*, pp. 72–75.

37. Manson, *Studies in the Gospels and Epistles*, p. 7.

38. Gottschalk, *Understanding History*, pp. 156–65.

39. A. R. C. Leaney, "Historicity in the Gospels," in *Vindications*, ed. Anthony Hanson (New York: Morehouse-Barlow, 1966), p. 120. To this may be added Mark 13:32; 15:34.

penter from Nazareth. To this could be added the opposition to Jesus from his family.[40] Also, the portrayal of the disciples is often embarrassing (e.g., when they are in unbelief, show cowardice, or have difficulty with Jesus' teaching). The request of the sons of Zebedee is surely authentic, as is Matthew 23:8, 10, which would seem to condemn the churches' own practice of having official teachers.

The Time Factor

The Expansion of Christianity

Jesus was probably crucified in A.D. 33.[41] As Christianity expanded from that time, it began as a religion immersed in Jewish culture; it eventually penetrated Gentile culture as the gospel was spread. Palestine in the first century had been influenced to some extent by Hellenism, and many Jews at that time were at least bilingual, speaking Aramaic and Greek.[42] By contrast, Hellenistic culture outside Palestine was not significantly influenced by Jewish thought-forms, nor did Gentiles speak Aramaic.

These features of first-century culture bear on the question of dating some of the materials in the New Testament. If a saying of Jesus or a christological title (e.g., "Lord") which shows Hellenistic influence is found in the New Testament, this is not necessarily a sign that the saying or title was created at a time when the church was predominantly Gentile. The saying or title could be early and attributable to Jesus himself, since Hellenistic influences were present in the Palestine of his day. On the other hand, if a saying or title translates easily from New Testament Greek back into Aramaic, or shows signs of Hebrew poetry or thought-forms, then such material is early. It would have originated at the latest in the early Palestinian church and at the earliest with Jesus himself. This will be important to keep in mind.

Paul's Letters

General Dating

Scholars disagree over how many of the New Testament letters attributed to Paul were really written by him, although a strong case can still be

40. Mitton, *Jesus,* p. 120.

41. See Harold W. Hoehner, *Chronological Aspects of the Life of Christ* (Grand Rapids: Zondervan, 1976), pp. 95–114.

42. For the influence of Hellenism on first-century Palestine, see I. Howard Marshall, "Palestinian and Hellenistic Christianity: Some Critical Comments," *New Testament Studies* 19 (April 1973): 271–87. On the language of Palestine in Jesus' day, see Philip Edgcumbe Hughes, "The Languages Spoken by Jesus," in *New Dimensions in New Testament Study,* ed. Richard N. Longenecker and Merrill C. Tenney (Grand Rapids: Zondervan, 1974), pp. 127–43.

made that all thirteen are authentic. In the last one hundred years or so, almost all critics have accepted Romans, 1 and 2 Corinthians, and Galatians. Today the situation is more conservative. It is safe to say that a standard liberal view of Paul's letters accepts at least seven to nine as authentic, Ephesians, 1 and 2 Timothy, and Titus being excluded (some would add Colossians and 2 Thessalonians).[43]

Thus, an objective historian would agree that we possess from seven to thirteen letters from the hand of Paul. Most of these letters are dated from 49 to 65. Two important features of Paul's letters should be mentioned at this point. First, they exhibit a high, advanced Christology (i.e., Jesus is not presented merely as a Jewish prophet who bears wisdom from God, but as God himself, the Lord of heaven and earth). This means that a concept of a divine Jesus was already present, at the latest, within sixteen to twenty years after the crucifixion. As Martin Hengel, one of the world's leading New Testament scholars, puts it, "the time between the death of Jesus and the fully developed christology which we find in the earliest Christian documents, the letters of Paul, is so short that the development which takes place within it can only be called amazing."[44]

Second, Hengel points out that we cannot detect any evolutionary development of Christology within Paul's letters themselves. His later letters have substantially the same Christology as his earlier letters. Thus, Paul's static Christology must have been largely completed *before* he began his great missionary journeys when he began to teach his christological views; that is, by 48. From Paul's letters we can infer that the picture of a fully divine, miracle-working Jesus was not one that developed several decades after his death. Indeed, a full-blown Christology was present no later than fifteen years after the crucifixion.

Creeds and Hymns

Paul's letters contain a number of creeds and hymns (Rom. 1:3–4; 1 Cor. 11:23 ff.; 15:3–8; Phil. 2:6–11; Col. 1:15–18; 1 Tim. 3:16; 2 Tim. 2:8; see also John 1:1–18; 1 Peter 3:18–22; 1 John 4:2).[45] Three things can be said about them. First, they are pre-Pauline and very early. They use language which is not characteristically Pauline, they often translate easily back into Aramaic, and they show features of Hebrew poetry and thought-forms. This means that they came into existence while the church was heavily Jewish and that they became standard, recognized creeds and hymns well before

43. See Guthrie for a defense of the Pauline authorship of all thirteen New Testament epistles attributed to Paul.

44. Martin Hengel, *Between Jesus and Paul* (Philadelphia: Fortress, 1983), p. 31. See pp. 30–47 for an excellent summary of the chronology of New Testament Christology.

45. See Habermas, *Ancient Evidence*, pp. 120–26; Hengel, *Jesus and Paul*, pp. 78–96.

their incorporation into Paul's letters. Most scholars date them from 33 to 48. Some, like Hengel, date many of them in the first decade after Jesus' death.

Second, the content of these creeds and hymns centers on the death, resurrection, and deity of Christ. They consistently present a portrait of a miraculous and divine Jesus who rose from the dead. Third, they served as hymns of worship in the liturgy of the early assemblies and as didactic expressions for teaching the Christology of the church.

In sum, the idea of a fully divine, miracle-working Jesus who rose from the dead was present during the first decade of Christianity. Such a view was not a legend which arose several decades after the crucifixion.

Galatians 1 and 2

All scholars agree that Galatians was written by Paul. Paul tells us that he received his understanding of who Jesus was and what he did from a supernatural experience within a year or two after the crucifixion. He also points out that he went to Jerusalem three years later and the apostles there agreed that his message of a divine Son of God who was crucified and rose from the dead was correct. There is no reason to doubt that Paul visited the apostles, since he has no clear motive for lying and, further, such a visit fits well with the Jewish practice of looking to authorized teachers of a rabbi's doctrines for controls on doctrinal purity. Thus, belief in a divine, risen Jesus was in existence within just a few years after his death.[46]

1 Corinthians 16:22

1 Corinthians was written (ca. 55–56) to a Gentile congregation with little Jewish influence. In closing the letter Paul used the phrase *maranatha*. This phrase uses the Aramaic word *mar*, which means "God" or "Deity."[47] It addresses Jesus as God and implores him to come quickly. Why would Paul use an Aramaic word of closing to a Greek-speaking congregation which did not understand Aramaic? The answer would seem to be that this had become a standard form of address by the time Paul had visited Corinth in 50. He communicated it to the Corinthians, so he knew they would understand it in his letter. Where did this form of address arise? It

---

46. The best defense for taking Paul's own word for the origin of his christological views—his encounter with the risen Christ on the Damascus road—is Seyoon Kim, *The Origin of Paul's Gospel* (Grand Rapids: Eerdmans, 1982).

47. See I. Howard Marshall, *The Origins of New Testament Christology,* Issues in Contemporary Theology series (Downers Grove: Inter-Varsity, 1976), pp. 97–110; C. F. D. Moule, *The Origin of Christology* (Cambridge: Cambridge University Press, 1977), pp. 35–46; Donald Guthrie, *New Testament Theology* (Downers Grove: Inter-Varsity, 1981), pp. 295–96.

would surely be in the early Jewish church. Thus, once again we have historical evidence that belief in a divine Jesus was not a late, Hellenistic view of a simple Jewish prophet from Galilee. Belief in a divine Jesus was early and originated in a Jewish context.

1 Corinthians 15:3-8

This passage is one of the earliest and most important of the pre-Pauline creeds in the New Testament and therefore it bears special mention.[48] Several features indicate that it is pre-Pauline:

1. The words *delivered* and *received* are terms descriptive of rabbinic treatment of holy tradition, indicating that this is holy tradition received by Paul.
2. Several primitive, early, pre-Pauline phrases are used ("the twelve," "the third day," "he was seen," "for our sins" [plural], "he was raised"). These phrases are very Jewish and early.
3. The poetic style is Hebraic.
4. The Aramaic *Cephas* is used; this was an early way of referring to Peter.

The formula is reserved and straightforward. It does not include speculation about how the resurrection took place or about details of the event itself. Thus, Jewish scholar Pinchas Lapide says, "This unified piece of tradition which soon was solidified into a formula of faith may be considered as a statement of eyewitnesses for whom the experience of the resurrection became the turning point of their lives."[49]

When should this tradition be dated? 1 Corinthians was written in 55 and Paul first visited the Corinthians in 50, so the formula precedes that date. It was already a formalized statement before Paul shared it with the Corinthians. Most scholars date it from three to eight years after Jesus' death. This date fits well with the mention of James and Cephas, who were also mentioned in Galatians 1:18-19. It seems likely, therefore, that this formula was given to Paul at the meeting which took place three to four years after the crucifixion. A date of three to eight years also fits well with the heavily Semitic flavor of the formula. Of course, the facts reported—

---

48. See Habermas, *Ancient Evidence*, pp. 124-27; Pinchas Lapide, *The Resurrection of Jesus: A Jewish Perspective*, trans. Wilhelm C. Linss (Minneapolis: Augsburg, 1983), pp. 97-100; R. H. Fuller, *The Formation of the Resurrection Narratives* (New York: Macmillan, 1971), pp. 9-49; Raymond E. Brown, *The Virginal Conception and Bodily Resurrection of Jesus* (New York: Paulist, 1973), pp. 81-96.

49. Lapide, *The Resurrection of Jesus*, p. 99.

the crucifixion and the resurrection experiences (if not the resurrection itself)—occurred before the stating of the formula.

From 1 Corinthians 15:3–8, therefore, we have a very early historical testimony to the resurrection of Jesus of Nazareth.

The Gospels

Until recent years, a fairly standard dating of the Gospels was this: Mark at 70, Matthew and Luke at 75 to 85, and John at 95. This dating was based on the belief that Mark was the earliest Gospel. It was also assumed that the Gospels were a result of a fairly long period when the Jesus tradition was circulated in various forms which would have taken time to develop and stabilize. But as we have seen in our discussion of Jewish oral tradition, there is no reason to doubt that many of the structural forms of the tradition came from Jesus himself or the early disciples. Further, there is no way of knowing how long it would have taken for a tradition to be put into forms, since there is no comparable first-century tradition which can clearly be dated at various stages of its development.

Moreover, the Gospels are given these dates because of Jesus' predictions of the fall of Jerusalem (70) in Matthew 24, Mark 13, and Luke 21. But again, this simply reflects an antisupernatural bias. Why could Jesus not have predicted this event? Scholars who deny this assume that the writer of Mark attributed these words to Jesus at a time when the events were imminent. But even if this is granted, or even if one grants that Luke's form of the statement has been shaped by reflection (and this need not be granted), the sayings still bear features in common with several Old Testament prophecies. If their form is a result of reflection, that reflection need not have been on an imminent event (the fall of Jerusalem in 70) but on Old Testament passages. Thus, these verses provide no clear indicators of their dating.

Even if these dates for the Gospels are accepted, the Gospels were still written during the time when eyewitnesses who had seen Jesus and had experienced his ministry were alive. One would, therefore, still be on good historical grounds for treating them as solid historical sources. But in recent years, there has been a trend in New Testament studies toward dating the Gospels earlier.[50]

50. The following present arguments for an early dating of the Gospels and other New Testament books: E. Earle Ellis, "Dating the New Testament," *New Testament Studies* 26 (July 1980): 487–502; John A. T. Robinson, *Can We Trust the New Testament?* (Grand Rapids: Eerdmans, 1977); *Redating the New Testament* (Philadelphia: Westminster, 1976); John W. Wenham, "Gospel Origins," *Trinity Journal* (old series) 7 (Fall 1978): 112–34. See the reply by Douglas Moo in *Trinity Journal* (new series) 2 (1981): 24–36; and the rejoinder by Wenham.

In order to understand what follows, a brief word is in order about the Synoptic problem.[51] The first three Gospels are called the synoptic Gospels and clearly have some sort of relationship among themselves. They have much in common in wording, sequencing, and inclusion of material. On the other hand, each Gospel has unique material. The Synoptic problem is the problem of stating what the literary relationship among the Synoptics is in such a way that their similarities and differences are explained. It is safe to say that there is no clear, acceptable solution agreed upon by all New Testament scholars. However, most would hold to what is called the four-source theory. According to this view, Mark is the first Gospel and Matthew and Luke used Mark in writing their Gospels—a stronger case being made for Lukan use of Mark than for Matthew's use of Mark. In addition, a Q source is postulated. Some scholars deny the existence of Q, and there is much in question about whether Q—if it existed—was an oral or written source and whether one or more versions of Q existed. Q is alleged to be that material which Matthew and Luke have in common but which is absent from Mark.

So, according to the four-source theory, Q and Mark predate Matthew and Luke. It should also be kept in mind that Luke and Acts are two parts of the same document; Luke precedes Acts slightly. This means that if one can date Acts, then Luke would have been written prior to Acts. And since Luke used Matthew and Mark, then Matthew and Mark are to be dated even earlier.[52] So a key to dating the Gospels is the date assigned to Acts.

Six arguments, taken together, provide a powerful case for dating Acts at 62 to 64. First, Acts has no mention of the fall of Jerusalem in 70, and this is quite odd since much of the activity recorded in Luke-Acts centers around Jerusalem. A large section unique to Luke focuses on Jesus' last movement to the Holy City, the resurrection appearances occur around Jerusalem (see Luke 24:13), and Jerusalem plays a key role in the structure

51. For an excellent brief summary of the Synoptic problem, see Robert L. Thomas and Stanley N. Gundry, *A Harmony of the Gospels* (Chicago: Moody, 1978), pp. 274–79. The standard defense of the priority of Matthew is William Farmer, *The Synoptic Problem* (New York: Macmillan, 1964). For a defense of the view that Matthew and Mark are independent of one another, see John M. Rist, *On the Independence of Matthew and Mark* (Cambridge: Cambridge University Press, 1978).

52. The conclusion that Luke relied on Matthew and Mark is independent of one's acceptance of the four-source theory. It seems clear from Luke's own testimony (1:1–4) that he used sources to compose his Gospel, and Mark was surely one of them. When Matthew's chronological order diverges from that of Mark, Luke follows Mark's order; when Matthew's chronology matches, Luke feels free to differ. This is explicable on the assumption that Luke had Matthew and Mark before him, even if Matthew and Mark are independent of one another.

Besides the volumes by Robinson, a helpful discussion which favors a pre-70 date for John is Leon Morris, *The Gospel of John* (Grand Rapids: Eerdmans, 1971), pp. 30–35. Still relevant is the classic argument for Johannine authorship of the fourth Gospel by B. F. Westcott, *The Gospel According to St. John* (1881; Grand Rapids: Eerdmans, 1950), pp. v–xxxii.

of Acts. The omission of any mention of the fall of Jerusalem makes sense if Luke-Acts was written prior to the event itself.

Second, no mention is made of Nero's persecutions in the mid-60s and the general tone of Acts toward the Roman government is irenic. This fits the pre-65 situation well. Neither the tone of Acts nor the omission of an account of Nero's persecutions can be adequately explained by saying it was an attempt to appease the Roman government. It was not the nature of the early church to appease anyone—witness conflicts with Judaism and the Pharisees which are recorded in Luke's writings.

Third, the martyrdoms of James (61), Paul (64), and Peter (65) are not mentioned in Acts. This is also surprising since Acts is quick to record the deaths of Stephen and James the brother of John, leaders in the early church. These omissions are even more surprising when one realizes that James, Peter, and Paul are the three key figures in Acts. The silence in Acts about these deaths makes most sense if, again, we assume that Acts was written before they occurred.

Fourth, the subject matter of Acts deals with issues of importance prior to the fall of Jerusalem in 70. The falling of the Holy Spirit on different people groups (Jewish, Samaritan, Gentile), the divisions between Palestinian Jews and Hellenistic Jews, Jewish-Gentile relations centering on circumcision and the law of Moses, and other themes make sense prior to 70. At that time Jewish Christianity was wiped out and the importance of a record of how Gentile pagan converts are to relate to Jews in the church would be much lower than the importance of such a record prior to 70.

Fifth, several of the expressions in Acts are very early and primitive. More will be said about this later. But the phrases *the Son of man, the Servant of God* (applied to Jesus), *the first day of the week* (the resurrection), and *the people* (the Jews) are all phrases that readers would understand without explanation prior to 70. After 70, they would need to be explained. These phrases, therefore, indicate that Acts was intended for an audience which would remember these terms and their usage.

Sixth, the Jewish war against the Romans (from 66 onward) is not mentioned in Acts. As Hugo Staudinger argues, "The Jewish war is an important part of the history of the early Church. The original followers in Jerusalem lose their significance through the war. With the destruction of Jerusalem Jesus' prophecy is moreover fulfilled. If Luke had been writing after 70, it would be incomprehensible that he should break off his narrative shortly before the fulfillment of Jesus' prophecy, and not indicate the fate of the followers in Jerusalem."[53]

---

53. Hugo Staudinger, *The Trustworthiness of the Gospels* (Edinburgh: The Handsel Press, 1981), p. 9. Many New Testament scholars have not accepted the early date for Acts because it implies an early date for

So a strong case can be made for dating Acts at 62 to 64. But this means that Luke should be dated just prior to that. Further, Matthew and Mark should be dated even earlier, perhaps from the mid-40s to mid-50s. The picture of Jesus presented in the Synoptics is one that is only twelve to twenty-nine years removed from the events themselves. And they incorporate sources which are even earlier.

A word should also be said about Q.[54] Q is usually dated from 35 to 50, the earlier part of the range being more probable according to our analysis. Q contains stories of miracles that Jesus performed and it also has a high Christology—Jesus is the divine Son of God, greater than all the Old Testament prophets and sages, who has unusual power. So if Q existed, it provides another early historical testimony to a divine, miracle-working Jesus.

The Historical Jesus of Radical Critics

New Testament critics have formulated several criteria for deciding which words of Jesus in the Gospels are actually his and which are later additions by the early church or Gospel writers.[55] By far the most accepted and most basic criterion is called the criterion of dissimilarity: an alleged saying of Jesus can be considered authentic only if it cannot be paralleled in early Judaism or the early church. In other words, if a saying of Jesus can be found in Jewish writings contemporaneous with Jesus, or in other parts of the New Testament, then the saying should not be accepted, since materials from either the Jewish or the Christian community could have been used to make up the saying. Such a criterion is surely too stringent. It is odd, to say the least, if a preacher does not preach in the idioms of his day. And it is also odd to say that such a discontinuity should be seen between Jesus and the early church.

So a great deal of material in the Gospels should be accepted as historically reliable even though it does not pass this criterion. On the other hand, if a saying *does* pass the criterion of dissimilarity, then it is certainly historical. When the criterion of dissimiliarity is applied to the sayings of Jesus, even the most radical of New Testament critics would accept some sayings as actually made by the historical Jesus (e.g., Matt. 11:16–19;

---

the Gospels. As France has noted: "It is tempting to suggest that the early date has failed to find widespread acceptance not because it is unconvincing in itself but because the results of its acceptance would be too uncomfortable!" See *The Evidence for Jesus*, pp. 120–21.

54. Marshall, *I Believe*, p. 159; Leopold Sabourin, *Christology: Basic Texts in Focus* (New York: Alba, 1984), pp. 15–28.

55. J. P. Moreland, "An Apologetic Critique of the Major Presuppositions of the New Quest of the Historical Jesus," unpublished Th.M. thesis, Dallas Theological Seminary, 1979, pp. 96–110; France, "Authenticity of the Sayings of Jesus."

18:23-33; 20:1-6; 21:28-31; 22:1-14; Mark 2:19; 10:15; Luke 9:62; 10:29-37; 11:2, 5-8, 20; 14:28-32; 15:11-32; 16:1-9; 18:1-8, 9-14).[56]

When these sayings are analyzed, they reveal that Jesus held a high view of himself. He had authority to forgive sins and welcome outcasts in God's name. In him God's kingdom had come, and he acts as if he stands uniquely in God's place. In other words, even if the most radical, stringent criterion is applied to the words of Jesus, one still gets a picture of a unique, supernatural Christ. It is open to someone to say, as Albert Schweitzer did, that Jesus was mentally deranged and had a mistaken view of himself. But apart from the difficulty of proving such a claim—after all, Jesus consistently behaves under pressure as one in complete possession of his faculties—the point can still be made that the picture of a divine supernatural Christ is not one which was developed long after Jesus' death and superimposed onto a simple religious prophet from Nazareth.

The Speeches in Acts 1–12

The evangelistic speeches in Acts 1-12 bear special mention.[57] These speeches have several features which indicate they are early records of events which occurred while Christianity was still young and which significantly predate Acts. In other words, they were sources already in existence when Acts was written and they were incorporated into the narrative of Acts.

For one thing, these speeches, in contrast to the speeches of Acts 13 and following, translate well into Aramaic. This is what one would expect if these record actual speeches given to Jewish audiences in the early days of Christianity.

Second, the speeches have a unique vocabulary, tone, style, and theology when compared to the rest of Acts. This points to the fact that in Acts 1-12, we are dealing with materials that were in existence before Acts was written. Third, the theology of these speeches is primitive; that is, it does not reflect a great deal of developed thinking, and many of the emphases were dropped later in the history of early Christianity. For example, the messiahship of Jesus is emphasized, not his deity (although they are compatible). Primitive phrases ("Jesus the Nazarene," "thy holy Child Jesus") are used in referring to Jesus. Further, a primitive concept of redemption is used: Jesus is seen in terms of his redemption of Israel as a nation.

56. See the excellent study by Royce Gordon Gruenler, *New Approaches to Jesus and the Gospels: A Phenomenological and Exegetical Study of Synoptic Christology* (Grand Rapids: Baker, 1982), chaps. 1-5.

57. See Stanton, *Jesus of Nazareth*, pp. 67-85.

Fourth, when one compares 1 Peter, Mark (which tradition says came from Peter), and Peter's speeches in Acts, the language, style, and emphases are almost identical. This makes sense if one assumes that all three actually refer to statements which came from Peter himself.[58]

Finally, Acts 1 and 2 indicate that the earliest preaching of the gospel took place in Jerusalem seven weeks after the crucifixion. This is historically probable, since there is no reason for inventing the seven-week interval. In fact, such an interval would have raised doubts; people would have wondered why the disciples waited seven weeks to preach the resurrection.

Several lines of evidence converge to show that the speeches in Acts 1–12 are early and that the probability that they are accurate pieces of history is high. And once again, we see that a unique view of Jesus, including his resurrection, was present very shortly after the crucifixion.

In sum, a good deal of evidence shows that the picture of Jesus in the New Testament was present only a few years after the ministry, death, and resurrection of Jesus. There simply was not enough time for a great deal of myth and legend to accrue and distort the historical facts in any significant way. In this regard, A. N. Sherwin-White, a scholar of ancient Roman and Greek history at Oxford, has studied the rate at which legend accumulated in the ancient world, using the writings of Herodotus as a test case. He argues that even a span of two generations is not sufficient for legend to wipe out a solid core of historical facts.[59] The picture of Jesus in the New Testament was established well within that length of time.

This chapter has brought together several pieces of evidence which cumulatively present an extremely strong case for believing that Jesus was truly the divine Son of God who performed miracles, died on the cross, and rose bodily from the dead. Such a belief is far from being unsupportable. It can be given strong historical validation, and one is well within his epistemic rights in believing the substantial historicity of the New Testament documents. Thus, the following statement by R. T. France seems to be correct:

> All this, and much more, comes to us from the gospels as a compelling portrait of a real man in the real world of first-century Palestine, and yet one who so far transcended his environment that his followers soon learned to see him as more than a man. It is a portrait which we have, in strictly historical terms, no reason to doubt; it is the philosophical and theological implications which cause many to question whether things can really have been as the gospels present them. But we have seen above sufficient reason to be

---

58. See E. G. Selwyn, *The First Epistle of St. Peter* (New York: Macmillan, 1946), pp. 33–36.

59. A. N. Sherwin-White, *Roman Society and Roman Law in the New Testament* (1963; Grand Rapids: Baker, 1978), pp. 186–93.

confident that the gospels not only claim to be presenting fact rather than fiction, but also, where they can be checked, carry conviction as the work of responsible and well-informed writers. The basic divide among interpreters of the gospels is not between those who are or are not open to the results of historical investigation so much as between those whose philosophical/ theological viewpoint allows them to accept the testimony of the gospels, together with the factuality of those records in which it is enshrined, and those for whom no amount of historical testimony could be allowed to substantiate what is antecedently labelled as a 'mythical' account of events.[60]

60. France, *The Evidence for Jesus,* p. 138.

6

The Resurrection of Jesus

Lhe resurrection of Jesus of Nazareth from the dead is the foundation upon which the Christian faith is built. Without the resurrection, there would have been no Christian faith, and the most dynamic movement in history would never have come to be. This chapter will investigate the evidence for the historicity of the resurrection. I do not mean to imply that Jesus' resurrection was merely the resuscitation of a corpse into a this-worldly existence. The New Testament presents the resurrected Christ as One who has been transformed into a different kind of existence. But this point can be, and has been, pressed to mean that there was no continuity between Jesus' body in the tomb and the risen Christ. The nature of Christ's resurrected body will be discussed later. But for now, let me say that by focusing on the historicity of the resurrection, I mean to imply that it was an event which was at once bodily and open to normal historical investigation.

We will consider three broad areas of evidence for the resurrection: the empty tomb, the resurrection appearances, and four key features of the early church which seem to presuppose the resurrection. We will then consider alternate explanations of the evidence.

The Empty Tomb

Arguments for the Empty Tomb

A Variety of Sources

A variety of sources in the New Testament testify to the empty tomb: Matthew 28:11–15 (the M material special to Matthew); Mark 16:1–8; Luke 24:1–12; John 20:11–18.[1] Apart from such explicit references to the empty tomb, the speeches in Acts and 1 Corinthians 15:3–8 presuppose an empty tomb, as I will argue later. Thus, there are several different witnesses to the empty tomb, Mark 16:1–8 and 1 Corinthians 15:3–8 being the earliest. The New Testament should not be treated as one single testimony to the empty tomb.

The Time and Place of the First Preaching

In the previous chapter it was pointed out that the speeches in Acts 1–12 are early and primitive. Many scholars agree that the seven-week time frame between the crucifixion and the first preaching of the resurrection in Jerusalem is historically accurate. There would be no clear motive for mak-

---

1. Murray J. Harris, *Raised Immortal: Resurrection and Immortality in the New Testament* (Grand Rapids: Eerdmans, 1985), p. 38.

ing up the seven-week delay and it could have been counterproductive, since people would wonder why there was a delay of seven weeks before the preaching.

It is highly probable, therefore, that the resurrection was preached in Jerusalem just a few weeks after the crucifixion. If the tomb had not been empty, such preaching could not have occurred. The body of Jesus could have been produced, and since it is likely that the location of Joseph of Arimathea's tomb was well known (he was a respected member of the Sanhedrin), it would not have been difficult to find where Jesus was buried. As Wolfhart Pannenberg has said, "Without having a reliable testimony for the emptiness of Jesus' tomb, the early Christian community could not have survived in Jerusalem proclaiming the resurrection of Christ."[2]

No Veneration at Jesus' Tomb

In Palestine during the days of Jesus, at least fifty tombs of prophets or other holy persons served as sites of religious worship and veneration.[3] However, there is no good evidence that such a practice was ever associated with Jesus' tomb. Since this was customary, and since Jesus was a fitting object of veneration, why were such religious activities not conducted at his tomb? The most reasonable answer must be that Jesus' body was not in his tomb, and thus the tomb was not regarded as an appropriate site for such veneration.

Some scholars have argued that certain features of Mark 16:1–8 show that this text was a liturgical legend used to proclaim Easter faith in the worship of the early Christian community, and that such a proclamation took place at the tomb of Jesus each Easter.[4] They argue that references to time ("the first day of the week . . . when the sun had risen" [Mark 16:2]) and place ("see the place where they laid him" [Mark 16:6]), as well as the centrality of the angelic creedal proclamation of faith ("He has risen, he is not here; see the place where they laid him" [Mark 16:6]), point to the liturgical function of this text.

E. L. Bode has shown that this view is "a most imaginative conjecture lacking solid foundation."[5] The references to time and place can just as well be understood as genuine historical remembrances, especially in light of a number of other indicators of historicity in the narrative. Further, if the reference to time in the Markan narrative indicated a Jerusalem liturgy, one

---

2. Cited in ibid., p. 39.

3. Edwin M. Yamauchi, "Easter—Myth, Hallucination, or History?: Part One," *Christianity Today* 4 (March 15, 1974): 4–16; Ulrich Wilckens, *Resurrection*, trans. A. M. Stewart (Atlanta: John Knox, 1978), pp. 8–9; Harris, *Raised Immortal*, p. 40, and p. 246 n. 5.

4. Walter Kasper, *Jesus the Christ* (New York: Paulist, 1976), p. 127; L. Schenke is cited in E. L. Bode, *The First Easter Morning* (Rome: Biblical Institute Press, 1970), pp. 130–32.

5. Bode, *The First Easter Morning*, pp. 130–32.

would expect the indications of time in the other New Testament accounts to agree more closely with that of Mark than they do. This would be so because the statement of the time would itself have had a special function in the early church. Finally, even if one grants that the Markan narrative functioned in the early church as liturgy and not as an apologetic (i.e., it was used in worship as a proclamation of faith rather than as an apologetic to prove faith in the resurrection), nothing whatsoever follows about the historicity of the narrative itself. One cannot infer historicity or lack of historicity from the function (or literary form) of a piece of literature alone. But in this case, if the narrative did not function as an apologetic for the resurrection (and it seems reasonable that it did), then that increases the probability that the narrative is reliable, since no apologetic motive was involved in fabricating the text.

It seems, then, that the lack of veneration at the tomb of Jesus is powerful evidence that the tomb was empty.

The Mutual Acceptance of the Empty Tomb

In the early speeches of Acts, no mention is made of the empty tomb. It should be recalled that these speeches are early and very Jewish and thus represent examples of resurrection preaching that took place in the Palestinian Jewish community at a time not far removed from the crucifixion. These speeches make no explicit reference to the empty tomb. As will be shown later, the Jews at that time believed that resurrection was bodily. Resurrection was not equated with a spiritual existence of a disembodied soul. Rather, resurrection involved the reanimation of the body. This reanimation need not be understood in crude terms, but it nevertheless involved some sort of continuity with the body a person had before death. There could be no resurrection of a person if that person's body was still in his tomb.

Why is the empty tomb not mentioned in these speeches? The best answer seems to be that the fact of the empty tomb was common ground between believers and unbelievers. Thus, there was no reason to mention it, especially since the early church did not usually use the empty tomb in itself as proof of the Christian message. The empty tomb could be interpreted in several ways; the Jews attributed it to the theft of Jesus' body by the disciples. So the fact of the empty tomb was not central in early evangelistic preaching to Jews. Instead, the proper understanding of the empty tomb is what is central, and this is what one finds emphasized in the Acts speeches. The Gospels are an attempt to complete the passion narratives of Jesus' trial, death, and burial with historical information about the person, deeds, and teachings of Jesus and are intended primarily for believers. The account about the empty tomb is included in the Gospels to describe what took place.

In sum, the absence of explicit mention of the empty tomb in the speeches in Acts is best explained by noting that the fact of the empty tomb was not in dispute and thus it was not at issue. The main debate was over why it was empty, not whether it was empty.[6] In Acts 2:29, Peter makes a reference to the fact that David's tomb was still with them. The implication seems to be that David was buried and remained in his tomb, but by contrast, Jesus did not remain in his tomb, as anyone listening to the speech could verify for himself (otherwise, the point of contrast between David and Jesus could not be made). This indirect reference to the empty tomb serves to underscore that no need existed for the early Christian preachers to make a major issue of the empty tomb. It was common knowledge which could be easily verified if such verification was needed.

The Presence of a Jewish Polemic

The only polemic offered by the Jews for which we have any historical evidence is the one recorded in Matthew 28:11–15. A number of scholars have pointed out that this polemic itself assumes that the tomb was empty.[7] This text could not have been written if, at the time of writing, there was not a Jewish counterargument to the Christian understanding of the empty tomb. But the Jewish polemic does not dispute that the tomb was empty; it gives an alternate explanation. This is a significant historical fact. The only explanations for the resurrection of Jesus for which we have evidence assume an empty tomb, regardless of whether the explanation is offered by a friend or a foe of Christianity. This is strong evidence that the tomb was in fact empty.

The Pre-Markan Passion Narrative

Because of the presence of Semitisms, personal names (e.g., Simon, Mark 14:37), and geographical references (e.g., Golgotha, Mark 15:22), many scholars take the geographic origin of the pre-Markan passion narrative to have been Jerusalem. This narrative clearly predates Mark, but when did it originate? William Lane Craig offers the following considerations which point to an origin prior to 36 to 38.[8] First, Paul's Last Supper tradition in 1 Corinthians 11:23–25 presupposes the pre-Markan narrative. 1 Corinthians 11:23–25 is holy tradition which Paul received well before he delivered it to the Corinthians when he visited them in 50. The passion

---

6. Harris, *Raised Immortal*, p. 40. For an alternate view, see Herman Hendrickx, *Resurrection Narratives* (London: Geoffrey Chapman, 1978), pp. 18–19.

7. Wilckens, *Resurrection*, pp. 45–46; Robert H. Stein, "Was the Tomb Really Empty?" *Themelios* 45 (September 1979): 8–12; Grant R. Osborne, *The Resurrection Narratives: A Redactional Study* (Grand Rapids: Baker, 1984), p. 219.

8. William Lane Craig, "The Empty Tomb of Jesus," in *Gospel Perspectives II*, ed. R. T. France and David Wenham (Sheffield: JSOT Press, 1981), pp. 190–91.

narrative, therefore, must have originated in the first few years in the Jerusalem church. Second, the passion narrative speaks of "the high priest" (14:53, 54, 60, 61, 63) without using his name. This seems to imply that Caiaphas was still high priest when the passion narrative was being circulated, since there was no need to use his name. Caiaphas was high priest from 18 to 37, which makes 37 the latest this tradition could have originated. Third, the order of the narrative corresponds with that of the pre-Pauline formula in 1 Corinthians 15, which is itself very early. This formula probably predates Paul's visit to Jerusalem in 36 to 38 (which is the most probable occasion for Paul to have received it). The tradition within the 1 Corinthians 15 formula obviously predates the time it was given to Paul, since it already would have been fixed, holy tradition before it was given to him.

Some scholars, such as R. H. Fuller, hold that the passion narrative originally ended with the account of the burial, and that the narrative about the empty tomb is a late addition which was included for apologetic reasons.[9] But the evidence for this is insufficient. First, Craig has pointed out that the accounts of Jesus' burial and the empty tomb have several verbal and grammatical similarities, indicating that they belong to the same source.[10] Second, several features of the burial account anticipate portions of the empty tomb account and would be incomplete without them. Mention of the stone anticipates the women's question about who would roll the stone away. The empty tomb account says "when the Sabbath was over," which assumes the burial account's statement, "the day before the Sabbath."[11]

The third and perhaps most important reason for holding that the empty tomb narrative was part of the original has been offered by Ulrich Wilckens.[12] Wilckens points out that tension is created in the passion account because God appears to have abandoned the just One. People in the early church, being predominantly Jewish, were steeped in the Old Testament (see the Psalms, in which cries for help are followed by hymns of praise for God's deliverance). Surely they would have wondered where God was when Jesus died. Why did he not vindicate him? To answer these questions about the faithfulness of God, the original narrative included as an essential component the narrative about the empty tomb. If the original narrative did not include the account of the empty tomb, it becomes un-

9. R. H. Fuller, *The Formation of the Resurrection Narratives* (New York: Macmillan, 1971), pp. 50–57. See also Günther Bornkamm, *Jesus of Nazareth*, trans. Irene and Fraser McLuskey (New York: Harper and Row, 1960), pp. 180–86.

10. William Lane Craig, *The Son Rises* (Chicago: Moody, 1981), p. 73.

11. For more features, see ibid., p. 73.

12. See Wilckens, *Resurrection*, pp. 27–44, especially pp. 42–44.

intelligible as to where God was when his righteous One needed him. Surely some mention of God's sovereign plan would have been included in the narrative prior to the account about the empty tomb. The lack of such an inclusion makes sense if the narrative about the empty tomb functioned to answer this question from the very first.

In sum, the pre-Markan passion narrative includes the account of the empty tomb as an essential ingredient, and since this narrative is quite early, it provides good evidence for an empty tomb.

No Other Burial Story Exists

If the burial account of Jesus is historically reliable, then the location of his tomb was well known. Given that to a Jew there could have been no resurrection without an empty tomb, then there would have been no preaching of a resurrected Christ had Jesus' tomb not been empty. The reliability of the burial account shows that persons in the early church could have examined Jesus' tomb; their belief about the bodily nature of resurrection shows that they would have examined Jesus' tomb.

If the burial account in the New Testament is not reliable, then it is surprising that other accounts are nowhere to be found. Why were there not several different accounts which tried to specify the details of the burial? No conflicting account is found anywhere, even among Jewish writings, where one would expect to find an alternative account. Further, if the New Testament account is false, why did not some fragment of the true account remain? The presence of just one account of Jesus' burial points to the fact that it must have been known to be accurate. No other account was made which could rival the true account.

The Jewish View of Resurrection

It is generally accepted that Jewish beliefs about the afterlife included the concept of a physical resurrection of the body.[13] This involved a continuity with the body that a person had before death. Jewish New Testament scholar Pinchas Lapide has examined the various schools of Jewish thought during and prior to New Testament times, and all schools agreed in holding to a notion of physical resurrection.[14] The Sadducees denied the resurrection altogether, but even they agreed that if there was a resurrec-

---

13. Bode, *The First Easter Morning*, p. 162; James D. G. Dunn, *The Evidence for Jesus* (Philadelphia: Westminster, 1985), pp. 66–67; Raymond E. Brown, *The Virginal Conception and Bodily Resurrection of Jesus* (New York: Paulist, 1973), pp. 113–15; Pinchas Lapide, *The Resurrection of Jesus: A Jewish Perspective*, trans. Wilhelm C. Linss (Minneapolis: Augsburg, 1983), pp. 44–65; John W. Drane, "Some Ideas of Resurrection in the New Testament Period," *Tyndale Bulletin* 24 (1973): 99–110.

14. Lapide, *The Resurrection of Jesus*, pp. 44–65; George E. Ladd, *I Believe in the Resurrection of Jesus* (Grand Rapids: Eerdmans, 1975), pp. 51–59.

tion, it would be bodily. Lapide concludes: "Any life in general was conceived of as bodily and spatial."[15]

James D. G. Dunn has pointed out that this view of the afterlife is confirmed by archaeological discoveries about some first-century Jewish customs. At the time of Jesus, it was customary to visit a loved one's tomb about a year after his burial to gather up the bones and put them in an ossuary. This practice was linked to the belief that the bones should be kept together, so that in the resurrection God could use them to reconstruct the body. The popular understanding of resurrection underlying this practice was that the resurrection body had some continuity with the body a person had before his death.

It is clear that the resurrection of Jesus was preached very shortly after his crucifixion, most likely within seven weeks. Given the contemporary beliefs about resurrection, the tomb of Jesus had to have been empty. Had there been no empty tomb, there would have been no belief in a resurrection and no preaching of the resurrection. Thus, the early preaching is evidence that the tomb was empty.

Historicity of the Empty Tomb

The pre-Markan passion narrative and accounts of the empty tomb and the pre-Pauline formula in 1 Corinthians 15 provide the earliest attestation to the empty tomb. In this section, we will investigate features of each text which underscore the historicity of the empty tomb.

Historical Features of the Pre-Markan Narrative

The Continuous Account of the Passion Narrative   Each part of the narrative would not make sense without the others and thus the narrative was most likely one unified piece prior to its inclusion in the Gospel. Further, the Gospels are in high agreement about the flow of these events. In contrast, there is a great deal of difference in reporting the appearances. The difference between the appearance narratives and the passion narratives can be explained by reference to the events themselves.[16] There is no smooth, continuous account of the appearances because the appearances themselves were unexpected, sporadic, and to different people on different occasions at different locations. By contrast, the events from the trial up to the discovery of the empty tomb were relatively well known and the general flow of those events is fixed. This means that the narrative recounting those events, which is early, is what one would expect if it were an accurate report of the events themselves.

15. Lapide, *The Resurrection of Jesus*, p. 56.
16. Craig, *The Son Rises*, p. 73.

The Reference to Joseph of Arimathea   Most scholars believe that Joseph of Arimathea was a real, historical person and that Jesus was actually buried in his tomb.[17] According to the Gospels, he was a member of the Sanhedrin, a group of seventy-one leaders whose members were very well known among the populace. No one could have invented a person who did not exist and say he was on the Sanhedrin if such were not the case. Almost everyone knew who was on the Sanhedrin. A fictitious character would have been more plausible if someone obscure had been chosen.

There was, then, a man named Joseph of Arimathea. There was no reason to make up the story that Jesus was buried in his tomb. For one thing, the only good motive for doing this would have been to give prestige and authority to a major leader in the church. But apart from the highly questionable assumption that the early church was led by men who were deceivers, there is no evidence that Joseph was a significant leader in early Christianity. Apart from a few other obscure references to him, he drops out of the picture. Several other candidates would have been better if the story about the tomb had been invented to enhance someone's leadership. And because Joesph was a public figure, people would have known him and the location of his tomb. If Jesus had not been buried in his tomb, this would have been all too easy to verify. So it would have been highly problematic to have mentioned such a public figure if someone were to fabricate the account.

In light of these difficulties, most scholars feel that it is highly probable that Jesus was, in fact, buried in Joseph's tomb. Incidental details about Joseph in the narrative confirm this fact. Joseph is called a rich man in the text, and archaeological discoveries have confirmed that only rich people owned the sort of tombs described in the burial account. Further, John tells us that Jesus' tomb was located in a garden and, again, archaeology has confirmed that this was characteristic of the tombs of wealthy or prominent people. Such details in the text are incidental remarks about which nothing is made.

The Accounts of the Tomb   Craig has pointed out that archaeological discoveries have confirmed the accuracy of the description of the tomb of Jesus.[18] Three different kinds of tombs have been discovered, but the description of Jesus' tomb indicates that it was either an acrosolia tomb or a bench tomb. Such tombs were scarce in Jesus' day and were reserved for rich and prominent people. Furthermore, near the traditional site for Jesus' grave, acrosolia tombs from Jesus' day have been found. Jesus' tomb was

17. Brown, *Bodily Resurrection of Jesus*, p. 113; Stein, "Was the Tomb Really Empty," p. 10; Bode, *The First Easter Morning*, p. 160; Craig, *The Son Rises*, p. 53.
    18. Craig, *The Son Rises*, pp. 55–56.

located in a garden, and one of the gates in the North Wall of Jerusalem was called the Garden Gate. Tombs of the Jewish high priests John Hyrcanus and Alexander Jannaeus were in that area, so it could easily have been a prestigious burial location.

The Presence of Women   The mention of women in the empty tomb and resurrection narratives indicates that the accounts have a high degree of probability of being historically correct.[19] This is true for several reasons. First, if someone were going to make up an account of the first witnesses to the empty tomb and the risen Christ, why would women be chosen instead of the disciples? This serves only to make the disciples look cowardly and the women look courageous. This would hardly enhance the leadership of the disciples in the early church. Second, the women are named specifically. If these women were not actual people, members of the early church would have wondered who knew these women and what happened to them. Third, three lists of women have been incorporated into Mark's account: 15:40, 15:47, and 16:1.[20] It is unlikely that any one list was made up from information in the others. Each seems to presuppose the other two, since each list contains unexplained material which becomes intelligible if a list is compared with the others. Thus, these three lists are early, different descriptions of the women.

The fourth and perhaps most important fact is that in first-century Judaism, a woman's testimony was virtually worthless. A woman was not allowed to give testimony in a court of law except on rare occasions. No one would have invented a story and made women the first witnesses to the empty tomb. The presence of women was an embarrassment; this probably explains why the women are not mentioned in 1 Corinthians 15 and the speeches in Acts, since these speeches were evangelistic. There was no reason to include in evangelistic messages an incidental detail which would cause the audience to stumble and not deal with the main point. The fact is included in the Gospels because the Gospels are attempting to describe what actually happened. No other explanation can adequately account for inclusion of this fact. This point can be pressed home even more if we recall that one of the women, Mary Magdalene, had been possessed by demons (Luke 8:2), a fact that would cast even more doubt on her veracity. It is no wonder that the disciples did not believe the women's report: "But these words seemed to them an idle tale, and they did not believe them" (Luke 24:11).

19. Bode, *The First Easter Morning*, pp. 160–61; Wilckens, *Resurrection*, pp. 37–39; Osborne, *The Resurrection Narratives*, p. 219; Craig, *The Son Rises*, pp. 59–61.

20. Wilckens, *Resurrection*, pp. 37–39; Craig, *The Son Rises*, pp. 59–61; Ben Witherington III, *Women in the Ministry of Jesus* (Cambridge: Cambridge University Press, 1984), pp. 9–10.

The Absence of Late Theological Reflection   Harris points out that there is
no evidence of late theological reflection in the empty tomb narrative. This
shows that the narrative is early, unadorned, and accurate.[21] The text is incredibly restrained, especially when compared to the apocryphal gospels.
No attempt is made to describe the resurrection or give details of how it
happened. There is no indication of joy on the part of the witnesses, only
surprise and fear. No attempt is made to introduce theological motifs
which came to have prominence later in the church: fulfillment of Old Testament prophecy, the dawning of the new age, Jesus' descent into hell,
christological titles applied to Jesus, reflection on the nature of Jesus'
corporeality.

In short, this narrative has not been changed. It is a primitive record
which does not indicate developed theological reflection.

The Absence of the Three-Day Motif[22]   From 1 Corinthians 15:4, we see
that the standard way of referring to the resurrection is by using the phrase
the third day. However, the empty tomb narrative does not use this phrase.
Instead it has the phrase *the first day of the week*. This phrase most likely
reflects an early account of the discovery of the tomb. It is kept in the narrative because it describes the time the women actually found the tomb
empty and the way this discovery was referred to. Furthermore, although
it is possible to harmonize the discovery of the tomb on the first day of the
week with the fact of Jesus' resurrection after three days, such harmonization is not easy.[23] Since the phrase *the third day* was a standard way of referring to the resurrection, the existence of a phrase in the narrative which is
hard to harmonize with it is best explained by the fact that the phrase *the
first day of the week* represents an early, accurate tradition.

The Difficulty of Harmonization   It is difficult to harmonize the empty
tomb and appearance narratives in the Gospels, though such a harmonization can be done.[24] As Dunn has pointed out, "The confusion between the
different accounts in the Gospels does not appear to have been contrived.
The conflict of testimony is more a mark of the sincerity of those from
whom the testimony was derived than a mark against their veracity."[25] The
differences can be best explained by treating them as different reports

---

21. Harris, *Raised Immortal*, p. 38; Craig, "The Empty Tomb of Jesus," p. 183.

22. Bode, *The First Easter Morning*, pp. 119–24, 156, 161–62.

23. See Harold W. Hoehner, *Chronological Aspects of the Life of Christ* (Grand Rapids: Zondervan, 1976),
pp. 65–74.

24. See Harris, *Raised Immortal*, pp. 69–71. For a fuller treatment, see the detailed study by John W.
Wenham, *Easter Enigma: Are the Resurrection Accounts in Conflict?* (Grand Rapids: Zondervan, Academie
Books, 1984).

25. Dunn, *The Evidence for Jesus*, p. 65.

coming from different points of view as described by different eye-witnesses.

The Presence of Semitisms   The presence of Semitisms in the narrative shows that it reflects an early Jewish account of an event which was itself witnessed by Jews on Jewish soil. The narrative is not influenced by Hellenistic mythology or religions. Mark refers to the day as *mia tōn sabbatōn* ("the first day of the week," 16:2). Matthew reports the presence of an angel who speaks in the name of God. The way this is reported reflects a Jewish way of speaking. These and other Jewish phrases show that the narrative is early.[26]

Other Details   Other details of the narrative lend weight to the historicity of the narrative. For example, Herman Hendrickx has pointed out the fact that "a group of women went to the tomb is in perfect agreement with the customs of the time."[27] Further, the reports about the fear and unbelief of the disciples are most likely accurate, since there would be no motive for disparaging them. Finally, the pace of the events surrounding the burial of Jesus is realistic, since Jesus died just prior to the beginning of the Sabbath and burials were not permitted on a Sabbath.

The Pre-Pauline Formula in 1 Corinthians 15

Craig has argued that the formula in 1 Corinthians 15:3b–5 testifies to the fact of the empty tomb.[28] He maintains that the phrase *he was buried* implies the empty tomb because it stands between Paul's mention of the death and the resurrection. The formula has four "that" clauses (that Christ died, that he was buried, that he was raised, that he appeared), and these clauses follow and highlight the general chronological order of Mark's narrative. In this formula, the burial seems to anticipate the resurrection, which would imply an empty tomb. In Paul's concept of baptism (Rom. 6:4; Col. 2:12) the act of immersion points forward to coming out of the water in newness of life. Paul himself parallels the sequence in baptism with the burial and resurrection of Jesus. And just as in baptism the same body is immersed and comes out of the water, so in the burial of Jesus the same body comes out in resurrection. So the burial points to the resurrection (and implies the empty tomb), according to Paul, and the presence of the phrase *he was buried* followed by the phrase *he was raised* would indicate an empty tomb. This is even clearer when we remember the Jewish nature of this formula and the Jewish view of resurrection.

---

26. Bode, *The First Easter Morning*, pp. 6, 50–51, 58, 71, 160.
27. Hendrickx, *Resurrection Narratives*, p. 15.
28. Craig, "The Empty Tomb of Jesus," pp. 173–82. See also Harris, *Raised Immortal*, pp. 9–14; C. F. Evans, *Resurrection and the New Testament* (London: SCM, 1970), pp. 41–56.

Craig also defends the view that the phrase *the third day* in this formula points to the empty tomb. Since no one actually saw the resurrection, how could it have been dated on the third day? Craig argues that the women found the tomb empty on the third day and the resurrection came to be dated on that day. So the phrase points to the empty tomb.

Since 1 Corinthians 15:3–8 is a very early formula, and since these two phrases ("he was buried" and "the third day") assume an empty tomb, then this text is further historical evidence for an early belief that the tomb was empty.

Explaining the Empty Tomb

An impressive case has been given for believing that Jesus' tomb was empty. How are we to explain this fact? Most New Testament scholars today who deny the bodily resurrection avoid a detailed treatment of naturalistic explanations of the empty tomb, preferring instead to try and show that belief that the tomb was empty was not early, or merely remaining agnostic about why it was empty. A sufficient case has already been made to show that belief that the tomb was empty was not a late addition but an early fact.

I will not attempt a detailed treatment of naturalistic accounts of the empty tomb because they have been adequately summarized elsewhere.[29] Almost no one of reputation today holds that Jesus did not die on the cross or that the disciples went to the wrong tomb. Jesus' grave site was well known, as I have already pointed out. Furthermore, if the enemies of Jesus had stolen his body, they could have produced it or alluded to the fact that they had taken it. No evidence exists that the Jews ever used this strategy against the early church. Their only counterargument implies that they did not take Jesus' body (see Matt. 28:11–15). No motive could possibly suggest itself for such a silence if, in fact, they had taken it. Finally, such explanations do not explain the certainty and dedication of the early believers.

Did Jesus' disciples steal the body and make up a tale about the resurrection? This suggestion is entirely implausible, and to my knowledge, no New Testament scholar, regardless of how skeptical he is about the supernatural elements in Christianity, considers this suggestion as remotely possible. But since this suggestion is often raised in popular audiences or in witnessing situations a few words of rebuttal may be in order.

For one thing, the disciples had nothing to gain by lying and starting a

29. See W. J. Sparrow-Simpson, *The Resurrection and the Christian Faith* (Grand Rapids: Zondervan, 1968), pp. 40–46; James Orr, *The Resurrection of Jesus* (London: Hodder and Stoughton, 1908), pp. 127–33; Josh McDowell, *Evidence That Demands a Verdict* (San Bernardino, Calif.: Here's Life, 1972), pp. 241–70; Gary R. Habermas, *The Resurrection of Jesus: An Apologetic* (Grand Rapids: Baker, 1980), pp. 26–33; Charles Anderson, *The Historical Jesus: A Continuing Quest* (Grand Rapids: Eerdmans, 1972), pp. 166–73.

new religion. They faced hardship, ridicule, hostility, and martyrs' deaths. In light of this, they could have never sustained such unwavering motivation if they knew what they were preaching was a lie. The disciples were not fools and Paul was a cool-headed intellectual of the first rank. There would have been several opportunities over three to four decades of ministry to reconsider and renounce the lie. Religion had its rewards for them, but those rewards came from a sincere belief that what they were living for was true.

Second, these men were Jewish theists. It may seem easy for a modern agnostic to think about making up a new religion for gain. But to a first-century Jew, such an act was tantamount to lying against the God of Israel, as Paul himself argues in 1 Corinthians 15:12–19. Lying against God and perverting his revelation would mean risking the damnation of one's soul to hell. Would such a person risk eternal torment for a few years of prestige as a leader of a new religion? The answer can only be no.

Third, the picture of Jesus was not in keeping with current conceptions of what the Messiah would be like (a theocratic ruler who would deliver Israel from Gentile oppression) and it would have been hard to convince others of its truth.

Fourth, much of the resurrection narratives bear unmistakable signs of historicity, as I have argued. The earliness of these accounts and the presence of hostile witnesses would have made a fabrication unlikely and dangerous.

Finally, if the empty tomb and resurrection was a fabrication, why did not at least one of the disciples break away from the rest and start his own version of Christianity? Or why did not at least one of them reveal the fraudulent nature of the whole enterprise? If bad motivation was involved in the fabrication, one is hard pressed to explain the continued unity of the early leaders, in light of the human tendency to want to promote oneself. The assumption that they were all committed to the truth of their message is the only adequate explanation of their continued unity and the lack of any revelation of fraud. Those who lie for personal gain do not stick together very long, especially when hardship decreases the benefits.

The tomb of Jesus was empty, and intellectual integrity requires one to admit that naturalistic explanations are simply inadequate. The most reasonable explanation of the empty tomb is the resurrection of Jesus from the dead.

The Resurrection Appearances

Almost no New Testament scholar today denies that Jesus appeared to a number of his followers after his death. Some scholars interpret these as subjective hallucinations or objective visions granted by God which were not visions of a physical being. But no one denies that the believers had some sort of experience. The skeptical New Testament scholar Norman Perrin admitted: "The more we study the tradition with regard to the appearances, the firmer the rock begins to appear upon which they are based."[30] Dunn, professor of divinity at the University of Durham, England, agrees: "It is almost impossible to dispute that at the historical roots of Christianity lie some visionary experiences of the first Christians, who understood them as appearances of Jesus, raised by God from the dead."[31] In this section, we will investigate some of the facts behind these claims.

The Nature of the Appearances

Several features characterize the New Testament descriptions of the appearances of Jesus. For one thing, they occur to several individuals. Some appearances were to a single person; one was to a group of five hundred. Second, they are reported to have taken place during a very specific period of forty days. After this they end abruptly, except for some appearances to the apostle Paul. Third, three Greek words are used to denote the appearances. The most important verb form is *ophthe*, which means "he appeared." This term probably implies seeing something which was objectively present outside the mind of the observer, though some have argued that it can also be used of a subjective vision. The former usage is more likely.[32] Fourth, the appearances do not happen just to believers. It is true that everyone who saw an appearance recorded in the New Testament became a believer, but they were not necessarily believers at the time of the appearance. Several of the Twelve were unbelieving even after one appearance. Paul and James (Jesus' brother) were not believers when they saw Jesus.

Several features of the risen Jesus surface when the New Testament data are examined.[33] First, the writers of the Gospels and Paul are agreed that Jesus appeared in bodily form. It should be granted that Jesus now had a spiritual body which was not entirely the same as his earthly body. But Jesus still had a spiritual *body*, and neither Paul nor the Gospel writers understand this to mean a purely spiritual being who can be seen only in the mind. This body could be seen and touched, and had continuity

30. Norman Perrin, *The Resurrection According to Matthew, Mark, and Luke* (Philadelphia: Fortress, 1977), p. 80.

31. Dunn, *The Evidence for Jesus*, p. 75.

32. Harris, *Raised Immortal*, pp. 46–49; Osborne, *The Resurrection Narratives*, pp. 221–72, 278. For the opposite view, see Brown, *Bodily Resurrection of Jesus*, pp. 90–91.

33. Harris, *Raised Immortal*, pp. 53–57; William Lane Craig, "The Bodily Resurrection of Jesus," in *Gospel Perspectives I*, ed. R. T. France and David Wenham (Sheffield: JSOT Press, 1980), pp. 47–74.

with the body laid in the tomb. The risen Christ was capable of eating (see Luke 24:41–43). Second, Jesus' body was no longer bound by space and time. It could be transported, appear, and disappear in a closed room without spatial approach or withdrawal. It could be materialized and localized at will. Third, Jesus could be touched and heard as well as seen. Finally, there was a continuity between Christ's body before the resurrection and his mode of existence after the resurrection. Although Jesus' post-resurrection body is suited for a different, heavenly mode of existence, a mode which may involve existing in a different sort of space (this suggestion is reasonable in light of current ideas in physics, with its talk of possible worlds which exist in different spaces), it nevertheless is continuous with the body in the tomb. The appearance narratives themselves show this continuity, since Jesus was recognized by his disciples and his body still had certain remains of his suffering.

The Evidence for Historicity

Features of the Appearance Narratives

Several features of the appearance narratives argue for their historicity.[34] First, we have in 1 Corinthians 15:3–8 an early testimony by Paul himself that he saw the resurrected Christ. This is strong evidence, for Paul was obviously sincere in his testimony and he understood the resurrection of Jesus as a bodily resurrection. Second, women were the first to see the risen Christ and, given the status of women as witnesses in first-century Judaism, this fact is hard to understand if it did not really happen. Third, early, primitive phrases ("the twelve," "Cephas") are used in 1 Corinthians 15 to report the appearances. These terms show that the reports are early and are not touched up to reflect later ways of speaking.

The reports of the appearances are difficult to harmonize and they are brief and sporadic. This not only shows that they are not contrived (since no attempt has been made to fit them into a coherent picture), but also is what one would expect if the reports are accurate. It was the nature of the appearances themselves to be brief, sporadic, intense moments when Jesus suddenly appeared and disappeared after a brief interlude. The reports of these events bear these features because that was the way the events themselves occurred. In the narratives, the disciples are slow to believe. This casts the leaders of the early church in a negative, unbelieving light, and thus the picture of them in these narratives would be counter-

---

34. Dunn, *The Evidence for Jesus*, pp. 69–71; Harris, *Raised Immortal*, pp. 62–63; Craig, *The Son Rises*, pp. 118–19; Gerald O'Collins, *The Resurrection of Jesus Christ* (Valley Forge: Judson, 1973), pp. 29–45.

productive to their authority and ministries. The accounts of their unbelief are most likely accurate. Furthermore, their unbelief makes sense when one realizes that the picture of the Messiah in Jewish thought in those days did not include the idea of a resurrection. As George E. Ladd has put it: "In light of these facts, the Gospel story is psychologically sound. The disciples were slow to recognize in Jesus their Messiah, for by his actions he was fulfilling none of the roles expected for the Messiah."[35]

Finally, the resurrection appearances are reported with extreme reserve. When one compares them with the reports in the apocryphal gospels (second century on), the difference is startling. In the Apocrypha, detailed explanations are given about how the resurrection took place. Gross details are added. For example, the Gospel of Peter (mid-second century) reports a cross coming out of the tomb after Jesus, and Jesus is so tall he extends above the clouds. Furthermore, several miracles and pronouncements are made which demonstrate that "all power in heaven and on earth" has been given to Jesus. But the New Testament accounts are subdued and do not include such fanciful descriptions.[36]

The Predisposition of the Disciples

The disciples were not predisposed to inventing the appearance stories or to having expectations of a resurrection which led to hallucinations.[37] It is hard to overestimate how crushed they were at the crucifixion. They were not interested in starting a new religion. Even if they were, the messianic expectations and the concepts of resurrection in first-century Palestinian Judaism would not have led to the belief that Jesus rose from the dead.

In this regard, four features of first-century Jewish beliefs about resurrection and the afterlife are especially important. First, in Jewish thought, the resurrection of the dead always occurred at the end of the world, and not at some point prior to the end. Second, there was no conception of isolated individuals rising from the dead. The resurrection was conceived as a general resurrection of all mankind. Third, the resurrection was conceived in a crude, physicalist way which involved a reassembling of the parts of the predeath body. No conception of a resurrection body fits the picture of Jesus' body with the unique features of its behavior. Fourth, Wilckens has pointed out that the Jewish understanding of visions contained two elements: they were understood as being visions of people directly translated to heaven and not raised from the dead, and in Jewish

---

35. Ladd, *I Believe in the Resurrection*, pp. 71–72.

36. Fuller includes the resurrection narratives in the apocryphal gospels (*Formation of the Resurrection Narratives*, pp. 189–97).

37. Ladd, *I Believe in the Resurrection*, pp. 50–73; Lapide, *The Resurrection of Jesus*, pp. 44–65; Wilckens, *Resurrection*, pp. 74–111; Craig, *The Son Rises*, pp. 129–31.

tradition, visions were always experienced by individuals and not by groups. More will be said shortly about the difference between translation and resurrection. But for now, it is important to point out that visions of Jesus are reported as having occurred to pairs or small groups. Jesus appeared to five hundred people at once, and the implication of the passage is clear: If the reader were skeptical, he could ask several of these people because they were still alive (see 1 Cor. 15).

Because of these features of Jewish belief, the disciples would not have had expectations or needs for wish-fulfillment which the resurrection of Jesus met. The resurrection was unexpected and it is reported in such a way as to be almost completely out of touch with what these men had been taught to expect from the time they were little boys. Thus, they would not have been in a position to have hallucinations, nor would they have made up such a culturally odd concept of the resurrection of Jesus. Such an account would have had a poor antecedent probability of being successfully promulgated.

Impossibility of Hallucinations to Explain Resurrection

Since the disciples would not have been in a frame of mind to expect a resurrection, they would not have been in a state of expectation and longing necessary for hallucinations to take place. But even if they had such hallucinations of Jesus, they would not have interpreted them to mean that he had been raised from the dead. Jewish beliefs at that time offered a much more accessible framework for understanding these experiences than the framework they chose, namely, Jesus' bodily resurrection. Both in the Old Testament and in Jewish literature other than the Old Testament, there were stories of people either being resuscitated or being translated (taken up directly) to heaven. The former was not considered a resurrection from the dead since it was individual, prior to the end of the world, and resulted in a person who could die again (the body was no different after the resuscitation than before it). Translations to heaven were considered entirely different from resurrections. A translation did not involve a bodily raising of a dead man, but a direct transporting to heaven.

It is a feature of hallucinations that they do not receive an interpretation which is entirely new. Instead, they combine (in a new way, perhaps) the beliefs already present in the collective subconscious of the person having the hallucination. These subconscious beliefs come from cultural indoctrination and reflect the beliefs of that culture. If the disciples had hallucinations, they would have interpreted them to mean that Jesus had been translated, not resurrected, and they would not have come up with the picture of Jesus' body which is presented in the appearance narratives. The most reasonable explanation for the interpretation they do give to their experiences is that Jesus really rose bodily.[38]

Dunn has made the point this way:

> The oddness and unexpectedness of the first Christian belief that God had raised Jesus from the dead should not be discounted. A belief that God had vindicated Jesus or exalted him to heaven after death would have been more understandable. But that they should conclude from these "sightings" (and the empty tomb) that God had actually begun the resurrection of the dead is without any real precedent. There must have been something about these first encounters (visionary or otherwise) which pushed them to what was an extraordinary conclusion in the context of that time. A careful jury would have to ask why the first Christians drew such an unusual conclusion. In the light of the considerations outlined above, the answer would be quite proper: A unique explanation for a unique event.[39]

The Psychology of Hallucinations

Certain features are true of people who have hallucinations which do not fit the accounts of Jesus' appearances.[40] First, hallucinations happen to persons who are high-strung, highly imaginative, and nervous. Second, they are linked in an individual's subconscious to his past beliefs and experiences. Third, it is extremely unlikely that two or more people would have the same hallucination at the same time. Fourth, they usually occur at particular places (places of nostalgia which create a reminiscing mood) and they recur over a long period of time.

None of these features adequately describe the New Testament experiences. Furthermore, the disciples were intelligent men who had several opportunities over the next few decades to reflect about the veracity of their experiences. It is hard to believe that Paul would not have reflected about his experience of Jesus in the light of the hardships he endured and the death he faced. A simple hallucination could not have transformed him or the others, nor could it have sustained their motivation for so long. This is especially true in light of the unexpected interpretation they gave to these experiences—the resurrection of Jesus.

---

38. Dunn, *The Evidence for Jesus*, p. 72, points out that one of Jesus' own symbols was his reference to his "coming on clouds of glory" as a heavenly figure. This image surely would have stirred the imagination of the disciples and would have provided a picture to interpret hallucinations they might have had. Yet nothing of this figure appears in the resurrection narratives.

39. Ibid, p. 73.

40. McDowell, *Evidence That Demands a Verdict*, pp. 258–59, 264. See also Osborne, *The Resurrection Narratives*, pp. 277–78.

Explaining the Appearances

Three explanations can be offered to explain these appearances apart from the one which accepts their veracity: the mythical interpretation, the subjective-hallucination theory, and the objective-vision theory. I have already argued against the first two. The third view holds that Jesus lived in spiritual form after his death and that God granted objective visions of Jesus to the disciples. These were true visions of an impression which came from God and were not merely subjective hallucinations. But they were not visions of physical events. It is beyond the scope of this chapter to give a detailed refutation of this view. But two brief points can be made. Even if this view is accepted, one must postulate a full-blown theism, including a view of Jesus which sees him as alive spiritually after his death, in order to adequately explain the resurrection appearances. This is not a very promising line of argument for an atheist. Second, the New Testament writers, including Paul, present Jesus as being raised bodily. Such a view squares with the data, explains the empty tomb, and fits in well with Jewish insistence on a bodily resurrection.

In sum, the most reasonable explanation for the appearances of Jesus after his death is the one which accepts their veracity.

Four Key Features of the Early Church

The Transformation of the Disciples

It is difficult to explain the transformation of the disciples without the resurrection. Lapide has put it this way:

> When this scared, frightened band of the apostles which was just about to throw away everything in order to flee in despair to Galilee; when these peasants, shepherds, and fishermen, who betrayed and denied their master and then failed him miserably, suddenly could be changed overnight into a confident mission society, convinced of salvation and able to work with much more success after Easter than before Easter, then no vision or hallucination is sufficient to explain such a revolutionary transformation. For a sect or school or an order, perhaps a single vision would have been sufficient— but not for a world religion which was able to conquer the Occident thanks to the Easter faith.[41]

Why did these men change? Why did they undergo hardship, persecution, pressure, and martyrdom? Consider James the brother of Jesus. Jo-

---

41. Lapide, *The Resurrection of Jesus*, p. 125.

sephus, the first-century Jewish historian, tells us that he died a martyr's death for his faith in his brother. Yet the Gospels tell us that during Jesus' life, he was an unbeliever and opposed Jesus. Why did he change? What could cause a Jew to believe that his own brother was the very Son of God and to be willing to die for such a belief? It certainly was not a set of lovely teachings from a carpenter from Nazareth. Only the appearance of Jesus to James (1 Cor. 15:7) can explain his transformation. As with James, so it is with the other disciples. One who denies the resurrection owes us an explanation of this transformation which does justice to the historical facts.

The Change in Key Social Structures in Judaism

In New Testament times and earlier, at least five religious and social beliefs formed the very core of Jewish corporate and individual identity. Centuries of dispersion and captivity by Gentile nations reinforced the social importance of these beliefs which were already valued for their religious content. These structures defined the Jews as a people and kept them from falling apart as a nation. They were major elements in education of the young, and the early converts to Christianity, including the disciples (most of the early church was composed of Jews for the first few years of its existence), would have been taught to cherish these structures from their youth.

First, there was the importance of the sacrifices. While obedience to the law was slowly eroding the centrality of the sacrificial system, nevertheless the importance of sacrificing animals for various sins was a major value in first-century Judaism. Second, emphasis was placed on keeping the law. Regardless of whether one was a Sadducee or a Pharisee, respect for the law of Moses and its role in keeping people in right standing with God was a major value. Third, keeping the Sabbath was important; several laws were formulated to help define Sabbath-keeping and to maintain its prominence. Fourth, clear-cut non-Trinitarian monotheism was a defining trait of the Jew. The Shema asserts that God is one, and this doctrine was non-negotiable. Specifically, there was no belief that God could ever become a man. Fifth, the Messiah was pictured as a human figure (perhaps superhuman, but not God himself), a political king who would liberate the Jews from Gentile oppression and establish the Davidic kingdom. No conception of a crucified messiah who established a church by raising from the dead was known.

The early church was a community of Jews who had significantly altered or given up these five major structures. What could possibly cause this to happen in so short a time? Suppose a person left the United States during the peak of the Reagan administration when there was a strong conservative shift in politics. Suppose further that he lost touch with the

U.S. for twenty years. Upon his return to the States, imagine that he picked up a history book which informed him that a radical Marxist was elected president after Reagan's last term in office. Such a radical sociological shift would demand an explanation.

The shift from Judaism to Christianity among the early Jewish converts is even more dramatic than the one imagined. Society did not change rapidly in those days. Jews would risk becoming social outcasts if they tampered with these five major beliefs, not to mention that they would risk the damnation of their own souls to hell. Why was such a change made in so short a time after the death of a carpenter from Nazareth—of all places[42]— who had suffered the death of a criminal on the cross, a death expressly detested among the Jews in their belief that "cursed is he who dies on a tree"? How could such a thing ever take place? The resurrection offers the only rational explanation.

The Sacraments of the Early Church

Two sacraments were prominent in the early church and both of them presuppose the resurrection of Jesus. The first sacrament was the Eucharist. The celebration of the Eucharist was an early practice (see 1 Cor. 11) which began no later than a few years after Jesus' death. This was not a gathering to mourn at Jesus' tomb; it was a celebration. Why would people celebrate the death of one they loved? They did not celebrate his life or teachings. They celebrated his death and his continued presence with them. Such an activity made sense only on the assumption of their certainty of Jesus' resurrection from the dead.

The other sacrament was baptism. Romans 6:1–6 and Colossians 2:12 demonstrate that the meaning of this sacrament was intimately linked to Jesus' death and resurrection. The practice of baptism in the early church was probably an adaptation of proselyte baptism practiced in Judaism. The change in meaning of the act of baptism by the church points to the resurrection as a necessary precondition for such a change.

The Existence of the Church Itself

What cause can be postulated to explain the fact that the Christian church transformed the world of the first century? The odds for its success were antecedently poor. Several religions existed in the first century and some of the elements of Christianity can be found in them. Why did Christianity succeed, especially when it was such an exclusivist faith which

---

42. Martin Hengel, *Crucifixion: In the Ancient World and the Folly of the Message of the Cross*, trans. John Bowden (Philadelphia: Fortress, 1977), pp. 5–7.

frowned on syncretism? What caused the church to get started? There never was a form of Christianity which did not emphasize the centrality of the death and resurrection of a divine Jesus.

The resurrection of Jesus is the explanation the church herself gave, and it is the only adequate one. Cambridge New Testament scholar C. F. D. Moule argues this way: "If the coming into existence of the Nazarenes, a phenomenon undeniably attested by the New Testament, rips a great hole in history, a hole of the size and shape of Resurrection, what does the secular historian propose to stop it up with?"[43]

Hellenistic Influences

Before concluding this chapter, a brief word regarding Hellenistic influences on the New Testament picture of the resurrection of Jesus may be helpful. One sometimes hears that the account of the resurrection of Jesus was the result of influence from mystery religions or Gnostic redeemer myths. It cannot be emphasized enough that such influences are seen by current New Testament scholars to have little or no role in shaping the New Testament picture of Jesus in general or the resurrection narratives in particular. Both the general milieu of the Gospels and specific features of the resurrection narratives give overwhelming evidence that the early church was rooted in Judaism. Jesus, the early church, and its writings were born in Jewish soil and Gentile influence was minimal.

Mystery Religions

There were several mystery religions in the ancient world.[44] These involved various mythical deities, such as Cybele and Attis, Dionysus, Adonis and Aphrodite, Tammuz and Inanna, and Isis and Osiris (also called Serapis). These religions involve various stories of dying gods who come back to life. Some have thought that these religions led the early church to fabricate similar explanations of Jesus' resurrection.

43. C. F. D. Moule, *The Phenomenon of the New Testament* (London: SCM, 1967), p. 3.
44. On the mystery religions, see J. Gresham Machen, *The Origin of Paul's Religion* (Grand Rapids: Eerdmans, 1925); Michael Green, ed., *The Truth of God Incarnate* (Grand Rapids: Eerdmans, 1977); John W. Drane, "The Religious Background," in *New Testament Interpretation: Essays on Principles and Methods*, ed. I. Howard Marshall (Grand Rapids: Eerdmans, 1978), pp. 117-25, and James D. G. Dunn, "Demythologizing—The Problem of Myth in the New Testament," pp. 285-307 in the same volume; Edwin M. Yamauchi, "Easter—Myth, Hallucination, or History? Parts I and II" in *Christianity Today* 4 (March 15 and March 29, 1974): 4-7, 12-16; Ronald H. Nash, *Christianity and the Hellenistic World* (Grand Rapids: Zondervan, 1984). On the influence of Hellenistic and rabbinic miracle stories on the New Testament, see Leopold Sabourin, "Hellenistic and Rabbinic Miracles," *Biblical Theology Bulletin* 2 (October 1972): 281-307.

Apart from the fact that the New Testament documents are early, Jewish, and written during the time of eyewitnesses, several things can be said against the thesis. First, Christianity is about a real historical person who lived and the material about him functions, among other things, to give a historical account of what he was like and who he was. The stories of the mystery religions were myths that served as reenactments each year. Such reenactments were associated with the yearly cycle of spring and the coming of new crops. So such stories never were intended to be historical narratives and did not function as such. Second, similarities between the accounts about Jesus and these religions are often apparent and not real. This becomes evident when one reads about the mystery religions. For example, in the Egyptian cult of Isis and Osiris, Osiris is killed and dismembered by the evil god Set. Isis discovers various parts of the body and places them back together in a casket. Magically, Osiris resuscitates in a crude sort of way. This is so mythical that one has to strain hard to see any significant parallels between Osiris and Jesus.

Third, differences far outweigh similarities. The mystery religions have a consort, a female deity who is central to the myth. They have no real resurrection, only a crude resuscitation. The mysteries have little or no moral context, fertility being what the mystery rites sought to induce. The mysteries are polytheistic, syncretistic legends unrelated to historical individuals. Fourth, the majority of sources which contain parallels with Christianity are dated after the Christian faith was established. This fact, coupled with the fact that the mystery religions were syncretistic, shows that if any borrowing went on, the mysteries borrowed from Christianity and not vice versa.

Gnostic Redeemer Myths

Others have argued that Iranian Gnostic redeemer myths influenced the formation of belief in the resurrection.[45] According to this view, prior to the New Testament there existed a full-blown Gnosticism which included a redeemer myth. This myth involved the belief in an original man (Urmensch) who fell from heaven and was ripped to shreds by demons. Parts of the original man are hidden in each man in the form of a spark of eternity. Demons attempt to put men to sleep so they will not recognize their heavenly origin, preexistent souls, and divine spark. So God sent a heavenly redeemer to come and impart secret knowledge to men about

45. For criticisms of the Gnostic redeemer thesis, see Nash, *Christianity and the Hellenistic World*, pp. 203–61; Edwin M. Yamauchi, *Pre-Christian Gnosticism: A Survey of the Proposed Evidences* (Grand Rapids: Eerdmans, 1973); Andrew K. Helmbold, "Redeemer Hymns—Gnostic and Christian," in *New Dimensions in New Testament Study*, ed. Richard N. Longenecker and Merrill C. Tenney (Grand Rapids: Zondervan, 1974), pp. 71–78.

their former state. After enlightening them, the redeemer returns to heaven.

Several objections make this view untenable. First, there is absolutely no evidence for a full-blown pre-Christian Gnosticism. The texts which describe a redeemer all were written after the New Testament (140 and later). So if borrowing did occur, it must have been by the Gnostics. Second, elements in the New Testament which were thought to be Gnostic are now seen to be Jewish, and some of them are rooted in the Old Testament. For example, John often talks of light versus darkness—a prevalent Gnostic theme. But this does not show he borrowed from Gnosticism. The motif could have come from the Old Testament. Further, this motif is now known to have been prominent at Qumran, a community of conservative Jewish ascetics (Essenes) which flourished just prior to and during New Testament times. The Essenes were concerned for ritual purity and were well within the mainstream of Jewish thought. Thus, the presence of such a motif in their writings was not due to Gnostic influence; the same holds true for John's writings.

For these and other reasons, most scholars today regard it a mistake to emphasize the importance of Hellenistic influences on the New Testament. Belief in Jesus' resurrection was born on Jewish soil and propagated by men nurtured in Jewish thought. In light of this fact, and the evidence given in this chapter, the most reasonable explanation for the data I have presented is the historical fact of the bodily resurrection of Jesus from the dead.

7

Science and Christianity

Is science a threat to Christianity? Is it possible to integrate the doctrines of Christian theology with the tenets of scientific thought? Is cre-

185

ation science a science, and if so, how does it compare with the general theory of evolution?

The interaction between science and Christianity has long been a subject of debate. In what may be the most authoritative work on the history of this interaction, historians of science David Lindberg and Ronald Numbers state that "for over a century scholars have debated the historical relationship between science and Christianity, some maintaining that the two have been mortal enemies, others that they have been allies, and still others that neither conflict nor harmony adequately describes their relationship."[1]

The purpose of this chapter is to examine important issues relevant to the question of the integration of science and Christianity in order to show that modern science has not demonstrated that religion is irrational, a matter of private subjective opinion, and so forth, whereas science is the paradigm of truth and rationality. First, we will explore different views about the nature of science itself. Should scientific theories be taken as true (or approximately true) and rational?[2] Or should they be taken in some other way? Second, we will examine some limits to science. Science cannot purport to be the *only* discipline that gives true and reasonable information about the world, and we will see why this is so. Third, different models of integration between science and Christianity will be investigated. Finally, we will consider the creation/evolution debate as an example of integration and focus on two questions: Is scientific creationism a science or is it religion? What are the major biblical and scientific issues involved in this debate?

The Debate About Scientific Realism

Most people untrained in the philosophy of science accept, explicitly or implicitly, a "realist" view of science. According to this view, good scientific theories are rational; indeed, science is the model of rationality, and

---

1. David Lindberg and Ronald Numbers, eds., *God and Nature* (Berkeley: University of California Press, 1986), p. 1. This book is arguably the best work to date on the history of the encounter between Christianity and science.

2. In the philosophy of science, laws ($PV=nRT$) and theories (such as the ideal gas theory) are usually distinguished from one another in one of three ways. Theories are said to have a higher degree of confirmation than laws, theories are broader than laws, or theories explain by using models whereas laws merely state regular relations between phenomena. I will not bother to distinguish the two and will sometimes use the terms interchangeably. For helpful introductions to the philosophy of science, see Carl Hempel, *Philosophy of Natural Science* (Englewood Cliffs, N.J.: Prentice-Hall, 1966); V. James Mannoia, Jr., *What Is Science? An Introduction to the Structure and Methodology of Science* (Washington, D.C.: University Press of America, 1980); R. Harré, *The Philosophies of Science* (Oxford: Oxford University Press, 1972); Del Ratzsch, *Philosophy of Science* (Downers Grove: Inter-Varsity, 1986).

good scientific theories are true, or at least approximately true, descriptions of the world. If a scientific theory says that some theoretical entity, perhaps an electron, exists, then it is rational to believe that electrons do, in fact, exist.

A realist understanding of science can contribute to an approach to the theology-science dialogue by implying that if science says something is true and Christianity seems to conflict with science, then Christianity needs to be adjusted. The result of this has been the idea that since science always defeats religion in their battles, then perhaps religion was never intended to be a factual, rational way of understanding the world, but rather a private guide for one's practical life.

On the other hand, if there is reason to doubt that scientific theories are rational or approximately true, then it is difficult to see how science could pose a threat to the truth and rationality of Christianity. Most debates between creationists and evolutionists assume scientific realism. After all, if one does not assume that evolutionary theory is true or rational, then why bother to argue against it or integrate Christian beliefs with evolutionary theory?

Today, a major battle is going on over scientific realism. A large number of respected philosophers, sociologists, and scientists reject scientific realism. In this section, I will survey some of the major positions taken in the debate about the nature of science. Though I myself lean toward some form of scientific realism, this survey will illustrate that many philosophers have raised serious arguments against it and have provided alternate accounts of science. This in turn should caution anyone who automatically thinks that just because science and Christianity "conflict," then Christianity must be the loser. For it may be that science as a discipline, or some particular theory of science, should not be viewed in realistic terms.

Consider the following diagram:[3]

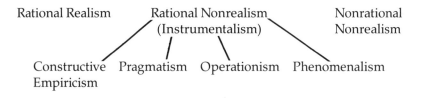

Rational Realism   Rational Nonrealism   Nonrational
                        (Instrumentalism)   Nonrealism

Constructive   Pragmatism   Operationism   Phenomenalism
Empiricism

3. I have taken the names for the basic categories from W. H. Newton-Smith, *The Rationality of Science*, International Library of Philosophy (Boston: Routledge and Kegan Paul, 1981), pp. 1–43. For other works by Christians who argue against science by opting for antirealism, see John Byl, "Instrumentalism: A Third Option," *Journal of the American Scientific Affiliation* 37 (March 1985): 11–18; Gordon H. Clark, *The Philosophy of Science and the Belief in God* (Nutley, N.J.: Craig, 1964). I differ with Byl and Clark in that I think rational realism is the best view. My point here is to show that rational realism is not a clear-cut winner, and thus scientific claims should be used with caution. One is justified in taking an eclectic view of science, adopting realism or antirealism on a case-by-case basis.

Rational Realism

Though it was a minority view in the first half of this century, scientific realism, or rational realism as I am calling it, is the majority view among current philosophers of science. Prominent realists are Ernan McMullin, Richard Boyd, W. H. Newton-Smith, and Karl Popper.[4] There are several different varieties of realism, but the core tenets of rational realism are these:

RR1. Scientific theories (in mature, developed sciences) are true or approximately true.

RR2. The central observational and theoretical terms of a mature scientific theory genuinely refer to things in the world. These terms make existence claims.

RR3. It is possible in principle to have good reasons for thinking which of a pair of rival theories is more likely to be more approximately true. Rationality is an objective notion and conceptual relativism (what is rational for one person or group should not necessarily be so for another person or group) is false.

RR4. A scientific theory will embody certain epistemic virtues (simplicity, clarity, internal and external consistency, predictive ability, empirical accuracy, scope of relevance, fruitfulness in guiding new research) if and only if it is approximately true.

RR5. The aim of science is a literally true picture of the world. Scientific progress tends to converge on truer and truer pictures of the world, where later theories usually refine and preserve the best parts of earlier theories and are closer to the truth than earlier theories.[5]

RR1 attempts to state that science is committed to some form of the correspondence theory of truth: a theory is true if and only if what it says about the world is in fact the way the world is. The theory-independent world is what makes a theory true. RR1 also assumes that the notion of approximate truth is a coherent one. Some theories can be *more* true than others.

RR2 is a semantic thesis about the nature of language and meaning. Since scientific theories have meaning and are stated in language, then a discussion of scientific theories will include issues relevant to a discussion

---

4. See Jarrett Leplin, ed., *Scientific Realism* (Berkeley: University of California Press, 1985).

5. For a variety of statements of realism, see Leplin, *Scientific Realism*, pp.1–7; Newton-Smith, *The Rationality of Science*, p. 43; Ratzsch, *Philosophy of Science*, pp. 85–90; Larry Laudan, *Science and Values: The Aims of Science and Their Role in Scientific Debate*, Pittsburgh Series in Philosophy and History (Berkeley: University of California Press, 1984), pp. 104–9.

of language in general; for example, debates about how terms get meaning and how they refer to something in the world. Consider the following two sentences:

1. Fido is brown.
2. The average family has 2.5 children.

In sentence 1, the term *Fido* is called a referring term. It refers to the dog Fido, an extralinguistic entity in the world, and says of him that he has the color brown. In sentence 2, the term *the average family* appears to function just as the name *Fido* does in sentence 1. However, "the average family" is not a referring term. No one would try to locate where the average family lives and count their children to make sure they have 2.5. Rather, "the average family" is a shorthand term for a set of mathematical operations. It says "add the number of children and divide by the number of families and you get 2.5."

Now consider this sentence:

3. Protons have positive charge.

RR2 says that the theoretical term *proton* is a referring term. Thus, if "proton" is in an accepted scientific statement like sentence 3, then this has ontological implications. Extralinguistic entities, protons, exist.

RR3 asserts that science is an objectively rational discipline and one can have objective reasons for accepting or rejecting a given scientific theory. RR4 adds that if a scientific theory has certain epistemic virtues, then it is objectively rational to believe that theory is approximately true, *because* it has these virtues. For example, if theory T is simpler than T_1 or if it explains more phenomena, gives more accurate predictions of empirical data, has more clearly defined terms, and so forth, then one should believe that T is truer than T_1. Further, if a theory is actually more true than any of its rivals, then one should expect it to eventually be better at predicting data, contain clearer terms, and so forth.

RR5 states that the aim of science is not just to have theories that work (i.e., that give us power over nature or help us have a useful picture for laboratory research). Rather, the aim of science is to discover truth. Science tries to tell us the way the world really is, and more recent scientific theories are more accurate pictures of the way the world is than their predecessors. Science converges over time toward a true picture of the world.

Several thinkers have rejected a rational realist understanding of science. The following is a sketch of some alternative understandings of the scientific enterprise.

Rational Nonrealism

There are several varieties of rational nonrealism, but they are all agreed that science is a rational discipline in an objective, nonrelativist sense of rationality and that theoretical terms in science do not refer to anything in the world and thus science does not give a true picture of real entities in the world which lie beyond what our senses tell us.

In order to understand rational nonrealism, it is important to keep in mind the distinction between truth and rationality. Something can be true without being rational. In fact something can be true even if no one has ever thought about it at all. For example, if protons really do exist and have positive charge, then this fact was true during the Middle Ages. But no one knew it was true, nor did anyone have any reason to believe it was true. Given the philosophical outlook of the Middle Ages, chemical change was explained in other ways (in terms of qualities, for example, and not in terms of atoms). Some of these explanations were reasonable (they explained certain phenomena and so forth) even though they were not necessarily true. The true explanation, given our modern assumption about the existence of protons, was not a reasonable one for someone in the Middle Ages to believe.

On the other hand, a rational belief is not necessarily a true one. When a jury finds someone guilty in light of the evidence, it is still possible that the person is innocent, even if the more reasonable view (on the basis of the evidence) is that he is guilty. Truth is an ontological notion and reasonableness is an epistemological notion. Truth does not change. Something either is or is not true. A rational belief can be changed when new evidence comes in.

Rational nonrealists hold that scientific theories are rational but do not give true descriptions of the deep structure of the world's hidden substances, particles, structures, or laws. Several varieties of rational nonrealism exist, but the following four are the most important ones.

Phenomenalism

Phenomenalism is a view which was more popular earlier in this century. Major proponents of one form or another of phenomenalism have been Benjamin Brodie, Ernst Mach, P. W. Bridgman, and A. S. Eddington.[6] Phenomenalism holds that scientific knowledge is about what we can see. Any thing or process which cannot be perceived cannot be supposed to exist for science. Second, the meaning of expressions which

---

6. See Harré, *Philosophies of Science*, pp. 69–89. An extended treatment of different forms of instrumentalism, including phenomenalism, can be found in Frederick Suppe, ed., *The Structure of Scientific Theories*, 2d ed. (Urbana: University of Illinois Press, 1977), pp. 6–241.

appear to be referring to unseen theoretical entities must be taken as referring to sensory experience. To clarify this, consider the following chart:[7]

Theoretical Term		Observational Term	
electron	mass	red	floats
electric field	kinetic energy	longer than	wood
atom	temperature	left of	water
molecule	gene	hard	weight
virus	charge	volume	iron

According to phenomenalism, the theoretical terms do not refer to entities that exist, but are either shorthand terms for a potentially infinite set of
actual or possible sensory experiences, or are rules for calculating certain
numerical ratios that will obtain after certain operations have been carried
out. For example, the word *hydrogen* does not refer to an atom which exists.
Rather, the word refers to a set of laboratory observations of colorlessness,
weight, and volume which follow when other observational data are recorded, namely, those data associated with a process of preparing hydrogen.

Laws of nature and theories are nothing but records of past experiences
which can be used to anticipate future experience. $2H_2 + O_2 = 2H_2O$ does
not mean that two molecules of hydrogen and one molecule of oxygen produce a real entity known as a molecule of water. Rather, it means that in the
past, two units of volume, weight, and odorlessness produced by certain
techniques have been added to one unit of volume, weight, and odorlessness produced by certain other techniques, and a wet, colorless substance
of one unit always follows.[8]

In sum, phenomenalism holds that science asserts the existence of ob-
servables only, theoretical terms refer to sets of actual or possible sensory
experiences, and laws or theories are summary statements of past sequences of sensory experience which allow one to predict future series of
sensory experiences.

Operationism

Operationism is a view closely akin to phenomenalism. Its major proponent has been Bridgman. According to operationism, theoretical terms
are shorthand devices, not for sequences or sets of sense experiences

7. Peter Achinstein offers a detailed explanation of observational and theoretical terms in *Concepts of Science: A Philosophical Analysis* (Baltimore: Johns Hopkins Press, 1968), pp. 157–201. See also Newton-Smith, *The Rationality of Science*, pp. 19–43.

8. In the early part of this century the French priest Pierre Duhem held the useful-fiction view, which is similar to phenomenalism. Theories are useful fictions which attempt to give us neat, orderly, elegant explanations of phenomena.

(phenomenalism), but for laboratory operations themselves. Theoretical terms are like the term *the average family*. They stand for a set of operations in the laboratory. For example, length is not an attribute that a physical body has; rather, it is defined as a set of operations of sliding rulers, marking coincidences, and counting how many operations one has made. The "length" of a room is nothing but the operation of taking a stick with thirty-six standard markings (call them inch markings), starting at one end of the room, and laying the stick end after end until one crosses the room, and recording all one's activities. Similarly, the statement that *x* amount of some acid neutralizes *y* of some base means that if one pours a certain measurement of one liquid (obtained by certain other operations) into a beaker and adds a certain measurement of another liquid, then certain measurements follow (the combined liquids change color when the volume measurements are done in a certain way).

Operationists deny that the theoretical entities of science really exist and that the laws of science are true descriptions of the underlying structure of the world. Theoretical entities and laws are just sets of laboratory operations and recorded numbers in a laboratory notebook.

Pragmatism

One of the leading philosophers of science is Larry Laudan, who holds to what can be called a pragmatic view of science.[9] According to Laudan, the aim of scientific progress is not to find truer and truer theories about the world. Rather, science merely aims to obtain theories that work (i.e., solve problems). Science aims to solve two broad kinds of problems. First, there are empirical problems. These are any problems about the natural world that strike us as odd and in need of explanation. The motion of the planets would be an example. Second, there are conceptual problems. Conceptual problems are difficulties with clarifying and harmonizing the theoretical concepts of a theory. Some conceptual problems are internal to a theory. For example, how can the nature of light be both a wave and a particle? Other conceptual problems involve harmonizing scientific concepts with concepts deemed rational by other disciplines such as theology and philosophy. For example, if one had philosophical reasons for believing that there was no such thing as action at a distance, then Newton's concept of gravity would involve an external conceptual problem.

So Laudan says that the aim of science is to solve problems, and this has little or nothing to do with truth. Further, some of the problems for science

9. See these four works by Laudan: *Science and Values; Progress and Its Problems: Toward a Theory of Scientific Growth* (Berkeley: University of California Press, 1977); "A Confutation of Convergent Realism," *Philosophy of Science* 48 (1981): 19–49; "Explaining the Success of Science: Beyond Epistemic Realism and Relativism," in *Science and Reality*, ed. James T. Cushing, C. F. Delaney, and Gary Gutting (Notre Dame: University of Notre Dame Press, 1984), pp. 83–105.

come from other disciplines. In fact, Laudan argues that there is no clear line of demarcation between science and nonscience. Thus, theological considerations are relevant to the rational assessment of a scientific theory, for they are examples of rational worldview beliefs which should be brought to bear on the rational appraisal of a scientific theory.

If science does not aim at discovering truth, but merely at solving problems, at explaining the world and making its workings seem less puzzling, then how does one know that he has a theory which solves a scientific problem? A theory solves a problem if it embodies certain epistemic virtues such as simplicity, predictive success, or conceptual clarity. Laudan lists dozens of theories in the history of science that explained facts, predicted new test results, accurately described phenomena, and so forth, but which were later found to be false. For example, various aether theories which postulated a medium through which light, heat, and electricity flowed embodied various epistemic virtues for a long time, even though we now believe these aether theories to be false. Furthermore, theories now believed by realists to be true for a long time lacked explanatory success, predictive ability, and so forth. For example, the chemical atomic theory in the eighteenth century was so unsuccessful that most chemists abandoned it, even though, according to current theory, it was approximately true.

In sum, Laudan holds that the aim of science is to obtain theories which solve problems. Theories which solve problems will embody certain epistemic virtues. Theories can embody these virtues without being true (or approximately true), and true (or approximately true) theories do not necessarily embody problem-solving virtues. Finally, Laudan argues that science is a rational discipline because it makes progress in solving its problems. It does not solve its problems because it is a rational discipline. Science gives us a better and better way of viewing the phenomena of the physical world such that the phenomena are less and less puzzling. We are able to predict phenomena, control and manipulate the world, and offer explanations for what happens, but none of these features of science requires that scientific progress converge on a true picture of the world. Science is rational not because it is true, but because it makes progress in explaining the world. It works.

Constructive Empiricism

Princeton philosopher Bas C. van Fraassen holds a view about science which he calls constructive empiricism.[10] Van Fraassen states, "Science

10. See Bas C. van Fraassen, "To Save the Phenomena," in Leplin, *Scientific Realism,* pp. 250–59; *The Scientific Image* (Oxford: Clarendon Press, 1980). For an evaluation of van Fraassen's views, see Paul M. Churchland and Clifford A. Hooker, eds., *Images of Science: Essays on Realism and Empiricism, with a Reply from Bas C. van Fraassen* (Chicago: University of Chicago Press, 1985).

aims to give us theories which are empirically adequate and acceptance of a theory involves a belief only that it is empirically adequate. This is the statement of the anti-realism I advocate; I shall call it constructive empiricism."[11]

Science does not aim at giving true descriptions of unseen theoretical entities. Rather, science aims at theories which accurately describe and predict empirical phenomena. Van Fraassen disagrees with the phenomenalist view that the *meaning* of a theoretical term is its actual and possible sensory experiences. The term *electron* means what the realist takes it to mean, an entity with negative charge. But even though science requires us to accept electrons, that is, to act *as if* electrons existed, we need not actually *believe* that they exist.

So constructive empiricism holds that science requires us to act as if theoretical entities exist, but in reality, all that this means is that such an assumption generates theories that work and are empirically adequate. We are not entitled to make the further claim that theoretical entities really exist and that science truly describes their properties.

Nonrational Nonrealism

Some philosophers of science not only deny realism, but also deny that there is some objective sense in which science is rational. Major figures in this group are Paul Feyerabend, N. R. Hanson, Hilary Putnam, and Thomas Kuhn.[12] Kuhn is, perhaps, the best-known example of this approach, so I will focus on his views.[13]

First, Kuhn holds that there is no such thing as neutral facts or data. Observation is theory-laden; that is, our perception of the world is not a perception of a mind-independent "given." The "world" we see is itself determined by our theories about the world. Two different people with different paradigms or theories actually see different things. Ptolemy *saw* a sun which revolved around the earth. Copernicus *saw* a stationary sun. They saw different worlds because they held different theories.

Second, rival theories or paradigms (Newton's views of mass, space, and time versus Einstein's) are incommensurable. This means that they cannot even be compared with each other to see which is more rational or closer to the facts. There are no theory-independent facts and there are no

11. Van Fraassen, *Scientific Image*, p. 11.
12. For a survey of this view, see Suppe, *Structure of Scientific Theories*, pp. 125–221. Putnam would no doubt argue with my classification of him, but it seems to me to be correct. See his *Reason, Truth, and History* (Cambridge: Cambridge University Press, 1981); "Why There Isn't a Ready-Made World," *Synthese* 51 (1982): 141–67; "Realism and Reason," *Proceedings and Addresses of the American Philosophical Association,* vol. 50, no. 6, pp. 483–98.
13. Kuhn's views are summarized and criticized in J. P. Moreland, "Kuhn's Epistemology: A Paradigm Afloat," *Bulletin of the Evangelical Philosophical Society* 4 (1981): 33–60.

theory-independent criteria (simplicity, predictive success, accuracy) which can be used to decide between two theories. Different theories describe different worlds and have their own internal criteria of rationality.

Third, the rational authority of science does not consist in a rational method of investigation but in a community of practitioners. Scientists are a culture of people and they arbitrarily set up the rules for what will and will not count as rational. What is rational for one culture is not necessarily rational for another culture. The distinction between rational and objective on the one hand, and irrational and subjective on the other, is an arbitrary distinction.

Fourth, the history of science is not a story of later theories refining and extending earlier ones as science converges more and more toward the truth. Rather, it is a history of paradigm shifts (successive replacements of one theory by another). Current theories are no more rational or true than earlier ones. They are just the ones that *our* community of scientists accepts.

Our brief survey of alternatives to rational realism allows us to draw three conclusions. First, rational realism has serious difficulties which have led a large number of thinkers to reject it.[14] Thus, even if some scientific theory seems to be well established and accepted by most scientists,

14. The major criticisms of realism are these: 1. Several past theories now believed to be false had several epistemic virtues, and several past theories now believed to be true (on realist grounds) failed to show epistemic virtues for a very long time. So truth is not related to the success of a theory. 2. Realists have not sufficiently clarified what it means for a later theory to refine and retain a former one. This lack of clarity allows realists to misread the history of science, which is mostly a history of replacement of theories, not refinements. If most past theories have been replaced, it is reasonable to expect current ones to be replaced. 3. Scientific disputes occur at three levels: facts (quantity, quality, and variety of facts), rules (double-blind experiments are preferred to single-blind ones), and aims or values (seek truth, simplicity, accuracy). A nonrealist view of science says progress comes from a coherence among these levels, not from a correspondence with the world. 4. Realist and antirealist views of science are empirically equivalent theories of the history of science itself, and thus are both able to explain the success of science. (These four points are covered in Laudan, *Science and Values*.) 5. Something is either true or false, and the notion of approximate truth is unclear and unhelpful. See Laudan, *Progress and Its Problems*, pp. 121–33. 6. Terms in a theory get their meaning from their role in the entire theory and they refer if an object satisfies the descriptive content of that term. But this means that all adjusted past theories were nonreferring, they are incommensurable with present theories, and present theories will probably be adjusted and thus shown to be nonreferring too. See David Papineau, *Theory and Meaning* (Oxford: Clarendon Press, 1979). Realists have responded with two alternative theories of reference. First, some offer a causal theory of reference. See Newton-Smith, *The Rationality of Science*, pp. 148–82. Second, some offer a partial-denotation theory of reference. See Hartry Field, "Theory Change and the Indeterminacy of Reference," *The Journal of Philosophy* 70 (1973): 462–81. 7. The breakdown of the observation/theory distinction means that we have no direct knowledge of a theory-independent world. See Thomas Kuhn, *The Structure of Scientific Revolutions*, 2d ed. (Chicago: University of Chicago Press, 1970); Newton-Smith, *The Rationality of Science*, pp. 19–43. 8. The history of science includes many empirically equivalent theories which cannot be decided by data. Such theories are underdetermined by the empirical facts. So realists cannot satisfy RR2 and RR3 simultaneously. See Paul Horwich, "How to Choose Between Empirically Equivalent Theories of the World," *The Journal of Philosophy* 79 (February 1982): 61–77. 9. The paradigm case of modern scientific success, quantum mechanics, is so difficult to take along realist lines (it is counterintuitive, it makes apparently contradictory assertions) that it is best to treat it in antirealist terms. What applies to the paradigm case of science

this is not in itself a good reason to assume that the theory is true or approximately true. Christians who try to integrate science and theology should not naively assume rational realism by holding that current science *must* be approximately true by definition and theology had better realize that. If some nonrealist version of science is true, then it may be that scientific theories merely provide useful solutions to certain empirical problems.

Second, even if one holds to some form of rational realism, as I do, one should still be cautious in accepting a current, established scientific theory as an approximately true description of the world. I do not see why one could not be an eclectic here. For example, someone could be a realist in geology, but a nonrealist in quantum physics. Suppose someone had good reason to believe that every event has a cause. If quantum mechanics denied this at the subatomic level, then one could be rational in taking a nonrealist understanding of quantum mechanics. Further, even if one were a rational realist in every area of science, one could still be cautious about accepting a current theory as clearly true. It has been said that one who marries current science is destined to be a widower soon. This seems to be an overstatement, but critics like Laudan have cited several examples of theories which have been successful in explaining data for a long time and later were found to be false. This should serve as a warning to beware of accepting a current theory as the absolute truth.[15]

Third, the boundary between science and nonscience is a difficult one to draw. Even if one could come up with an acceptable definition of science which separated it from other disciplines, it would still not follow that intellectual problems in those other disciplines are irrelevant to the rational assessment of a scientific theory. As Laudan argues, some conceptual problems outside science, such as philosophical or theological problems, *are* relevant to the rationality of science. For example, if the arguments against the possibility of an actual infinite are good arguments, then they count against any scientific cosmology which postulates an actually infinite past, regardless of the fact that they are "philosophical" arguments. If there are good philosophical arguments for the existence of the soul,

---

applies to the rest of science. As physicist Richard Morris puts it, "No one really understands the meaning of quantum mechanics." See Richard Morris, *The Nature of Reality* (New York: McGraw-Hill, 1987), p. 216. See also Ernan McMullin, "A Case for Scientific Realism," in Leplin, *Scientific Realism*, pp. 8–40.

15. In chapters 1 and 2, I have used scientific evidence in the cosmological argument (the second law and the big bang) and the design argument (cosmic singularities, studies on the origin of life). This is in keeping with my own position as a rational realist. But because rational realism may be false as a general position, or as a proper way to take some specific scientific theory, I have used science tentatively, and not as a conclusive argument. I rest the cosmological and design arguments on philosophical considerations, not scientific ones, though I have supplemented them with concepts from science if it seems reasonable to do so.

as was argued in chapter 3, then they count against any form of scientific materialism.

So even if rational realism is true, it is not a clear-cut winner in the debate about the nature of science. Therefore, one should not automatically assume that the only solution to tensions between science and theology is to take a realist view of the scientific theory in question. But suppose one adopts some form of rational realism regarding science. How then should one relate science to Christianity? In the remainder of this chapter, let us assume that rational realism is true, and continue to clarify the relationship between science and Christianity in light of that assumption.

The Limits of Science

Recently I attended an evening gathering where I was introduced to a man finishing his doctorate in physics from Johns Hopkins. When he learned that I am a philosopher and theologian, he began pointing out to me that science is the only discipline that is rational and true. Everything else is a matter of mere belief and opinion. He told me that if something cannot be quantified or tested by the scientific method (whatever that means), it cannot be true or rational.

Unfortunately, this opinion is widely shared in Western culture. Science is believed by many to be the only field which is interested in truth and in which beliefs can be rationally assessed. But however widely this opinion may be held, it is nonetheless patently false. There are several severe limits on science, even when it is construed along rational realist lines.

Science and Self-Refutation

For one thing, the statement "only what can be known by science or quantified and empirically tested is rational and true" is self-refuting. This statement itself is not a statement *of* science. It is a philosophical statement *about* science. How could the statement itself be quantified and empirically tested? And if it cannot, then by the statement's own standards, it cannot itself be true or rationally held.

Another way of putting this is to say that the aims, methodologies, and presuppositions *of* science cannot be validated *by* science. One cannot turn to science to justify science any more than one can pull oneself up by his own bootstraps. The validation of science is a philosophical issue, not a scientific one, and any claim to the contrary will be a self-refuting *philosophical* claim.

The Presuppositions of Science

In order for science to be seen along rational realist lines, several philosophical views which are necessary presuppositions of science must be held. First, one must hold that the senses are reliable and give accurate information about a mind-independent physical world and not merely information about my successive *sense impressions*. There are two major philosophical theories of perception: perceptual realism, which states that objects in the world are the immediate objects of perception, and representative dualism, which holds that the immediate objects of perception are sense images of the world in the minds (or perhaps, brains) of perceivers. Representative dualists are divided into those who, like John Locke, believe a mind-independent physical world *causes* our sense impressions to occur, and those who, like George Berkeley, deny the existence of a mind-independent world. These three views are empirically equivalent; that is, they each entail the same sense of empirical experience. The dispute among them is a philosophical one and rational realism cannot be true if Berkeley's view is correct.

Other assumptions ground the truth and rationality of science. Science must assume that the mind is rational and that the universe is rational in such a way that the mind can know it. Science must assume some uniformity of nature to justify induction (i.e., science must assume that one can legitimately infer from the past to the future and from the examined cases to unexamined ones of the same kind). Just because hydrogen and oxygen combine to form water in all past or examined cases, why should we assume that the same will happen in future or unexamined cases? Science seems to assume the existence of universals and the uniformity of nature to justify such inductive inferences from the examined members of a class to all the members of a class (past and future), but these assumptions cannot themselves be justified inductively. The justification of induction is a philosophical issue.

Science also assumes that the laws of logic are true, that numbers exist (since scientific theories seem to assert, for instance, that water is H_2O, where twoness is just as much a constituent of water as oxygen is), that language has meaning, and that some terms refer to things in the world (since scientific theories are themselves examples of language and thus are involved in problems of general semantics), that truth exists and involves some sort of correspondence between theories and the world (assuming rational realism to be true).

Further, science assumes certain moral, epistemic, and methodological values. Regarding moral values, science assumes that experiments should be reported honestly and that truth-telling is a moral virtue. Regarding epistemic virtues, science assumes that theories ought to be simple, accurate, predictively successful, and so forth. Regarding methodological values, science often values such things as disinterestedness, organized skepticism, and procedural rules (e.g., "prefer double blind experiments to single blind experiments," "prefer theories which make bold new predictions to those which merely explain past data retrodictively," or "make sure to calibrate instrument x with standard y").

Another area outside science is the existence of boundary conditions. For example, Newton's laws of motion tell us that the velocity of a bullet can be described as follows: $v = v_0 + \frac{1}{2}at$, where v is the velocity at time t, v_0 is the initial velocity, and a is the rate of acceleration. The value of v_0, however, is not settled by the equation. It is a boundary condition. The initial velocity depends on the gun, not this equation of motion. Some boundary conditions are just given in the cosmos. The mass of a proton, the rate of expansion of the big bang, the existence of the big bang itself—in short, all cases of genuine brute givens not subsumable under higher laws—are boundary conditions for science. They are givens which cannot be accounted for by science.

These and other presuppositions are necessary to ground science as a rational discipline which gives us approximate truth about the world. But these are philosophical assumptions or brute givens which cannot themselves be verified by science itself without begging the question.[16]

One final point should be made. No generally accepted definition of what science is is agreed on by a majority of philosophers of science. Several alleged characteristics of science (repeatability, observability, empirical testability) have been offered, but none of them has succeeded. There are examples of good science which fail to have these characteristics and there are examples which most would want to call nonscience which have them. Consider observability. The existence and nature of magnetic fields cannot be observed even in principle (only the effects can be observed). But magnetic fields are surely part of the theoretical entities of science. On the other hand, the debate over universals (entities such as redness, humanness, or triangularity which can allegedly be in more than one place at the same time) between nominalists who deny their existence and realists who affirm their existence is an example of a nonscientific, philosophical issue. But some realists have appealed to observation in support of their case by pointing out that one can *see* that two apples have the same color by merely looking at the apples.

The point is that science is just not a discipline that is isolated from other

16. A major point of Laudan's *Science and Values* is that realist and antirealist understandings of science can both offer explanations of the success of science through its history and that the debate between them is a philosophical one. Thus, the truthfulness of science is an issue discussed at the philosophical level. Science does not justify its own aims, goals, and values by a scientific method. See also John Kekes, *The Nature of Philosophy* (Totowa, N.J.: Rowman and Littlefield, 1980), pp. 147–63.

fields of knowledge in such a way that it fits into a neat compartment. There are some cases of what most people would consider to be science, but there does not seem to be an adequate definition of science which covers all the cases. Even if one were to emerge, the adequacy of the definition of science would not itself be a scientific issue but a philosophical one, and thus such a definition would itself illustrate the limits of science.

Models of Integrating Science and Theology

Assuming that rational realism is true, how are science and theology to be integrated? There are at least five different models for integrating science and theology.[17]

Difference in Essence

Science and theology are concerned with two distinct and separate realms, the natural and the supernatural. Thus, science and theology cannot, even in principle, come into conflict. For example, science focuses on the natural world by trying to describe the nature of atoms. This is not a theological issue. On the other hand, theology focuses on issues in the supernatural realm of existence: on the existence and nature of God, angels, values, the proper view of the Eucharist, and so forth.

There is some truth to this view. It is hard to see why theology would be interested or able to make a pronouncement on the way that pressure, temperature, and volume interrelate in a mole of hydrogen gas. Further, it is hard to see how science could help to settle the question of the extent of the atonement, the security of the believer, and so forth. But the first view is inadequate as a total position on the integration of theology and science, for there are several examples where the two do, in fact, describe the same world. Science makes biological statements about birds, and theology says that they are creations of God. The Bible describes certain acts of God (e.g., the flood), and signs of its presence should appear in the geological record regardless of whether one thinks of the flood as a large, local one or a universal one. Both science and theology speak about the origin of the cosmos, man, and life in general. So this first view may be partly correct, but it needs to be supplemented by other views of integration, for it is inadequate by itself.

17. See A. R. Peacocke, *Creation and the World of Science* (Oxford: Oxford University Press, 1979), pp. 1–49; A. R. Peacocke, ed., *The Sciences and Theology in the Twentieth Century* (Notre Dame: University of Notre Dame Press, 1981), pp. ix–xvii; Ratzsch, *Philosophy of Science*, pp. 132–49.

Difference in Approach

Science and theology are two distinct, noninteracting approaches to the same reality. There are two different versions of this position. First, some argue that science and theology describe the same reality, namely, the universe and its contents, but they differ in method.[18] Theology starts with faith in revelation, involves receptivity and commitment, and is based on personal involvement in living the truth. Science involves active observation of the universe and objectivity and detachment, and makes no demands on the scientist. This dichotomy seems to be false. Both science and theology start with facts from either general or special revelation, form and test hypotheses, and involve epistemological objectivity (the rationality of theological systems or theories in science is a matter of publicly assessable evidence and rationality is not, in the final analysis, a mere matter of psychological subjectivity and commitment).

A second version of the second view, called the complementarity view, is associated with Donald M. MacKay, Richard Bube, and others. This position was discussed in chapter 3 in the context of the mind/body problem, so we need not describe it in detail here. Two features of this position should be noted. First, theological aspects of phenomena and scientific aspects of those phenomena are different levels of explanation involving their own vocabulary and so forth. A psychological account of conversion describes it differently than a theological account. Second, theology focuses on the *why* and *who* of a phenomenon; science focuses on the *what* and the *how*. Theology says that God is the director of evolution for the purpose of glorifying himself and creating man to love. Science tells us how evolution happened and what actually took place in the sequence of things.

The complementarity view has some value. Theologians themselves distinguish between primary and secondary causes, the former being direct miracles (e.g., the resurrection) where God intervenes immediately in the natural world and interrupts natural processes, and the latter being cases where God uses natural processes to accomplish his purposes by working through them. It is true that God is equally involved in both kinds of causation. God may use a pastor to help reparent a new believer, and the growth that takes place could be described in both psychological and theological terms; the two descriptions would not compete but would be complementary.

But the complementarity view is inadequate as a total view for at least two reasons. First, ontologically it is hard to take the Bible on its own terms

18. See Nigel M. de S. Cameron, "Science versus Religion," *Themelios* 8 (September 1982): 23–27.

without seeing in some of its statements an account of what the world is like and how God brought things about. For example, the Bible seems to clearly teach some form of substance dualism and freedom of the will, and if this is so, then the Bible would rule out the possibility of a complete physicalist and deterministic account of human behavior.[19] Similarly, the Bible teaches that the cosmos has not been in existence for an actually infinite past and it teaches that there is a discontinuity between man and animals. It may be difficult to state precisely what constitutes that discontinuity, but the fact of such a discontinuity is clear in the biblical text.[20]

Second, cases where God uses primary causes (immediate, direct miraculous acts of God—the parting of the Red Sea, the resurrection, the creation of man) provide important epistemological evidence for the rational justification of Christian theism. Surely these processes involved natural features. God may not have literally scooped up dust to form man. But the Bible implies that gaps do in fact exist in natural explanations, and the existence of such gaps is a part of the case for God. Jesus himself said that the truth of his words rested on his works, and he did not mean merely their messianic nature, but also that the miraculous nature of his deeds authenticated who he was.[21] If such deeds could be accounted for without gaps at a natural level, how could they provide *evidence* for the supernatural level? If no gaps exist, then it may still be reasonable to believe in a deistic God, but it would not be reasonable to believe in the God of Christian revelation. He is a God of primary causes and that fact is not diminished by his use of secondary causes.

Theology Foundational for Science

Theology provides the metaphysical foundation for science and helps to ground the latter by explaining the necessary preconditions of science. Theology asserts that there is an external world made by the same being who made our sensory and rational faculties and who gave us epistemic and moral values. Theology also asserts that creation was a free act of God, and thus one cannot deduce what the world must be like by a logical de-

19. I remain unimpressed with recent Christian writers who deny that substance dualism is taught in the Bible. They often identify substance dualism with Cartesian dualism, but Thomistic dualism is a better dualist model for integration with the Scriptures. See chapter 3 for more on this issue.

20. See Charles Feinberg, "The Image of God," *Bibliotheca Sacra* 129 (July 1972): 235–46.

21. Both the Old and New Testaments contain examples where evidence is cited for the truth of a religious claim, evidence which cannot adequately be described from a naturalistic point of view because it has gaps at that level which help make the theistic interpretation of that evidence rationally persuasive. See Bernard Ramm, "The Apologetic of the Old Testament," *Bulletin of the Evangelical Theological Society* 1 (Fall 1958): 15–20; W. Harold Mare, "Pauline Appeals to Historical Evidence," *Bulletin of the Evangelical Theological Society* 11 (Summer 1968): 121–30.

duction from some first principle about the nature or motives of God. Rather, one must use some sort of inductive method, since creation was free and the world is contingent.

Again, with certain qualifications this view has some merit to it. Although it is certain that too much has been made of the warfare between science and theology where theology is seen as the constant loser, too much has been made of the fact that science owes its existence to Christian theology.[22] It is probably more accurate to say that science owes its existence as a rational, truth-seeking enterprise to philosophy, for it is really philosophy and not theology which discusses the necessary presuppositions for science. Having said this, the main features of Christian theology—the rationality of the world, the existence of value, the reliability of the mind and senses—are surely consistent with these presuppositions of science, and it may even be argued that a Christian worldview offers a better explanation of why the world is such that science is possible than any rival worldview (Theravada Buddhism, for example, denies the existence of an enduring self to know the world and an enduring, real world to be known). So theology may lend support to science. And science may be most compatible with a Christian worldview. But this latter point is not easy to establish.

So science does rest on philosophy, and it may be best accounted for within the contours of a Christian worldview. At the very least, the presuppositions of science are consistent with Christian theology. But that cannot be all there is to the integration of science and theology, for the two do seem to make interacting and competing claims. So the third view is inadequate as a total view of integration.

Science Delimitative of Theology

Science provides the boundaries within which theology must work. Theology can do its work only after consulting science, for science is the best paradigm of knowledge we have. Therefore, science can dictate to theology what its limits must be, but not vice versa. For example, science has shown that the general theory of evolution is a fact and therefore any view of theology which contradicts this fact is false. Theology can only speculate within the bounds of science by embracing some sort of theistic evolution.

For a person who believes that it is true and reasonable to hold to the inerrancy of Scripture, as I do, this view is not an acceptable model of integration.[23] In a way, this whole chapter is an argument against this view. But three things can be briefly said against it here. First, recall that even if one

---

22. See Lindberg and Numbers, *God and Nature.*
23. See J. P. Moreland, "The Rationality of Belief in Inerrancy," *Trinity Journal* 7 (Spring 1986): 75–86.

accepts rational realism, one cannot be dogmatic about being a rational realist in light of the difficulties raised against it. The authority of science as a source of truth about the world has been weakened in recent years precisely because of the complexity of the debate over realism, and to that extent, the authority of science to dictate boundaries to theology has been weakened.[24]

Second, the Christian worldview has a wide variety of arguments in its favor. Suppose someone is convinced that Christianity is true for some of the reasons offered in this and other apologetic works. That person could be rational in rejecting the general theory of evolution for reasons outside science, even if evolution is rationally justified when science is considered alone (and this is itself questionable). The rationality of a worldview is a multifaceted affair, involving scientific, historical, and philosophical considerations. It is difficult to see why science should be singled out for the role of dictator in worldview assessment, since worldviews are broad paradigms which must take into account all the facets of life. It is hard to falsify a worldview by some crucial experiment, and science does not seem adequate to dictate to other avenues of inquiry what must or must not be rationally embraced at the level of worldview. Science is an important part of worldview assessment, but it is only one part. The rationality of accepting any scientific hypothesis involves bringing rationally justified external conceptual problems to bear on that hypothesis, even if those problems do not come *from* science.

Third, the history of science shows an incredible list of cases where science has changed its views and replaced former theories. Admittedly, some theories are retained in and refined by new ones, but others are replaced and drop out altogether as false and outdated. I do not know what percentage of theories in the history of science has been replaced or what percentage has been refined. But scientists themselves are reluctant to say that current science will resemble the science of two hundred years from now, and the history of science lends support to this attitude. Thus, even if science conflicts with theology at some point, that does not by itself mean that science should be the dictator and theology should work only within the bounds of science.

Interactive Approaches to the Same Reality

Science and theology are interacting approaches to the same reality. Occasionally they make competing, interacting claims about the same reality

---

24. For an application of this point to evolution, see John C. Greene, *Science, Ideology, and World View: Essays in the History of Evolutionary Ideas* (Berkeley: University of California Press, 1981).

in such a way that theology sometimes implies that gaps will exist in scientific accounts at those points where God intervened.

This fifth view seems to be correct if one is going to let biblical revelation speak for itself, allowing of course for appropriate hermeneutical issues to have a proper role in ascertaining what the Bible is genuinely asserting in a given instance. This view can be integrated with the first, second, and third views to form a full model of integration between science and theology. By allowing the fifth view to be a part of that model, and by adopting a rational realist view of science, the possibility arises that science and theology will make conflicting truth claims. An example of this is the creation/evolution debate. We will examine some salient features of this debate as an example of how to integrate science and theology. But first, a criticism raised against the fifth view should be considered.

Various thinkers, religious and otherwise, have criticized the fifth view because they believe it implies a "God-of-the-gaps" strategy. The "God-of-the-gaps" strategy is allegedly a bad strategy because it appeals to actions by God to explain gaps in our scientific understanding, and the history of science has shown that theology always loses when this happens, since science eventually comes up with a naturalistic explanation for the gap. Thus, a "God-of-the-gaps" strategy discredits theology because it limits theological explanations to a smaller and smaller number of gaps which merely plug up our scientific ignorance.

Five things can be said in response to this objection. First, a proper view of the integration of science and theology is not limited to view 5 alone, but includes views 1 through 3 as well. Thus, the view I am defending does not limit theological explanation to gaps in scientific knowledge. An eclectic view allows for different realms of existence, different kinds of explanation of the natural world, and primary and secondary causes.

Second, it is debatable that theology has always lost battles to science. The history of the interaction between science and theology is a complicated business and a "warfare" metaphor is ultimately too simplistic to describe this history. But even in those cases where science *was* in conflict with theology, it is not clear that theology always loses. For example, years ago some theologians predicted that the fossil record would show systematic gaps, that the universe was temporally finite, that a behavioristic account of human beings would not succeed, that some form of catastrophism was needed in geology, and that anthropologists would discover a widespread belief in a supreme Being among the cultures of the world. It is also arguable that biblical revelation implies the nonreducibility of biology to chemistry and physics and the inadequacy of atomism in accounting for biological phenomena. This is because the Bible would seem to imply that living organisms fall into natural kinds and have natures or essences which define what they are (see Gen. 1:11; 1 Cor. 15:35–41). If this is so, then an ontology of substances and qualities would seem to follow; that is, the essential qualities of living things could not be reduced to quantities. It is generally agreed that atomism has failed as an adequate version of physicalism, though the reducibility of biology is still being questioned.

In the cases cited, theology seems to have won against the scientific views which competed with these theological claims. I do not know what a full comparison between theological claims and scientific claims in conflict would look like. But the cases cited suggest that if a comparison would be made of simultaneous theories held in both domains, then cases would exist where the scientific theories have been falsified and the theological views confirmed.

Third, even if the number of gaps in science is small and getting smaller, this does not prove that there are no gaps at all. It begs the question to argue that just because most alleged gaps turned out to be explainable in scientific terms, then all alleged gaps will turn out this way. After all, what else would one expect of a gap but that there would be few of them? In this regard, gaps are like miracles. By their very nature, they are in the minority, for two reasons. God's usual way of operating is through secondary causes. Primary causes which generate gaps are special acts of God. For example, Genesis 1 says that God delegated to living things themselves the ability to reproduce after their kinds. Regardless of where one locates gaps in this process where God created directly, such gaps are in the minority. Second, the epistemological value of a miracle or a gap arises only against a backdrop where the miracles or gaps are rare and unexpected. It is in the contrast with the usual that a miracle or a gap obtains evidential value for being a direct act of God.

Fourth, a "God-of-the-gaps" argument can be used against science itself. Most past scientific theories have been replaced or falsified, and therefore a pessimistic induction from the history of science would seem to imply that current science will not be successful for long either. Past scientific theories are often like cases where God was used inappropriately to explain gaps. They were shown later to be inadequate. In my opinion, the history of discarded theories in science warrants caution in accepting too readily a current theory. But it does not warrant a view which rejects all scientific theories. Similarly, past cases of inappropriately appealing to God to explain a gap should warrant caution. But such cases do not warrant a view which rejects all uses of God in scientific explanation, especially in those cases where ultimate boundary conditions are being discussed (since they are outside the bounds of science) or in those cases where careful biblical exegesis gives us reason to expect a primary cause from God was in operation. In these latter cases, it is not our ignorance of science that causes us to appeal to God, but knowledge of the biblical text.

Finally, in some cases the gaps may be getting worse rather than better with the advance of science. This seems to be the case in research about the origin of life. The more we learn about the complexity of the organic materials necessary for life and their complex interdependence, and the more we learn about conditions on the early earth, the more implausible a strictly naturalistic account becomes. Scientists one hundred years ago were not aware of the immensity of the problems in the spontaneous generation of life from some primordial soup. But today some scientists feel these problems are overwhelming. In this regard, the following statement by scientists Charles B. Thaxton, Walter L. Bradley, and Roger L. Olsen makes the point well:

> One characteristic feature of the . . . critique needs to be emphasized. We have not simply picked out a number of details within chemical evolution theory that are weak, or without adequate explanation *for the moment*. For the most part this critique is based on crucial weaknesses intrinsic to the theory itself. Often it is contended that criticism focuses on present ignorance. "Give us more time to solve the problems," is the plea. After all, the pursuit of abiogenesis [the origin of life from nonlife] is young as a scientific enterprise. It will be claimed that many of these problems are mere state-of-the-art gaps. And, surely, some of them are. Notice, however, that the sharp edge of this critique is not what we *do not* know, but what we *do* know. Many facts have come to light in the past three decades of experimental inquiry into life's beginning. With each passing year the criticism has gotten stronger. The advance of science itself is what is challenging the notion that life arose on earth by spontaneous (in a thermodynamic sense) chemical reactions.[25]

If one assumes a rational realist view of science, one must come up with a way of integrating science and theology in order to maintain an internally consistent Christian worldview. An eclectic model of integration is the most adequate. It recognizes that sometimes the two disciplines are concerned with two distinct realms, sometimes they are noninteracting approaches to the same realm which provide answers to different kinds of questions, sometimes theology provides an adequate worldview consistent with the necessary philosophical presuppositions of science, and sometimes they are interacting, competing approaches to natural phenomena. When theology and science relate in this last way, caution must be urged to guard against using God to merely cover our scientific ignorance.

25. Charles B. Thaxton, Walter L. Bradley, and Roger L. Olsen, *The Mystery of Life's Origin: Reassessing Current Theories* (New York: Philosophical Library, 1984), p. 125.

But when ultimate boundary conditions are being considered or cases where careful biblical exegesis seems to indicate that a gap should be expected, then God can be used to explain such cases. The objection that this involves a poor "God-of-the-gaps" strategy fails to be convincing.[26]

Let us now consider an example of integration—creation and evolution. Three issues need to be explored. First, is creation science a science or is it religion? Second, what biblical issues are involved in understanding the Christian doctrine of creation? Third, what scientific issues are involved in the debate about evolution?

Creation and Evolution

Creation Science

The first thing we must do is give a sufficient working definition of creation science. In December 1981, a creation/evolution trial (*McLean v. Arkansas*) was held in Little Rock, Arkansas.[27] The following definition of creation science was given:

> "Creation-science" means the scientific evidences for creation and inferences from those scientific evidences. Creation-science includes the scientific evidences and related inferences that indicate: (1) Sudden creation of the universe, energy, and life from nothing; (2) The insufficiency of mutation and natural selection in bringing about the development of all living kinds from a single organism; (3) Changes only within fixed limits of originally created kinds of plants and animals; (4) Separate ancestry for man and apes; (5) Explanation of the earth's geology by catastrophism, including the occurrence of a worldwide flood; and (6) A relatively recent inception of the earth and living kinds.

This definition is adequate for our purposes, but two qualifications must be made. First, some evangelical scholars do not believe the Bible teaches that the flood of Noah was a universal flood, but rather a flood that extended far enough to include the human race.[28] It is beyond our present purposes to debate this issue, but it should be pointed out that the basic

26. For a fairly balanced discussion of the integration of science and theology which leaves (tentative) room for interaction and gaps, see Ernan McMullin, "How Should Cosmology Relate to Theology?" in *The Sciences and Theology in the Twentieth Century*, ed. A. R. Peacocke (Notre Dame: University of Notre Dame Press, 1981), pp. 17–57.

27. Excellent coverage of the trial can be found in Norman L. Geisler, *The Creator in the Courtroom* (Milford, Mich.: Mott Media, 1982).

28. See Bernard Ramm, *The Christian View of Science and Scripture* (Grand Rapids: Eerdmans, 1954), pp. 156–69. For a criticism of this view, see Henry M. Morris, ed., *Scientific Creationism*, updated ed. (El Cajon, Calif.: Master, 1985), pp. 250–55.

debate between creation and evolution does not involve the existence of a universal flood. The nature of the flood is a secondary issue which gains importance depending on one's perception of the strength of the exegetical evidence for one's view and the centrality of the flood in one's system of integration.

Second, the age of the earth or universe is not a central issue in the debate between creation and evolution either.[29] More will be said about this later, but for now, suffice it to say that the main point of contention between creationists and evolutionists is the adequacy of the general theory of macroevolution to explain the origin of life in general, man in particular, and the development between the first living things and man.

Is creation science as it was defined in the Arkansas law a science? It is, and to see this, it might be best to consider the major criticisms which have been raised against the scientific status of creation science.[30] It is difficult to settle the question by offering a definition of science, for as Laudan points out, "few authors can even agree on what makes an activity scientific."[31] However, we can try to spell out many of the characteristics that most philosophers believe mark off most cases of scientific activity as being scientific. These characteristics will be examined by focusing on attempts to show that creation science is faulty in some important way. Keep in mind that our purpose is not to show that creation science does, in fact, explain the scientific data adequately. I do believe it does. But our purpose here is the more modest one of trying to show that creation science is really science. Six objections are often raised in an attempt to show that creation science is a religion and not a science.

1. *Creation science uses a religious concept ("God") and therefore it is a religion and not a science.* This objection fails because "God" is not necessarily a religious concept. When "God" functions as a religious concept, it is used to promote religion as its principal or primary effect, it is involved in moral and spiritual exhortation, and it is surrounded by ritual and other forms of

29. General discussions of dating can be found in Frederic Howe, "The Age of the Earth: An Appraisal of Some Current Evangelical Positions, I and II," *Bibliotheca Sacra* 142 (January 1985): 23–37; 142 (April 1985): 114–29. A summary of evidences for a recent earth is contained in Morris, *Scientific Creationism*, pp. 131–70. For a critique of evidence for a recent earth, see Walter L. Bradley, "The Trustworthiness of Scripture in Areas Relating to Natural Science," in *Hermeneutics, Inerrancy, and the Bible: Papers from the ICBI Summit II*, ed. Earl D. Radmacher and Robert D. Preus (Grand Rapids: Zondervan, 1984), pp. 285–317.

30. See Norman L. Geisler, "Is Creation-Science Science or Religion?" *Journal of the American Scientific Affiliation* (September 1984): 149–55; Davis Young, "Is 'Creation-Science' Science or Religion?—A Response," *Journal of the American Scientific Affiliation* (September 1984): 156–58; Larry Laudan, "Commentary: Science at the Bar—Causes for Concern," *Science, Technology and Human Values* 7 (Fall 1982): 16–19; Michael Ruse, "Response to the Commentary: Pro Judice," *Science, Technology, and Human Values* 7 (Fall 1982): 19–23; Larry Laudan, "More on Creationism," *Science, Technology, and Human Values* 8 (Winter 1983): 36–38; Philip Quinn, "The Philosopher of Science as Expert Witness," in *Science and Reality*, ed. James T. Cushing, C. F. Delaney, and Gary Gutting (Notre Dame: University of Notre Dame Press, 1984), pp. 32–53.

31. Laudan, "Commentary," p. 18.

religious devotion. The simple fact is that "God" may be a mere philosophical concept or theoretical term denoting an explanatory theoretical entity needed in some sort of explanation, much like the terms *quark* and *continental plate*. For example, in Aristotle's philosophy God was an entity, the existence of which served to explain, among other things, the existence of motion in the cosmos. But Aristotle did not worship the unmoved Mover of his philosophical system. Isaac Newton appealed to the existence of God in order to help explain planetary motion, arguing that God occasionally nudged the planets. Newton's appeal was later falsified (this was a "God-of-the-gaps" argument unsupportable by exegetical evidence). But that is not the point. The point is that "God" was not a religious concept here but a theoretical one, for "God" was not the object of worship or a means of moral exhortation in Newton's theory, but a mere explanatory entity.

2. *"God" is an illegitimate term in science, not because it is religious, but because it is supernatural, and science explains by using natural laws.* Four things can be said against this objection. First, this seems to beg the question in favor of a naturalistic explanation of origins, since it seems to imply that a proper explanation *must* be a naturalistic one. But surely even an atheist would agree that, in the absence of a case for contradictions among God's attributes, the existence of God is logically possible. God *could* exist and he *could have* created life in general and man in particular. But if science cannot in principle recognize this possibility because of its naturalistic assumptions, then science would be necessarily false if creationism is true. Any discipline which could not, even in principle, discover the truth, is surely faulty.

Second, scientists of other generations recognized that God was a legitimate source of explanation in science (and some do today, including some who are not theists), so why should we be required to accept a definition of science which would arbitrarily rule out as nonscience all the cases in the history of science where God was appealed to as a theoretical entity?[32]

Third, it is far from clear that "God" is being used as a supernatural concept in any way inappropriate to science. It is possible to distinguish operation science (which focuses on the regular, recurrent operation of the universe or, in theological terms, secondary causes) from origin science (which focuses on singular events [the origin of the universe, life on earth] which, in theological terms, are primary causes which are not regular).[33] Origin science does, in fact, postulate first causes as brute givens. For example, the existence of the mass/energy of the big bang, or of other cosmic

---

32. For repeated documentation of this, see Lindberg and Numbers, *God and Nature*.

33. See the excellent work by Norman L. Geisler and J. Kerby Anderson, *Origin Science: A Proposal for the Creation-Evolution Controversy* (Grand Rapids: Baker, 1987).

constants used in the design argument are examples (see chap. 2). "God" in creation science merely means "a first cause who resembles a rational agent more than matter." What is unscientific about this?

Finally, scientists have long understood the difference between establishing the existence of a phenomenon and explaining it by a natural law. Charles Darwin (allegedly) established the existence of natural selection nearly a half a century before the laws of heredity helped to explain it. If, contrary to fact, there had been no natural laws to explain natural selection, Darwin's achievement would still have been scientific.[34] Similarly, one could establish the existence of a first cause with explaining that cause by subsuming it under natural laws. This is not unscientific, even if that first cause resembles a person. The science of psychology explains things in terms of desires and intentions of persons and there is no good reason to banish such explanations from science.

3. *Creation science is a theory derived from the Bible and is therefore not a scientific theory.* This objection is an example of the logical fallacy known as the genetic fallacy. The genetic fallacy is the mistake of confusing the origin of a claim with its evidential warrant and undermining the claim by calling attention to its origin. What is relevant to the rationality of a claim is the evidence for that claim. The medieval practice of alchemy was the basis for the modern discipline of chemistry, but that would hardly be a good objection to raise against the rationality of chemical theory. It makes no difference whether a scientific theory comes from a dream, the Bible, or bathroom graffiti. The issue is whether independent scientific reasons are given for the theory. Creation scientists clearly offer reasons for creation science. Whether these reasons are adequate is another matter. But scientific reasons are offered and that is all creation science needs to count as science.

4. *Creation science makes no predictions and is not empirically testable.* It is true that some tenets of creationism are not testable in isolation from other claims (e.g., the claim that man emerged from a direct act of God). But as Laudan has argued, this "scarcely makes Creationism 'unscientific'. It is now widely acknowledged that many scientific claims are not testable in isolation, but only when embedded in a larger system of statements, some of whose consequences can be submitted to test."[35]

Scientific creationism makes a large number of predictions which can be tested. For example, scientific creationism predicts that the fossil record will lack clear transition forms and will show systematic gaps. Flood geolo-

---

34. Most philosophers of science deny a covering law model of scientific explanation as the only or even the best way to describe explanation in science. See Harré, *Philosophies of Science*, pp. 53–58, 168–83. See also Peter Achinstein, *The Nature of Explanation* (New York: Oxford University Press, 1983).

35. Laudan, "Commentary," p. 17.

gists predict that porphyrins should be commonly found in sedimentary rocks.[36] Many other examples could be cited.[37] It is false that scientific creationism makes no empirically testable predictions.

5. *Creation scientists are narrow-minded and hold their theory so tenaciously that it causes them to be closed to a revision of their theory.* Three problems can be raised with this objection. First, the argument is, at best, an ad hominem criticism against some (alleged) personality defects of creation scientists. But what does that have to do with creation science as a theory? Would it matter if all Newtonians were Marxists? Surely this would not count against the scientific status of Newtonian theory. In fact, creation science could be tested, or even taught for that matter, by an evolutionist. And an evolutionist could hardly be accused of narrow-mindedly embracing creation science.

Second, many scientists in other areas of science have shown resistance to scientific change, as Kuhn and others have pointed out. In fact, in many cases it is the presence of a small band of "rebel" scientists—like creation scientists—which helps others to overcome their bias in favor of a prevailing theory. Third, it is not true that creation scientists do not refine their views. Creation scientists have changed several features of their model when they are compared with their counterparts of one hundred years ago. So evidence *does* cause them to refine and review their theories.

6. *Creation science does not rely on positive evidence to support its case, but rather relies on problems in evolutionary theory. But just because some version of evolutionary theory is problematic, this does not mean creationism is true. Some other form of evolutionary theory may be adequate.* This objection is false because creation science *does* involve predictions which give positive evidence for creation science. Some of the predictions already listed would be examples of this. Those working on extending and clarifying creation science should continue to spell out more positive test implications of their theory. But it is wrong to say that no positive evidence has been found to support creation science.

Second, if there is a small number of currently available rival hypotheses, then if one of those hypotheses is falsified or weakened, this *does* offer support to its rivals. The logical possibility of some unknown future theory emerging does not refute this point, for one must work with the major rivals at hand.

Consider the following case. The neo-Darwinian version of macroevolution holds that evolutionary change comes about in a large number of sequential steps involving very small changes at each point along the

36. David McQueen, "The Chemistry of Oil Explained by Flood Geology," *Impact* 155 (May 1986): i–iv.
37. Morris, *Scientific Creationism*, pp. 8–13; Lane Lester and Raymond G. Bohlin, *The Natural Limits to Biological Change* (Grand Rapids: Zondervan, Academie Books, 1984), pp. 172–75.

way. But the fossil record simply has not offered what neo-Darwinism predicts. Millions of fossils have been discovered, and a very small number of controversial transition forms have been found. Neo-Darwinism predicts that thousands and thousands should be found.

Currently, three options are open to scientists in their attempt to explain the fossil record. First, one could choose to reaffirm neo-Darwinism, but add some ad hoc hypothesis explaining the absence of transition forms. For example, neo-Darwinists sometimes argue that because transition forms are not clearly superior in the struggle for survival, they would not last long and thus would leave few fossils. Second, one could embrace a different version of evolutionary theory called punctuated equilibrium.[38] According to this view, evolutionary change occurs rapidly and is followed by long periods of stasis where no change occurs. Thus, the fossil record does not teem with transition forms, for there were none. Third, one could embrace scientific creationism and argue that there are no clear transition forms because there were none.

Proponents of punctuated equilibrium argue that the absence of a large number of transition forms tends to falsify neo-Darwinism, for even if transition forms were not superior in the struggle for survival, one would still expect to see more of them in the fossil record than we do see (if neo-Darwinism were true). This seems to me to be a good argument. The fossil record tends to falsify neo-Darwinism, and because of this, it tends to support punctuated equilibrium. But what is sauce for the goose is sauce for the gander, and I see no reason to hold that the fossil record does not similarly support scientific creationism because it tends to falsify neo-Darwinism. In fact, one *could* argue that punctuated equilibrium is itself an ad hoc strategy to save some form of Darwinism. In any case, if a small set of rival hypotheses exists, then when one is weakened, the others are supported even though it is logically possible that an entirely new theory will be forthcoming in the future. If advocates of punctuated equilibrium can appropriately argue in this way, and I think they can, then there is no good reason why scientific creationists cannot use the same argument.

In sum, none of the major objections against the scientific status of scientific creationism succeeds. This, coupled with the fact that no generally accepted definition of science is agreed on by a majority of philosophers of science, implies that it is implausible to hold that scientific creationism is not a science. Opinions to the contrary are either uninformed or represent mere bias.[39]

---

38. For a discussion of the difference between neo-Darwinism and punctuated equilibrium, see Lester and Bohlin, *Natural Limits to Biological Change,* pp. 65–148.

39. It is interesting to read Quinn's article, "Philosopher of Science as Expert Witness," with this point in mind, particularly his treatment of philosopher Michael Ruse.

Biblical Issues in the Doctrine of Creation

The main purpose of this section is to argue that there are sufficient problems in interpreting Genesis 1 and 2 to warrant caution in dogmatically holding that only one understanding is allowable by the text. To show this, I will first list, without much comment, various ways biblical scholars have taken Genesis 1 and 2 and then state certain exegetical issues involved in understanding these verses.[40]

Different Interpretations of Genesis 1 and 2

Literal Interpretations   First, the six-day-creation view of Henry M. Morris and Duane T. Gish holds that Genesis 1 and 2 are talking about the original creation of the world ex nihilo, that the six days are twenty-four-hour periods, and that the creation of the cosmos is recent, perhaps ten to twenty thousand years ago.[41] In support of this last point, proponents argue that while it is true that biblical genealogies often list only important people and leave names out, one abuses this if he holds that Adam was created a million years ago. Surely there were not that many gaps in the genealogies.[42] The cosmos was created six days prior to Adam, and thus is recent.

Second, the six-day-re-creation view of Bruce Waltke holds that Genesis 1:1 is a topic sentence for the creation narrative which begins at Genesis 1:2.[43] The Genesis text does not describe the original creation of the world ex nihilo (which is clearly taught in other places of Scripture), but rather describes God's re-creation of the world from a state of chaos and, perhaps, judgment described by the words *formless and void*. (Isaiah 45:18 states that God did not create the world in this state.) We are not told why the world is in this state in Genesis 1, but it may be that Satan fell after the original creation, and in Genesis 1 and 2, God is bringing salvation to the world by bringing order out of chaos in his re-creation. The days of re-creation are six twenty-four-hour days.

Third is the six-revelatory-day view of Bernard Ramm and P. J. Wise-

---

40. For more on this, see Stephen Barnett and W. Phillips, "Genesis and Origins: Focus on Interpretation," *Presbyterian Journal* (February 6, 1985): 5–10; L. Duane Thurman, *How to Think About Evolution*, 2d ed. (Downers Grove: Inter-Varsity, 1978), pp. 115–26; Pattle P. T. Pun, *Evolution: Nature and Science in Conflict?* (Grand Rapids: Zondervan, 1982), pp. 240–71; Ronald Youngblood, ed., *The Genesis Debate* (Nashville: Nelson, 1986).

41. See Morris, *Scientific Creationism*.

42. Still relevant on the question of the nature of biblical genealogies is W. H. Green, "Primeval Chronology," in *Classical Evangelical Essays in Old Testament Interpretation*, ed. Walter C. Kaiser (Grand Rapids: Baker, 1972), pp. 13–28.

43. See Bruce Waltke, *Creation and Chaos* (Portland, Ore.: Western Conservative Baptist Seminary, 1974).

man.[44] The days of Genesis 1 are literal twenty-four-hour days, but they are days of revelation, not days of creative activity. The events described on the first day are not events God did in a twenty-four-hour period, but the things God revealed to Adam or Moses in a twenty-four-hour period. Some other creation accounts in the ancient Near East had twenty-four-hour revelatory days and this is the proper way to understand the Genesis text.

Fourth is the gap theory of Thomas Chalmers.[45] Genesis 1:1 describes the original creation of a perfect world. Between Genesis 1:1 and 1:2 there is a huge period of time during which Satan fell and brought destruction to the world. Genesis 1:2 describes the earth in this fallen state by saying that "the earth *became* formless and void." Genesis 1:2 and following describe the re-creation of the earth in six twenty-four-hour days which chronologically follow Genesis 1:1 and the gap of time between 1:1 and 1:2 (much of the fossil record is alleged to have taken place during this gap when Satan destroyed the earth). Few scholars hold the gap theory any more.

Progressive Creationism Progressive creationists hold that theistic evolution—the view that the general theory of macroevolution is true and was a process directed by God—is scientifically and biblically inadequate.[46] God intervened at certain points in the process of creation and acted directly. Evolutionary change is limited to change in lower levels of taxonomic classification. Progressive creationists may differ over exactly how often God intervened, but as far as I can tell, they all agree that God created directly at the three points where the Hebrew word *bārā'* is used—the creation of heaven and earth, the creation of animal life, and the creation of man. Most progressive creationists hold that God intervened more often than this.

Progressive creationists also disagree that the days of Genesis are literal twenty-four-hour days, preferring instead to take them as long, unspecified periods of time. Progressive creationists try to steer a middle course between six twenty-four-hour-day creationists and theistic evolutionists.

There are at least three varieties of progressive creationism. First, there is the day-age version which holds that the six days are six consecutive, nonoverlapping periods of time. In each "day," God created the life specified during that day through a combination of direct acts and the use of

44. See Ramm, *Christian View of Science and Scripture*, pp. 149–56; P. J. Wiseman, *Clues to Creation in Genesis* (London: Marshall, Morgan, and Scott, 1977).

45. For a statement and critique of the gap theory, see Ramm, *Christian View of Science and Scripture*, pp. 134–44; Morris, *Scientific Creationism*, pp. 231–43.

46. See Robert C. Newman and Herman J. Eckelmann, *Genesis One and the Origin of the Earth* (Downers Grove: Inter-Varsity, 1977), pp. 57–88; Gleason L. Archer, Jr., *A Survey of Old Testament Introduction* (Chicago: Moody, 1964), pp. 181–88.

secondary causes and normal processes which he guided. As with the other two varieties of progressive creationism, adherents of this view wish to limit the scope of evolutionary change to those observed within micro-evolution.

The second variety of progressive creationism is called the overlapping day-age view. This view takes the "days" as six long periods of time which overlap each other. In the day-age view, God did not begin the work of creating the things listed on the second day until he was finished with all the things he did on the first day. The overlapping day-age view allows for the possibility that the second day began sometime during the first-day period and thus the days overlap. One period of time does not need to be complete before the next one begins.

The third variety of progressive creationism is called the alternate day view. This position allows for overlapping days, but differs as to when God's direct creative activity took place within each period of time. The alternate day view holds that each overlapping period of time was begun with a literal twenty-four-hour day within which God did all the direct creating. The remainder of that period was a time when God unfolded, through natural processes, the work he did during the first twenty-four-hour day of that period.

The Religious Allegory View   This view holds that theistic evolution is true and that Genesis 1 and 2 is a religious myth designed to teach that the world owes its existence to God. Genesis 1 and 2 are not to be taken literally nor do they have anything whatever to say about the process God used in accomplishing his work. Science describes the process.

This view fails to take the biblical text seriously, and therefore is not an option for an evangelical. There is no indication in Genesis 1 and 2 that the text is poetical. Rather, it reads like history in the same way that the rest of Genesis reads when it describes the partriarchs.

Five Exegetical Issues

The Hebrew Word Bārā'   The Hebrew word *bārā'*, often translated "to create," occurs 33 times in the Old Testament, including Genesis 1:1, 1:21, and 1:27. The Hebrew word *āśāh* occurs 624 times in the Old Testament and is usually translated "to make." *Āśāh* sometimes refers to a direct miracle of God, sometimes a created process. (Zechariah 10:1 says that God makes the storm clouds which give rain.) Human beings are sometimes the subject of the verb.

Bārā' has only God as its subject. *Bārā'* is used interchangeably with *āśāh* in Genesis 1:26, 1:27, and 1:31. *Bārā'* does not just mean "to create out of nothing." It can also mean "to transform, build, shape, or fashion some new thing out of materials which already exist." Perhaps a good definition of *bārā'* would be "to be newly fashioned by God." There is no doubt that the Bible teaches that God created the world out of nothing. The point is that creation ex nihilo cannot be inferred from the mere presence of *bārā'*. It would seem best to see the Genesis 1 and 2 narrative, with its use of *bārā'* and *āśāh*, as referring to creative acts of God in which he used direct, primary causes as well as directing natural processes.

The Hebrew Word Yôm   Is the word *yôm* ("day") used in Genesis 1 and 2 for a twenty-four-hour period or can it be used for an unspecified period of time as well? How should we understand it in the creation narrative? Those who take it as a literal twenty-four-hour period offer at least four arguments:

1. When *yôm* is used in the Pentateuch with a numerical adjective (this happens two hundred times), it always means a literal twenty-four-hour day.
2. Evening and morning are usually associated with *yôm* as a twenty-four-hour period.
3. Exodus 20:9–11 compares our Sabbath rest with the sixth day, and since the former is a twenty-four-hour period, so is the latter.
4. *Yôm* occurs nineteen hundred times in the Old Testament, and only sixty-five of these uses do not refer to literal twenty-four-hour periods.

Those who hold that the word refers to a long, unspecified period of time argue as follows:

1. The narrative of Genesis 1 and 2 is unique and should not be compared naively with the rest of Genesis. This is especially true regarding the nature of time, for during the first three days there was no sun, moon, or night.
2. There are exceptions to the rule, including Psalm 90:4–6 where *yôm* is used in conjunction with evening and morning but does not mean a twenty-four-hour period.
3. The emphasis of the teaching about the Sabbath rest is that it occurs on the *seventh* day, not on how long that day is. Seven is a number of perfection in Scripture and the Sabbath year is another example where the concept of rest on the seventh unit is meant to show the appropriateness of the rest, not the duration of the rest. Further, Hebrews 4 teaches that the Sabbath rest is continuing.
4. Positive support for the extended period of time rests on Genesis 2:4, where the word *day* is used for the whole period of time. This metaphorical use sets the appropriate grid for understanding the other

uses of *yôm* in the narrative (cf. Isa. 4:2). Further, it is argued that the events of the sixth day, as expanded in Genesis 2, involve too much activity (naming the animals) for one twenty-four-hour period. When Adam finally recognizes that God has made him a woman, he says "this is now," which is better rendered "here now at last." This Hebrew phrase implies the passage of a long duration of time in which Adam was waiting, but a twenty-four-hour period hardly fits this.

Ancient Near Eastern Chronology   Ancient Near Eastern historical or biographical accounts did not always follow a rigid chronological sequence. Sometimes they diverge and follow a topical order. For example, sometimes Matthew will offer a teaching of Jesus during one of his speeches which is on the same topic but out of order chronologically. This is not an error, for it was the nature of ancient biography to sometimes cover things in a topical way. Matthew does not state things Jesus did not do or say; he just tries, occasionally, to list his views on a given topic together. Chronological order was usually the backbone of a narrative, but topical arrangement could be followed on occasion.

In light of this, some argue that it may be wise to take the general chronological order of events in Genesis as attempting to teach chronology (regardless of whether the order records six twenty-four-hour days or six periods of time), but to allow for some of the order to be governed by topical considerations. This can be abused, but with due caution one should not press the chronology of details too far.

The Structure of the Narrative   The structure of Genesis 1 is in large measure set by the theme of "formless and void" stated in verse 1. The chapter unfolds with this state of affairs in mind, and it shows how God filled the formlessness and structure in days 1–3, and the voidness with content in days 4–6. Day 4 gives content to the structure created on day 1, day 5 gives content to the structure created on day 2, and day 6 gives content to the structure created on day 3 (see table 2).

Table 2

	tōhû Universe without structure: form given	**bōhû** Universe without content: fullness given	
God first develops a structure that will support life (days 1–3)	Day 1 (1:2–5)	Day 4 (1:14–19)	God fills the structure with life that is derived from and dependent upon that structure (days 4–6)
	Day 2 (1:6–8)	Day 5 (1:20–23)	
	Day 3 (1:9–13)	Day 6 (1:24–31)	
	Day 7 (2:1–3)		

Thus, the order and structure of the narrative are determined in part by a literary theme. This does not mean that the events recorded are not historical. Indeed, they are, for one can record historical events which are woven around some literary theme. But the chronological order of the narrative may be motivated in part by literary issues and not strictly by chronological issues. Again, this can be abused, but some argue that caution in pressing the chronological details is warranted by the presence of a literary motif which may have helped set some of the structure of the narrative.

The Purpose of the Narrative   The purpose of Genesis 1 and 2 must be set against the backdrop of the Pentateuch as a whole. The Pentateuch seeks to introduce the nation of Israel to its origin and election by God. To do this, the Pentateuch seeks to record actual historical events which led up to Israel's election. The purpose of Genesis 1 and 2 is to introduce the sovereign ordering of creation which is good and in which God can rest. Thus, one should treat this narrative as straightforward history which teaches theology and involves a general chronological outlook. It would be against the purpose of the narrative to diverge too far from chronological order since it is attempting to explain the events which led up to Israel's election. Some details may be sequenced according to topical or literary considerations, but the general sequence should be treated chronologically.

Another purpose of Genesis 1 and 2 is that the creation account functioned as a polemic against other ancient Near Eastern religions. In other religions, the creation of the world was a crudely depicted immoral affair. In these religions, life is rekindled each spring by copulation between certain deities; their seed falls to earth and sparks life. Genesis 1 and 2 emphasize that the world owes its existence to Yahweh and it is utterly distinct in its being from him. It also emphasizes that God delegated to created kinds the ability to generate seed which would reproduce after that kind. Thus, Genesis 1 and 2 does say something about the processes God uses in creating and sustaining life.

In sum, several complicated exegetical issues are involved in understanding Genesis 1 and 2. The text should be taken as recording actual history with a basic chronological order, though the presence of topical or literary motivations should give us pause in attempting to be too detailed or precise in discerning that chronological order. The narrative indicates a mixture of direct creation and divinely guided natural processes. The exegetical problems should cause us to allow the possibility that several different understandings of the text, within the framework of inerrancy, are genuine contenders. The date of the creation is a difficult question, but on exegetical grounds alone, the literal twenty-four-hour-day view is better. However, since the different progressive creationist views are plausible exegetical options on hermeneutical grounds alone, then if science seems to point to a universe of several billions of years, it seems allowable to read Genesis in this light. It would be wrong to let science elevate an understanding of Genesis which is not antecedently plausible on hermeneutical grounds alone. But in this case, an old cosmos seems allowable. On the other hand, it does not seem possible to hold to a great antiquity for man. Even with gaps in the genealogies, it seems that Adam and Eve would be recent, surely within fifty thousand years, probably earlier. In any case, Christians should continue to promote various paradigms of Genesis 1 and 2 which do not do damage to the text. There are too many difficult exegetical issues for dogmatism and infighting among us.

Scientific Issues in the Creation/Evolution Debate

We can only sketch in outline form some of the main issues which have been raised against the general theory of evolution. It is important to distinguish macroevolution from microevolution. Microevolution involves observable changes within lower levels of classification which give rise to variations. A moth may develop the ability to blend in against a black background, but it is still a moth. Macroevolution is the general theory that all life arose from nonlife in some prebiotic soup (where chemical reactions plus some form of energy gave rise to the first life), and all life evolved from the first life up to Homo sapiens. Creationists agree with microevolution but disagree with macroevolution. Their criticisms are varied, but three areas of debate are central.[47]

The Myth of the Prebiotic Soup

Four major criticisms have been leveled against the abiogenesis of life from a prebiotic soup.[48] First, there is no geological evidence for concentrated organic pools on the early earth. Even if there were such pools, dilution processes would have held the build-up of complex organic molecules to a level far too small for life to evolve. Second, evidence is accumulating that the early earth's atmosphere contained oxygen and was not a reducing atmosphere. The organic reactions thought necessary for the build-up of complicated organic molecules will not occur in the presence of oxygen. Furthermore, the oldest rocks on earth date from 3.8 to 3.98 billion years

47. In addition to the works by Thaxton, Bradley, and Olsen, Morris, Lester and Bohlin, and Thurman, other critical evaluations of evolution can be found in Michael Denton, *Evolution: A Theory in Crisis* (London: Burnett Books, 1985); Duane T. Gish, *Evolution: The Challenge of the Fossil Record* (El Cajon, Calif: Master, 1985); John Wiester, *The Genesis Connection* (Nashville: Nelson, 1983); Gordon Rattray Taylor, *The Great Evolution Mystery* (New York: Harper and Row, 1983); Michael Pitman, *Adam and Evolution* (London: Rider and Company, 1984).

48. The best work on the problems with the biochemical evolution of life is Thaxton, Bradley, and Olsen, *The Mystery of Life's Origin*. See also Robert Shapiro, *Origins* (New York: Summit, 1986).

ago and the earliest life is present as far back as 3.81 billion years. This means that life had only 100 to 170 million years to evolve, a mere instant in geological time. The absence of a reducing atmosphere makes this problem even worse.

Third, in the last twenty-five years of experiments which attempt to synthesize organic compounds under the conditions supposed to have obtained on the early earth, two problems arise. First, if life can be likened to an encyclopedia in complexity and information, then the best we have done is to synthesize a compound which carries the complexity and information of the word *ME*. The jump from ME to an encyclopedia is so far and speculative that the relevance of progress so far is questionable. Further, the little progress we have made has come from illegitimate spectator interference. The reactants at a certain stage of a synthesis experiment must be quickly withdrawn, isolated from the environment, cooled, and added to a new environment. These steps are hard to conceive of without a person intervening at just the right time. It is difficult to conceive of a natural mechanism to accomplish what spectator interference accomplishes.

Fourth, the evolution of life from nonlife runs into problems with the second law of thermodynamics. Second-law calculations show that such a reaction is immensely improbable by chance, roughly one chance in $10^{40,000}$. Self-ordering tendencies in matter are not adequate to overcome these odds or generate the information needed for living molecules from the simple order of inorganic materials resting on clay catalyses. Further, the fact that the earth was an open system does not refute the second-law argument, for raw energy cannot bring order or information out of chaos any more than one can form a Boeing 747 by dropping a bomb on a machine shop. Raw energy needs a blueprint (such as DNA) to direct it and an energy-converting mechanism (such as the digestive system in animals) to convert the form of energy so it will be usable. But blueprints and energy-converting mechanisms are themselves produced only by life, so the process is in a catch-22.

Problems in the Fossil Record

Two features of the fossil record lend support to creationism and argue against neo-Darwinism.[49] The latter predicts that the fossil record should show millions of transition forms intermediate between the various forms of life they ancestrally link together. But this is not the case. For one thing, the fossil record reveals what is called the Cambrian explosion. The Cambrian period of the geological column (dated at around 570 million years ago) reveals a sudden explosion of all marine invertebrates which appear

49. See Gish, *Evolution*, and Lester and Bohlin, *Natural Limits to Biological Change*, pp. 65–148.

fully formed, unchanged to the present, and without a fossil record of ancestors before them or transitions among them.

Second, whenever we have the opportunity to observe an organism through successive periods of geological time, we find that it appears fully formed, that it has no clear ancestors, that there are no bridges between it and other organisms, and that it does not change even though the species must have lived through numerous environmental changes. This evidence has led may evolutionists to abandon neo-Darwinism and opt for punctuated equilibrium—the view that organisms evolve abruptly without several, gradual transitional forms, and that this sudden change is followed by a long period of stasis or lack of change. But punctuated equilibrium appears to be empirically equivalent to creationism as far as the fossil record goes. Both seem to imply the same data, and it can be argued that punctuated equilibrium is either an ad hoc addition to save macroevolution or a replacement of evolutionary theory preceding it and not a refinement of evolutionary theory.

Millions of fossils have been found and there are only a handful of possible transition forms (e.g., the *Archaeopteryx* and the famous horse series). But these examples are all questionable (evolutionists can be found who argue against each example), and in light of the incredible absence of transitional forms, it seems best to see them as fitting the general pattern.

Problems in the Extrapolation
from Micro- to Macroevolution

Finally, some have argued that there are problems in extrapolating from evidence for microevolution to macroevolution.[50] Microevolution is observable but macroevolution is not. Macroevolution faces incredible probability odds against it and there seem to be built-in limits to change in genetic material. Sometimes the rate and degree of change in the morphological or physiological features of organisms is independent of genetic change (as measured by nucleotide substitution in DNA). But the latter is supposed to account for the former according to macroevolution. Finally, it is hard to see how small changes could be beneficial to an organism. Some structures (the eye or a four-ventricle heart) are helpful only when the whole structure is in place. An incipient structure would not be operable.

In light of these and similar arguments, it is fitting to close with a quotation from scientist Michael Denton:

The overriding supremacy of the myth [of Darwinian evolution] has created a widespread illusion that the theory of evolution was all but proved one

---

50. The works by Thurman, Pun, Lester and Bohlin, Denton, Taylor, Thaxton, Bradley, and Olsen, and Morris all criticize the extrapolation from microevolution to macroevolution.

hundred years ago and that all subsequent biological research—paleonto-logical, zoological and in the newer branches of genetics and molecular biology—has provided ever-increasing evidence for Darwinian ideas. Nothing could be further from the truth. The fact is that the evidence was so patchy one hundred years ago that even Darwin himself had increasing doubts as to the validity of his views, and the only aspect of his theory which has received any support over the past century is where it applies to micro-evolutionary phenomena. His general theory, that all life on earth had originated and evolved by a gradual successive accumulation of fortuitous mutations, is still, as it was in Darwin's time, a highly speculative hypothesis entirely without direct factual support and very far from that self-evident axiom some of its more aggressive advocates would have us believe.[51]

Is science a threat to the truth and rationality of Christianity? How should the Christian integrate science and theology into a consistent worldview that is rationally satisfying? The purpose of this chapter has been to discuss some of the key issues involved in these and related questions. In light of our discussion, it is safe to say that science has not shown Christianity to be false or irrational and that several helpful principles have been offered to facilitate a deeper understanding of the interface between science and the Christian faith.

51. Denton, *Evolution*, p. 77.

8

Four Final Issues

In the first seven chapters, several arguments have been marshaled which present a cumulative case for the truth and rationality of the Christian worldview.[1] If these arguments are successful, then there are good reasons to hold that the Christian faith is true. Nevertheless, when one attempts to present Christianity to others, they often raise objections which seek to discredit the rationality of Christianity. It would be impossible to catalogue all the objections which people can raise in discussions about Christianity.[2] However, certain issues come up frequently. In this chapter, four questions which fit this category will be addressed.

---

1. Two brief treatments of how to rationally assess a worldview are Norman L. Geisler and William Watkins, *Perspectives* (San Bernardino, Calif.: Here's Life, 1984), pp. 231–42; Keith Yandell, *Christianity and Philosophy* (Grand Rapids: Eerdmans, 1984), pp. 272–85.

2. Two objections I will not consider are the problem of evil and difficulties in the attributes of God. Regarding the former, see Norman L. Geisler, *The Roots of Evil* (Grand Rapids: Zondervan, 1978), and Alvin Plantinga, *God, Freedom, and Evil* (New York: Harper and Row, 1974). Regarding the latter, see Ronald H. Nash, *The Concept of God* (Grand Rapids: Zondervan, 1983), and Richard Swinburne, *The Coherence of Theism* (Oxford: Clarendon Press, 1977).

The Visibility of God

The following objection is often raised: "If only I could see God, I would believe in him. If he would appear to me now, I would accept his existence. But since neither I, nor anyone else, can sense God with the five senses, then belief in his existence is unreasonable." Underlying this objection is the principle that in order for someone to be rational in believing that P exists, that person must be able to sense P with the five senses.

This objection and the principle which underlies it are rather crude forms of empiricism.[3] At first glance, the objection may seem to be a reasonable one. After all, why believe in something that one cannot sense? Yet on further inspection it becomes clear that this viewpoint has serious difficulties. For one thing, the view is self-refuting. The proposition "I can believe in only what I can see" cannot itself be seen. Thus, if the proposition is believed, one could not believe that the proposition itself existed. In the first third of this century, a group of philosophers known as logical positivists held that the only propositions which were cognitively meaningful were ones true in virtue of the meanings of the terms of the proposition alone (as in "all bachelors are unmarried males") or those which were empirically verifiable. Propositions in ethics (e.g., "love is a virtue") and religion (e.g., "God loves the world") were condemned as meaningless. But the positivist criterion could not itself be empirically verified and thus it was self-refuting. There are no strict positivists around any longer in professional philosophy.

One could try to escape this objection by identifying the position with the physical sentence itself which expresses it, and go on to say that one *can* see the sentence. But the proposition expressed by the sentence "I can believe only what I can see" is not identical to that sentence. The sentence is such-and-such inches long and colored black. These properties do not hold true of the proposition itself. It would seem, then, that the view is self-refuting, for it rules out the possibility of believing that the view itself exists.

Second, several things exist and cannot be seen. The great majority of thinkers in the history of Western thought have embraced one or more of these nonempirical entities: values, propositions, numbers, sets, persons, one's own thoughts, the laws of logic. For example, I know that my own thoughts exist, but I have never seen one of them. But if I can believe in only what I can see, then I must deny the existence of my thoughts or try to

3. Several forms of empiricism have existed in the history of philosophy, and Aristotle, Aquinas, Locke, Berkeley, Hume, Carnap, and Ayer could all be called empiricists. Obviously, some forms of empiricism are compatible with theism. By "crude empiricism" I have in mind the more extreme forms of empiricism which a nonphilosopher who has "empiricist" leanings may hold.

reduce them to physical entities or observable behavior. To date, all such reductions have failed, and the best explanation for my mental life is to embrace the existence of nonphysical entities called thoughts which can be in my mind. The history of philosophy is filled with the existence of nonempirical entities, and it has not sufficed in arguing against them to simply point out their nonempirical nature. Such a strategy is question-begging.

This last point leads to a third objection to the view that one can believe something exists only if it can be sensed. This view commits a category fallacy. A category fallacy is the fallacy of assigning to something a property which applies only to objects of another category. For example, it is a category fallacy to state the color of the note C. Sounds are not colored. Similarly, it is a category fallacy to fault colors for not having a smell, universals for not being located at only one place, and God for not being an empirical entity. God, if he exists at all, is by definition (in orthodox Christianity) an infinite Spirit. It is not part of the nature of a spirit to be visible empirically as a material object would be. It is a category fallacy to ascribe sensory qualities to God or fault him for not being visible. This is faulting God (an invisible Spirit) for not being a visible object.

Fourth, some objects which can be partly visible are not completely visible. If one believes in only what he can see, then he cannot believe in the existence of whole physical objects. We see only the surfaces of objects. We do not see whole, three-dimensional objects in their entirety. Earlier in this century, empiricists like Rudolf Carnap recognized this problem and tried to reduce physical-object statements (there is a red ball in the corner) to an infinite number of actual or possible sense-datum statements (if you walk to the corner, you will see a red, round color patch). Carnap was never able to reconstruct the world of regular objects. An object is not identical to an infinite number of experiences of that object.

In the seventeenth century, the British empiricists John Locke and George Berkeley debated the existence of a world of material objects. Locke held that we see our sense images of these objects, but he went on to assert that there were mind-independent objects "out there" which cause our sense images. Berkeley denied this latter claim, asserting that we see only our images. One may side with Locke against Berkeley and believe that the external world exists. But this decision cannot be based on sense experience itself. The theories of Locke and Berkeley are empirically equivalent; that is, they both entail the same sensory experiences. To choose between them, one must use a principle: "objects continue to exist when they are not observed." But such a move abandons the position that one can believe only what one sees. For this second principle is believed but not seen.

So if one holds that objects exist and cause our sensations of them, he must do so on the basis of some principle other than that of crude empiricism. And if he holds that the objects which exist are three-dimensional ones and not just surfaces, he must hold this on the basis of some principle other than crude empiricism. If one believes in only what he sees, then he cannot believe in full-blooded, mind-independent physical objects.

Fifth, there may be other ways of seeing apart from sensory seeing. There may be some form of rational intuition or numinous intuition which enables one to see nonphysical objects. "Intuition" here means "being directly aware of" as opposed to just thinking about something. Some philosophers believe that moral values can be seen or intuited directly. Furthermore, in numinous experiences—direct awareness of a holy, good Person—people claim to see God. These forms of perception may be nonexistent. But they are not clearly so. And if they do exist, then it may be possible to "see" God by some form of awareness other than sensory perception. More will be said about this later.

Sixth, it is often the case that we believe in the existence of things because we infer their existence to explain some group of facts. In these cases, these entities are believed to exist even if they cannot be seen even in principle. For example, many theoretical entities of science are postulated even though one could never see them. Magnetic fields are an example. Another example is the existence of other minds.[4] How do we know there are other minds? We do not see them as we do material objects. It may be that we infer that others are embodied persons and not just robots because we observe an analogy between their bodily behavior and our own. We know that our own behavior is a result of our minds, so theirs must be too. One can infer the existence of God from his effects in a way similar to that in which we infer the existence of other minds or theoretical entities.[5] In all three cases, we believe in the existence of things which cannot be seen.[6]

In sum, there are at least six major objections against the view which asserts that one can believe in something only if it can be sensed. So this position fails as a serious challenge to theism.

God as a Psychological Projection

Some thinkers, Karl Marx, Ludwig Feurerbach, Sigmund Freud, and Bertrand Russell among them, have argued that belief in God is not ratio-

4. Alvin Plantinga has argued that our knowledge of God is similar to our knowledge of the existence of other minds in *God and Other Minds: A Study of the Rational Justification of Belief in God*, Contemporary Philosophy series (Ithaca, N.Y.: Cornell University Press, 1967).

5. This is the main point of Stanley L. Jaki's Gifford Lectures in *The Road of Science and the Ways to God* (Chicago: University of Chicago Press, 1978). I (and Jaki) am assuming some form of scientific realism here.

6. It might be said that we have seen Christ and therefore we have seen God in some sort of visual, sensory way. But this is not quite correct. People saw Christ's humanity but inferred his deity from his works and words.

nal, for God is merely an objectification of purely human ideals, wishes, and needs.[7] Humans have a need for a father figure to meet needs and calm fears, so they project a concept of God outside themselves and reify that concept. But since this is how we come to have our concept of God, it is not rational to believe that such a being exists.

Several things can be said in response to this problem. For one thing, it can be turned on its head and used against the atheist. Psychologist Paul Vitz has argued that atheism is a result of a desire to kill the father figure (in Freudian language) because one wishes to be autonomous. Thus atheism is itself a form of projective denial. If one is going to give an account of religious belief or antibelief in terms of some theory of projection, then it would seem that atheism is a more likely candidate for projection than theism. In the history of mankind, theists have overwhelmingly outnumbered atheists. Further, conversions to Christianity fail to fit some tight control group, for converts come in all kinds of personality types, at different states in life (happiness, sadness), and different circumstances in time, place, culture, and education. Although I cannot prove it, I suspect that atheists fit a more tightly defined group than do theists, and it may be that other factors which help to define the class of atheists (for example, absent or passive fathers) may be key psychological causes for why people embrace atheism.

Second, it does not really matter how a belief is generated (whether by projection or denial) if the question at issue is the *truth* of the belief. In fact, the atheist who faults belief in God because our concept of God originated in fear commits what is known as the genetic fallacy. The genetic fallacy is the fallacy of confusing the origin of a belief with its epistemological warrant, and faulting the belief because of its origin.[8] Where a belief comes from is a different matter than why one should believe it. The former involves the psychology of discovery, the latter the epistemology of justification. I learned the multiplication tables from my second-grade teacher, Mrs. Fred, and I believe that they are correct. But it would be foolish to hold that I cannot be certain that $2 \times 2 = 4$ because Mrs. Fred was an evil person.

So it is an example of the genetic fallacy to fault the truth or rationality of theism due to the origin of the idea of God, even if one grants that the idea of God came from fears (which I see no good reason to accept). However

---

7. See John H. Hick, *Philosophy of Religion*, 2d ed. (Englewood Cliffs, N.J.: Prentice-Hall, 1963), pp. 31–36.

8. It may seem that my argument in chapter 3 regarding the self-refuting nature of physicalism is an example of the genetic fallacy. There I argued, among other things, that if all of our thoughts are byproducts of physical causes, then we could not have rationality. But this is not an example of the genetic fallacy, for in order for there to even be such a fallacy, one must be able to distinguish the process of origin of a belief (including the psychology of discovery) from the rational justification of that belief. But if *all* the factors which cause our beliefs are physical, then such a distinction is itself impossible, for there would be no rational factors or rational agents which could be affected by them.

theists come up with their beliefs about God, they offer independent reasons for that belief which stand on their own and must be evaluated in their own right. A psychological account of the origin of an idea comes in *after* philosophical argumentation. Thus, a theist who is convinced that the case for God is good might ponder why a number of university professors are not believers. One could argue that perhaps something about the sociology of the university or the psychology of most professors has caused them to reject theism. But this form of argument cannot be used in place of rational assessment of the pros and cons of the case itself.

Third, R. C. Sproul has pointed out that the biblical God is not the sort of being one would want to project.[9] The biblical God is holy, demanding, omnipotent, omniscient (thus capable of knowing me through and through even when I do not wish to be known), awesome in wrath and justice, and so forth. If one were going to project a god to meet one's needs, a being much tamer, much more human, much more manageable would be a better candidate. In fact, the Bible itself recognizes such a style of projection, and calls it idolatry. But the biblical picture of God does not mirror the collective consciousness of Israel nor is it the type of being someone would think up on his own. Idols are better candidates for projection than is the biblical God.

Finally, Christian thinkers have argued that what people really need exists.[10] If one has a fundamental desire (a natural need which is grounded in one's human nature), then there is an object which exists as the object of that need. For example, humans have a real need, based on their nature, to obtain food and water. Now it may be the case that some specific person cannot meet that need, perhaps because he is in the desert. But still, water and food exist to meet this need. Further, people have a real need to transcend the finite. There is a real need for God. Therefore, there is an appropriate object of that need—God himself.

Several things can be said against this argument. One can deny that there is such a thing as human nature or natural desires. One can deny that natural desires always have objects which meet those desires, and one can deny that the need for God is a *natural* desire, arguing perhaps that it is a learned desire. On the other hand, proponents of the argument can point out that if there is no such thing as human nature in humans, then it is hard to explain the unity of the class of humans. What unites them and separates them from other living things if not a common nature? And it does seem true that for most natural needs, the presence of the need *is* correlated with a real object which can meet that need. Finally, the univer-

9. See R. C. Sproul, *The Psychology of Atheism* (Minneapolis: Bethany Fellowship, 1974).

10. See Norman L. Geisler, *Philosophy of Religion* (Grand Rapids: Zondervan, 1974), pp. 79–82; C. S. Lewis, *The Weight of Glory, and Other Addresses* (Grand Rapids: Eerdmans, 1949), pp. 1–15.

sality of the desire to transcend the finite and seek some sort of supreme Being does suggest that this desire is grounded in being a human being and is not a result of socialization, though the exact form that the desire takes may be. In any case, it is far from clear that the desire for God in the face of life's uncertainties is an argument against God's existence. It may even be evidence that God exists.

Religious Experience

Religious experiences of various kinds play an important role in Christian life and witness. It is certainly possible to make too much of religious experience (e.g., by resting the entire case for Christianity on one's changed life), but it is also possible to make too little of religious experience (by arguing that it is merely subjective). Donald Evans has captured the current climate of opinion when he asserts that "[a certain epistemological perspective] pervades academic thought in general today. This perspective excludes the possibility of any direct awareness of spiritual reality."[11]

Is religious experience valuable in building a rational case for Christianity? I believe it is. This section will defend this claim by analyzing two different types of arguments from religious experience. But first, a word should be said about what religious experience is. There are several kinds of religious experiences.[12] Some are monistic, involving a union between the subject and the One. Others are clearly theistic in nature, involving an awareness of some sort of personal Being who is separate from the subject, holy, and so forth. These experiences are often called numinous experiences, and they may or may not involve visual or auditory sensations. Some religious experiences involve seeing a normal object "as if" it were religious (when one sees the sky as God's handiwork). Some religious experiences involve seeing an unusual public object or person (e.g., the resurrected Jesus).

Each type of religious experience enters the case for Christian theism in its own way. Rather than analyze each type of religious experience, let us

11. Donald Evans, "Can We Know Spiritual Reality?" *Commonweal* 13 (July 13, 1984): 392.

12. See C. Stephen Evans, *Philosophy of Religion*, Contours of Christian Philosophy series (Downers Grove: Inter-Varsity, 1985), pp. 78–81; Richard Swinburne, "The Evidential Value of Religious Experience," in *The Sciences and Theology in the Twentieth Century*, ed. A. R. Peacocke (Notre Dame: University of Notre Dame Press, 1981), pp. 182–96; Gary Gutting, *Religious Belief and Religious Skepticism* (Notre Dame: University of Notre Dame Press, 1982), pp. 141–77; Peter Moore, "Mystical Experience, Mystical Doctrine, and Mystical Technique," in *Mysticism and Philosophical Analysis*, ed. Steven T. Katz (New York: Oxford University Press, 1978), pp. 101–31. For fuller treatments, see William James, *The Varieties of Religious Experience* (New York: Modern Library, 1902); Evelyn Underhill, *Mysticism* (New York: New American Library, 1955).

concentrate on what we have called numinous experience. The term *numinous experience* comes from Rudolf Otto's classic work on religious experience, *The Idea of the Holy*. A numinous experience is one in which the subject (allegedly) has some sort of direct apprehension of a personal Being who is holy, good, awesome, separate from the subject, and One upon whom the subject depends in some way for life and care. Such experiences are common to an overwhelming number of people and they are often life-transforming in a number of ways. Numinous experiences form the basis of most personal testimonies which are offered today by believers on behalf of their faith. Let us now evaluate the evidential value of numinous experiences by focusing on two different ways they enter into arguments for the truth of Christian theism.

The Causal Argument

Sometimes numinous experiences are used in what can be called causal arguments for God. In this case, a person cites certain experiences of spiritual power and transformation, his changed life, his new ability to handle problems in a way not available to him before his conversion (or before some special numinous experience after conversion), and postulates God as the best explanation for his change. God becomes an explanatory hypothesis to account for the facts of the believer's transformation.

The best-known example of this sort of argument is William James's famous work, *The Varieties of Religious Experience*. James analyzed several different kinds of people who had had a variety of religious experiences and concluded that the best explanation for their changed lives was the hypothesis of a genuine spiritual Reality which caused those changes. James states his conclusion this way:

> When we commune with it [spiritual Reality, i.e., God], work is actually done upon our finite personality, for we are turned into new men, and consequences in the way of conduct follow in the natural world upon our regenerative change. But that which produces effects within another reality must be termed a reality itself, so I feel as if we had no philosophic excuse for calling the unseen or mystical world unreal. . . . God is real since he produces real effects.[13]

Obviously, the value of the causal argument rests in the ability of the God hypothesis to explain the data more adequately than (or at least as adequately as) other hypotheses. It is possible to argue that all such experi-

13. James, *Varieties of Religious Experience*, pp. 506–7.

ences are merely psychological or perhaps the result of sociological factors like peer pressure. One could hold that some sort of placebo effect is going on; that is, the changed lives of believers are due to the *belief* that God is there, not the fact that God is really there.

Three things can be said in favor of the God hypothesis. First, the religious claim does not deny that a changed life involves psychological and social factors. Rather, it is claimed that such changes are *more than* psychological and social. The believer need not deny that the data can be described using terms from psychology and sociology. After all, the religious believer is still a person and he worships in a community. The claim is that psychological and sociological explanations cannot adequately capture *all* the features of religious transformation.

This point must be kept in mind. I was once lecturing in a psychology of religion class and a student challenged the God hypothesis by pointing out that my conversion had certain features in common with what happens to someone when he feels loved by another human. Thus, he argued, one can reduce religious phenomena to mere psychological phenomena. But just because religious transformation has a psychological and sociological component, it does not follow that such components are all there is to it. Religious transformation need not be less than psychological and sociological to be more than psychological and sociological. It begs the question in advance to assume that such experiences *must* be merely psychological and sociological. Scholars, among them Evelyn Underhill and James, have argued that when one does a painstaking analysis of religious experiences, they exhibit properties all their own (e.g., a new zeal for holiness and self-sacrifice) and a power which cannot be reproduced in its intensity or longevity by other forms of experience.

Second, attempts to reduce religious transformation to the psychological or sociological must assume that there is a common causal factor, or perhaps a small number of causal factors, which is responsible for such transformation. However, such a strategy becomes less and less plausible as the diversity increases in the nature and scope of religious transformation. The larger the group of those who experience religious transformation, and the greater the increase in diversity among those experiencing such transformation, the more difficult it is to find a common psychological or sociological cause to explain such phenomena.

Religious change exhibits an incredible variety in and quantity of those experiencing it, and such variety and quantity argue for the God hypothesis, since the working of God seems to be the major, perhaps only, constant factor at work in such experiences. Religious transformation has occurred for thousands of years, in primitive cultures and advanced ones, in young people and old people, in those well educated and those without education, in cool, calm people and emotional, hysterical people, in those in a religious culture and those in an atheistic culture. Such differences in time, place, upbringing, temperament, and age are good evidence that the common causal factor in such cases is God.

Finally, religious transformation in Christianity is tied to objective events (the resurrection) and an objective interpretive grid (the Bible) which render such transformation probable. If Christ is risen from the dead and scriptural promises for a new life are true, then one has a basis for predicting that certain patterns of life change will occur. When such cases of change do in fact happen, they serve as positive confirmations of the Christian hypothesis which predicts them. Thus, such transformation is rooted in and predicted by objective, historical data, and its reality serves to confirm the truth of those data. If Christianity claimed that Christ was alive and promised certain benefits of transformation upon conversion, and if such benefits never occurred, this would tend to disconfirm such claims. On the other hand, the reality of these benefits of transformation confirm that hypothesis. So religious transformation need not be evaluated strictly on its own merits, but against the backdrop of the hypothesis of the resurrected Christ as well.

The Direct-Perception Argument

The Argument

Suppose that there was a table before you and you could see the table. Now suppose that someone asked you how you really knew that the table was there. It may be, he could point out, that an evil spirit is causing you to suppose that you see a table, or perhaps there are some undetected mirrors in front of you which are projecting a picture of a table before you which you merely take to be a table. What could you say?

You could point out weaknesses in the other hypotheses and argue that the most reasonable explanation for your sensations is the fact that a real table exists and causes your sensations. On the other hand you could simply point out that you see the table directly. In this latter view, the theory of perception it expresses is called perceptual realism, the view that the immediate objects of my perceptual experiences are things in the world—normal material objects. Perceptual realism contrasts with a second theory of perception called the sense-data theory or representative dualism. This view was embraced by René Descartes, Locke, Berkeley, and David Hume. Representative dualism holds that the immediate objects of my perceptual experiences are my sense impressions of things in the world, not those things themselves. I *infer* the existence of mind-independent material objects as the *cause* of my sense impressions, but I do not directly see those objects. I directly see my sense impressions in my mind.[14]

The argument from religious experience from direct perception claims that, occasionally, God himself is directly perceived or apprehended by a nonsensory form of seeing. In such cases one directly experiences God himself. As Job 42: 5–6 states, "My ears had heard of you but now my eyes have seen you. Therefore I despise myself and repent in dust and ashes" (NIV). This sort of argument seeks to show that there is a close analogy between the religious form of perception in numinous experience and the sensory form of perception in visual experience, and since we know the latter to be cognitive and (usually) veridical, there is justification for taking the former to be cognitive and (usually) veridical.[15]

The case for the causal form of the argument from religious experience rests on showing that the God hypothesis is a better causal explanation than any other reasonable hypothesis. The case for the direct-perception form of the argument from religious experience rests on showing that there is a close analogy between visual, sensory perception and mystical, numinous perception. To show this, let us consider some traits of normal, sensory perception, the perception of a red table.

Sensory Perception

At least seven features characterize normal acts of sensory perception. First, certain conditions must be met, both in and out of the perceiving subject, if the perception is to be possible. The perceiving subject must not be blind or even colorblind, must have his eyes open and be concentrating, and so forth. Concerning conditions outside the subject, the lights must be on, there must be no other objects between the subject and the table, the subject must be within, say, a mile of the table to see it, and so on.

Second, sensory perception possesses a noetic structure. Such experiences have intentionality; that is, they are *about* or *of* objects which usually exist independently of the experience itself. Some philosophers contrast experiences with a noetic structure with those which do not have a noetic structure. An (alleged) example of the latter would be an experience of pain or depression, which is not an experience of some object which is taken to exist.[16] Experiences with a noetic structure (e.g., visual experi-

14. Evans, *Philosophy of Religion*, pp. 81–88, seems to assume that a perceptual realist will not use the causal argument. But I see no reason why he cannot use both the causal and the direct-perception arguments. An entity can be both a theoretical one (argued to as a hypothesis) and an observational one at the same time.

15. One of the best articles on this subject is William J. Wainwright, "Mysticism and Sense Perception," in *Contemporary Philosophy of Religion*, ed. Steven M. Cahn and David Shatz (New York: Oxford University Press, 1982), pp. 123–45.

16. I disagree that pains are not intentional and therefore without objects. But my disagreement here is not relevant to the point at issue. For I still hold that pains are not cognitive, as thoughts are. For a list

ences) are experiences *of* objects which are taken to exist outside the subject and which usually do exist.

Third, sensory perception exhibits what is called a fulfillment structure.[17] Among other things, a fulfillment structure includes law-like relations which obtain between and among successive experiences of the object which lead one from a vague experience to a clear experience of that object. The exact nature of these law-like sequences is dependent, in part, on the nature of the object which offers itself through different modes of presentation, depending on how it is viewed. An illustration may help clarify what is meant here. Suppose a person is seeing a table from a half a mile away. At that distance, he may see an object but not be able to tell that it is a table. As he approaches the table, the successive experiences he has of the table replace one another in normal ways appropriate to acts of seeing a table. The table is seen as larger and larger, the color becomes brighter, and so on. Once one is at the table, it may appear as a circle viewed from overhead, an ellipse from an angle, and a straight line with legs from the side. These different experiences replace one another in law-like ways appropriate to the perception of a table. As one moves one's head from overhead to the side of the table, the circle should pass through the ellipse and into the line. These are some of the different modes of presentation that the table possesses. It should not be a part of this sequence that one suddenly sees the table moving its legs. Such an experience is not a part of the series of sequences involved in viewing a table.

Fourth, visual perception should be approached by what Richard Swinburne calls the principle of credulity—in the absence of special considerations (e.g., the subject is on drugs, he is colorblind) it is a principle of rationality that if it *seems* to a subject that x is present, then probably x *is* present; what one seems to perceive is probably so.[18] An experience of perceiving a table carries its own conviction that the table is really "out there." If one seems to see some object, then there is at least prima facie evidence for the existence of that object, and in the absence of some relevant evidence which defeats the claim that the object exists, the experience counts as evidence for the object.

Fifth, sensory experience exhibits a public aspect and a private aspect. The objects of such experiences are public in the sense that tables are mind-independent entities which can be seen by several people at the

---

of at least sixteen traits of numinous experience with an emphasis on the object of such experiences, see C. P. M. Jones, "Mysticism, Human and Divine," in *The Study of Spirituality,* ed. Cheslyn Jones, Geoffrey Wainwright, and Edward Yarnold (Oxford: Oxford University Press, 1986), pp. 17–24.

17. See Dallas Willard, *Logic and the Objectivity of Knowledge: Studies in Husserl's Early Philosophy* (Athens, Ohio: Ohio University Press, 1984), pp. 205–55.

18. See Swinburne, "Evidential Value of Religious Experience," pp. 185–90; Gutting, *Religious Belief and Religious Skepticism,* pp. 146–53; Yandell, *Christianity and Philosophy,* pp. 30–36.

same time. On the other hand, no one else can have *my* experience of the table. The having-of-the-experience is private and cannot be shared; the object of the experience is public and can be seen by many simultaneously.

Sixth, sensory perception admits of a part/whole distinction in the object of perception. One need not see all of the table to genuinely see the table. For example, one cannot see the back side of the table. But just because one can see only part of the table, it does not follow that the table cannot be truly grasped in perception. One need not exhaustively see an object in its entirety to see it truly. Furthermore, one need not see some part of the object correctly to be justified in claiming to see the object itself. For example, one may see the top of a round table as an ellipse, or one may see the red leg as slightly orange, and he would still be seeing the table. There is a line to be drawn here. If one claimed that the table was running and barking, or that it was a round square which was red and green all over at the same time, then his claim to see a table would be better understood as a hallucination.

Finally, there are public checks for sensory perception. One can ask others if there is a table in the room, one can have someone else describe the color, and so on. A variety of means exist whereby one could check his perception and have it confirmed or disconfirmed.

Numinous Perception

I agree with a number of scholars who argue that numinous perception exhibits the same features which characterize sensory perception. For one thing, numinous experience involves conditions within and outside of the subject. In most cases, the subject must be "looking" for God, he must be seeking, and he must be willing to respond. He must develop, through practice and discipline, an ability to "recognize" God's voice, and so on. Conditions outside the subject are important as well. Most mystical writers state that places of quiet or solitude are helpful, certain kinds of music can facilitate an awareness of God, certain forms of group prayer where people are genuinely seeking God can allow one to be aware of God directly.

Second, numinous perception exhibits cognitive structure; that is, it is described by those who have it in intentional terms such that "the sense of immediacy or objectivity of what is apprehended in mystical experience comes across very strongly in mystical writings and mystics stress that it persists long after the experience is over."[19] In numinous experiences

19. Moore, "Mystical Experience," p. 125.

themselves, there is a constant claim that the experiences are awarenesses of an object which is given in the perceptual acts.

Third, numinous experiences show a fulfillment structure where law-like relations obtain among sequences of apprehension and the Object of the perceptions exhibits different modes of presentation. The initial stage of awareness of God frequently involves an awakening of the self to a vague sense of God's presence accompanied by intense feelings of joy and exaltation.[20] This is often followed by a clearer apprehension of God's beauty and holiness with a concomitant awareness of one's own sin and guilt. Eventually, perception becomes clearer to the point that spiritual work is done on the self in that it becomes more unified, whole, and at peace. Further, God has several attributes. So it is possible to apprehend different modes of presentation with God. Just as a table could appear circular from one angle and elliptical from another, so numinous perception can fasten onto different aspects of God as he is experienced in different ways in different conditions (grief, celebration, guilt).

Fourth, the principle of credulity would seem to apply to numinous experience. In the absence of any special conditions (use of drugs, nitrous oxide, alcohol) the experience itself carries some presumption of evidence in favor of the veridicality of the experience. This is especially true when one considers that many individuals who have experienced numinous awareness are intelligent, self-examining, rational people not prone to emotionalism.

Fifth, numinous experiences show a public and private aspect. There is no sufficient reason for taking these experiences as private in a way that sensory experience is not private. In religious awareness, the having-of-the-experience is private in the sense that no one else could have *my* experience of God. But it does not follow that the object of such an awareness in private is not in any sense relevant to epistemological considerations. Others may experience the same Object at the same time I do, whether they are in the same group as I am or somewhere else. The Object of numinous awareness can be attended to by several persons at once, and is in this sense just as public as a table.

Sixth, the Object of numinous awareness enters into those experiences in a part/whole way. One need not exhaustively perceive God to be genuinely aware of him. One can truly apprehend God's attribute of love even if that apprehension does not fully experience that love and even if it does not experience some other attribute of God at that time. Further, different degrees of vagueness may explain the different descriptions given to the Object of numinous experience. It may well be that God is experienced in

20. See Underhill, *Mysticism*, p. 169.

some cases of numinous experience in different world religions (there is a clear tendency in monistic meditation to describe the Object of such awareness in personal terms). This does not mean that such awarenesses are veridical and it certainly does not mean that they would bring salvation. Christianity teaches that salvation comes only through faith in Christ. But just as a red table is being experienced by a person even though he is colorblind and describes the table as a brown ellipse, so God may be the real object of some numinous experiences (one could not rule out other spiritual beings such as demons as appropriate objects in these cases) even though the descriptions are not completely accurate. At some point, a line would be crossed where we would no longer say that God is being perceived. If one ascribes barking and a tail to the table we would say that the subject is hallucinating. Similarly, if one ascribes contradictory or monistic properties to God, we would not say that God is not being attended to accurately in these cases but rather that he is not being attended to at all.

Finally, there seem to be several public checks available to the subjects of numinous experiences by which one can validate the truthfulness of those experiences. We should not expect these tests to be identical to those used in visual sensory perception. The nature of the object of perception and the faculty used in perception (the eyes as opposed to a faculty of spiritual apprehension) should determine the nature of the relevant tests for veridicality. At least seven tests have been offered to distinguish true from false perceptions of God.[21]

First, if the experience is about an internally contradictory object (such as a Being who is both personal and impersonal) or if the experience is somehow self-refuting (such as the experience that I am not a real self who can have experiences), then the object does not exist (compare this with the denial of the existence of square circles in visual perception).

Second, do the experiences show similarities with those of mystics who are considered to be exemplars of numinous apprehension (e.g., Isaiah, Moses, Saint Francis or Saint Teresa of Avila)? These people demonstrated themselves to have been seeking God and trying to see him; to have mastered certain disciplines or skills which are important conditions for religious perception (fasting, solitude, various kinds of prayer); to embody those character traits which are important preconditions of religious perception (such as purity of heart, devotion, kindness).

Third, if an experience of God is veridical, one would expect certain other experiences to usually follow: those having such experiences would be likely to have them again; other individuals should be found who have

---

21. See Evans, *Philosophy of Religion*, pp. 92–95; Gutting, *Religious Belief and Religious Skepticism*, pp. 150–53; Wainwright, "Mysticism and Sense Perception," pp. 126–28.

milar experiences (especially when the same skills are mastered and
ame character traits are present); those having such experiences will
.ided in their efforts to lead morally better lives.

Fourth, the consequences of such experiences should be good for the
mystic in the long run (such as edifying to his outlook on life, unifying to
his personality, empowering to his devotion to God and others).

Fifth, the consequences of such experiences should be good for others.
Do his experiences tend to cause him to build others up and help them, or
do they make him self-centered?

Sixth, the depth, the profundity, the "sweetness" of the experience
counts as evidence for its genuineness. On the other hand, the insignifi-
cance or silliness of the experience counts against it.

Seventh, does the experience conform to an objective body of revelation, Holy Scripture, which can in turn be validated by means other than
numinous claims (fulfilled prophecy, historical arguments) to keep from
arguing in a circle?[22]

In sum, it seems that there are several reasons for holding that there is a
close analogy between sensory perception and numinous perception.
And since we know that the former is (usually) veridical, there is good reason to take the latter as (usually) veridical.

Moral Relativism

The existence of moral absolutes—objective moral values which are real
and true for all men regardless of whether any person or culture believes
them to be true—enters into discussions of the existence of God at several
levels. They figure into a refutation of physicalism as a worldview (since
they are not themselves physical entities), they are used in arguments for
God as the ground of morality, and they are part of the discussion about
the meaning of life.

Many people reject the existence of moral absolutes, opting for some
form of moral relativism. In turn, moral relativism elicits arguments by absolutists defending the existence of object morality. These debates often do
not get at central issues because the nature of moral relativism is left unclear. This section will clarify five different forms of relativism and argue
against each one.[23]

22. One difference between perceiving God and seeing a material object is that God is a person. Thus,
one's ability to perceive him depends on his willingness to disclose himself. One could be in a state which
fulfills the proper perceptual conditions and yet God might not make himself known. God is more illusive
as an object of perception than a purely passive object.

23. For surveys of ethics which include good discussions of relativism, see John Hospers, *Human Conduct* (New York: Harcourt, Brace, and World, 1961); Tom Beauchamp, *Philosophical Ethics: An Introduction to*

Cultural or Descriptive Relativism

Cultural relativism is the descriptive, factual thesis, often made by anthropologists and sociologists, that different societies do, in fact, have disparate views on basic ethical judgments. A basic ethical disagreement is one which remains when all the factual issues are agreed upon, and two cultures mean the same thing by the same ethical concept, but disagree as to whether acts done on the basis of that concept are right or wrong.

An example may help to clarify what a basic ethical disagreement is. Consider two cultures, A and B. Suppose A holds that it is a virtue to kill the elderly when they reach a certain age. Culture B holds that such an act is immoral. This appears to be a case of moral disagreement over the principle "do not murder." However, if the different facts about the belief systems of A and B are stated, the disagreement may be seen as factual and not moral. Suppose that A believes that one takes his body into the afterlife and must hunt, fish, and so on, in that body. One's happiness and safety in the afterlife would depend upon the condition of his body at death. Society B has no such belief about the afterlife. With this factual clarification, it becomes clear that both societies could agree about the basic moral principle "do not murder," but due to factual disagreements, they would disagree about what constitutes a case of murder. Society A sees the act of killing the elderly as a case of beneficence, a case of morally appropriate life-taking (just as some today would argue regarding capital punishment, self-defense, or war).

A Jehovah's Witness who refuses blood transfusions could be accused of being guilty of suicide by one not sharing the belief that such transfusions are wrong. Both parties could agree that "suicide is wrong" expresses a true, basic ethical judgment, but differ (due to factual beliefs about the nature of blood transfusions) about what constitutes suicide. So both factual and basic moral considerations are relevant to discerning the nature of prima facie moral differences. Cultural relativism holds that when the relevant factual considerations are included, cultures do in fact differ over basic ethical judgments.[24]

Two things should be pointed out about cultural relativism. First, cultural relativism is not a *moral* thesis at all. It is not a statement *of* morality, but a statement *about* morality. Cultural relativism is a descriptive factual

---

Moral Philosophy, ed. Kaye Pace (New York: McGraw-Hill, 1982); Fred Feldman, *Introductory Ethics* (Englewood Cliffs, N.J.: Prentice-Hall, 1978); Bernard Williams, *Morality: An Introduction to Ethics* (New York: Harper and Row, 1972). More technical is Michael Krausz and Jack Meiland, eds., *Relativism: Cognitive and Moral* (Notre Dame: University of Notre Dame Press, 1982). For a defense of moral relativism, see Robert Arrington, "A Defense of Ethical Relativism," *Metaphilosophy* 14 (July/October 1983): 225–39.

24. Scripture teaches that people are morally responsible for holding to certain factual beliefs, especially the content of the gospel.

thesis which entails no substantive moral thesis. In particular, it does not follow from cultural relativism that there are no moral absolutes that are true for all men, nor does it follow that these absolutes cannot be known. Different cultures differ over the shape of the earth and the cosmos. But from the mere fact that cultures differ, nothing whatever follows about whether the earth has a shape or whether this shape can be known.

Second, cultural relativism may even be weak as a descriptive thesis. When due consideration is given to factual clarification, cultures exhibit a widespread agreement in basic ethical values. As Lewis pointed out in *The Abolition of Man*, no culture has valued cowardice in battle, general dishonesty, and so forth. So while some difference may exist after factual issues are considered, there is still widespread agreement over basic ethical judgments. This agreement can be used as part of an argument for some sort of natural law, or put more theologically, general revelation, which *can* be known by most men and is, in fact, known by most men.

Normative Relativism or Conventionalism

Normative relativism is a substantive moral thesis which holds that everyone ought to act in accordance with his own society's code. What is right for one society is not necessarily right for another society, and an act is right if and only if it is in keeping with the code of the agent's society. According to normative relativism, society A may have in its code the principle "adultery is morally right" and society B may have in its code the principle "adultery is morally wrong." A and B mean the same thing by "adultery," "right," and "wrong," and thus these societies genuinely differ over the rightness of this moral principle.

Several things can be said against normative relativism. For one thing, it is difficult to define what a society is, and even if that can be done, it is difficult in many cases to identify the morally relevant society. Some acts are done in more than one society at the same time. Suppose there is a community of fairly wealthy, sexually liberated adults who hold that adultery is actually a virtue (since it is a sign of escape from sexual repression). Now suppose there is a community ten miles away which is more conservative and has in its code "adultery is wrong." If a man from the first society, Jones, has intercourse with Mrs. Smith, a member of the second society, at a motel halfway between the two societies, which society is the normative one?

Second, moral agents can be members of more than one society at the same time. Suppose Fred is an eighteen-year-old college freshman who is a member of a social fraternity and a member of a Baptist church. His social fraternity may hold that it is morally obligatory to get drunk at parties, the university may hold that such acts are not obligatory but are at least permissible, and the Baptist Church may hold that such an act is morally forbidden. It is hard to tell which society is the morally relevant one. So these objections point out that even if we have a clear notion of what constitutes a society (and this is a difficult task), we still have the problem that some acts are done in more than one society by people who belong to more than one society.

Third, normative relativism suffers from an objection called the reformer's dilemma. If normative relativism is true, then it is impossible in principle to have a true moral reformer who changes a society's code and does not merely bring out what was already implicit in that code. For moral reformers, by definition, *change* a society's code by arguing that it is somehow morally inadequate. But if normative relativism is true, an act is right if and only if it is in the society's code; so the reformer is by definition immoral (since he adopts a set of values outside the society's code and attempts to change that code in keeping with these values).[25] It is odd, to say the least, for someone to hold that every moral reformer who ever lived—Moses, Jesus, Gandhi, Martin Luther King—was immoral by definition. Any moral view which implies that is surely false.

Fourth, some acts are wrong regardless of social conventions. It is wrong to torture babies regardless of whether a society agrees that this is wrong. The Nazi war crimes were wrong regardless of the fact that they were morally acceptable to that society's code.[26] It is possible that some day every culture in the world will agree that torturing babies is morally permissible. There is no logical contradiction in such a view. But this fact would not make such an act right in spite of what normative relativism says.

Fifth, it is difficult to see how one society could blame another one. According to normative relativism, I should act in keeping with *my* society's code and person *s* should act in keeping with *his* society's code. Any view which rules out the possibility of criticizing another society fails to capture our basic intuitions about the consistency and universalizability of morality.

One could respond to this objection by pointing out that society *A* may have in its code the principle that one *should* criticize acts of murder regard-

---

25. It is possible for a society to have in its code a principle which states "follow the teachings of moral reformers." This may appear to solve the reformer's dilemma, but it does not. For one thing, what does it mean to say that the reformer is moral if not that he keeps the rest of the code? But if that is what makes him moral, then how can he change it and still be so? Further, it is hard to see how the justification of a reformer boils down to the existence of such a principle in that society's code. Could not there be a moral reformer in a society without such a principle in its code? Finally, the presence of such a principle in a society's code would place all the other moral principles in jeopardy, for they would be temporary principles subject to the whims of the next moral reformer. And what would happen if two reformers taught different principles at once? How could this principle decide between them without assuming some absolute standpoint?

26. See John Warwick Montgomery, *The Law Above the Law* (Minneapolis: Bethany Fellowship, 1976).

less of where they occur. So members of A *could* criticize other societies. But such a rule reveals an inconsistency in normative relativism. Given this rule and the fact that normative relativism is true, members of A seem to be in the position of holding that members of B ought to murder (since *their* code says it is right) and I ought to criticize members of B because *my* code says I should. Thus, I criticize as immoral members of B and at the same time hold their acts should be done. If I do criticize members of B, such criticism seems to be arrogant and unjustified, since normative relativism rules out the possibility that *my* society is really the correct one which has grasped the true essence of an absolute moral law.

Finally, if one asks about the moral status of the principle of normative relativism itself, then it seems that normative relativism is really an absolutist position and not a genuine relativist one. For most proponents hold that one *ought* (in the robust, morally absolutist sense of that term) to embrace normative relativism. Surely normative relativists do not wish to merely say that it is true (morally obligatory) for normative relativists only, and that absolutists are not morally obligated to be normative relativists. For they *argue* for their view and imply that one (epistemologically) ought to embrace it and (morally) ought to live in light of it. In this case, normative relativism is being offered as a moral absolute.

Metaethical or Conceptual Relativism

Metaethical relativism is an even more radical thesis than normative relativism. According to normative relativism, cultures A and B *mean* the same thing by moral terms such as "right" and wrong"; they just differ over whether some particular act *is* right or wrong. But A and B can at least compare moral principles and differ over their judgments about them.

According to metaethical relativism, the *meanings of moral terms of appraisal* such as "right" and "wrong" are themselves relative to one's society. Put metaphysically, there is no such property as rightness. Rather, rightness is a relation between an act and a society. Put linguistically, the statement "x is right" is shorthand for the statement "x is right for society A." The very meaning of "right" is "right for society A."

Metaethical relativism suffers from some of the same problems that were raised against normative relativism—problems of defining a society and determining the relevant society for the act and the agent, the reformer's dilemma, and the fact that some acts (torturing babies) are wrong regardless of what societies mean by "right" or "wrong." But metaethical relativism suffers from an additional objection which makes it wildly implausible. According to normative relativism, two societies, A and B, can at least differ over moral commitments. A can say that some act is right and B says that this same act is wrong. It is even possible, though it may be arrogant and inconsistent, to *criticize* members of B if I am a member of A. But I can at least hold that the two societies do in fact differ over a moral issue.

Metaethical relativism, however, rules out the very possibility of two societies ever having a moral difference. Suppose A says that "murder is right" and B says that "murder is wrong." According to metaethical relativism, these two statements are incomplete translations. What is really being said by A is "murder is right to us in A"; B is affirming that "murder is wrong to us in B." In this case, no dispute is occurring, for both of these statements could be true. The untranslated statements make it appear that A and B are having a genuine conflict. But the translated statements express what is really going on, and these reveal that societal conflict is not even possible. Both statements are true and no conflict can occur. Any moral theory which rules out the *possibility* of cross-cultural moral conflict is surely mistaken, for it is a basic feature of the moral life that societies do in fact differ. Thus, moral statements cannot mean what metaethical relativists tell us they mean.

Ethical Skepticism

Ethical skepticism is the thesis that no one's ethical beliefs are true or rational. There are two main varieties of ethical skepticism: an epistemological version and an ontological one. The epistemological version does not state that there are no objective moral values which are true. It merely holds that even if such values exist, we can never know what they are. Perhaps, so the argument could go, crude empiricism is true. In this case, moral values may *exist*, but since we can know things only through the senses, no one could ever *know* which moral values are true nor could anyone ever have a rational belief one way or the other about any moral claim.

Two things can be said about the epistemological version of ethical skepticism. First, it seems to be false. Some moral statements can be known (torturing babies is wrong) and one is not obligated to give a criterion for how one knows this to be so before one can claim to know it.[27] One need not always have a criterion for knowing something *before* he can claim to know it. Otherwise, one would need a criterion before one could claim to know the first criterion, and so on. This would be an infinite regress that is vicious. Some things can be known simply and directly. I know that I exist and that the external world is real, and I do not need a criterion for how I know these facts. I know clear cases of red and clear cases of orange

27. See Roderick Chisholm, *The Problem of the Criterion* (Milwaukee: Marquette University Press, 1973).

without having a criterion for how to judge borderline cases where it is hard to tell if the sample is more red or more orange. In fact, any criterion I use for borderline cases would be ones surfaced from observing my clear cases of knowledge without such a criterion.

Similarly, some claims can be known directly in ethics and criteria can be used from these claims to judge more problematic cases. So some ethical statements can be known to be true directly and simply. The epistemological version of ethical skepticism is often motivated by some form of naive scientism (the view that only what science claims can be known to be true). But apart from the fact that such a claim is self-refuting (how could *it* be construed as a scientific claim that could be tested), and apart from the fact that science is itself committed to the existence of values (the epistemological value that simple theories are probably correct and the moral value that test results should be reported honestly), some moral principles can be known with more certainty than some scientific claims. I know that torturing babies is wrong more surely than I know that quarks exist. It is possible, even likely, that future physics will do away with quarks or radically change what they are thought to be, but it is difficult to think of future circumstances which could revise the rationality of the claim to know that torturing babies is wrong.

The ontological version of ethical skepticism claims that there is no moral knowledge because no objective, absolute moral values exist. There are at least four varieties of the ontological version of ethical skepticism. One could hold it because one was a metaethical relativist. We have already considered that option. One could hold it because one held to emotivism, private subjectivism, or ethical naturalism.

These last three views have already been explained and criticized in chapter 4, so we need only review them here. Emotivism is the view that moral statements do not state moral facts, but are emotive utterances ("murder! ugh!"). Emotivism implies that moral statements can be neither true nor false and are noncognitivist in nature. Emotivism is inadequate as a moral theory, for it rules out the possibility of moral disagreement, it fails to account for how moral judgments can occur in the absence of any emotions whatever, and it cannot explain how some moral statements can stand in logical relations with other moral statements (if I have a duty to do x, then this fact entails that I have a right to do x), since emotive utterances do not bear logical relations to other emotive utterances.

Private subjectivism is the view that "murder is wrong" states a private psychological fact about the person holding the view ("I dislike murder"). Private subjectivism denies the possibility of *moral* knowledge, for it denies the existence of distinctively *moral* properties and statements. Private subjectivism fails as a moral theory because it rules out the possibility of moral conflict (one person can dislike murder and another like it), and there do seem to be irreducibly moral properties (people have the property of good-ness or worth and acts can have the property of rightness).

Ethical naturalism reduces moral properties and statements to natural scientific properties which could be verified scientifically. For example, it replaces "good" in "loving my neighbor is good" with "tends to produce pleasure rather than pain," "tends to enhance survival value," and the like. Survival value and pleasure can be measured and (allegedly) are natural properties. Ethical naturalism denies the existence of distinctively *moral* knowledge by denying the existence of distinctively moral properties and statements which cannot be reduced to nonmoral properties and statements. Ethical naturalism fails as a moral theory because, among other things, every alleged reduction of a moral property to a nonmoral one fails. For example, the identification of "x is good" with "x tends to produce more pleasure than pain" is false, for there are examples of mor-ally good acts which do not tend to produce more pleasure than pain (cases of surgery that failed even though the surgeon did his best), and there are cases of morally bad acts which do tend to produce more pleasure than pain (cases where a person gets pleasure from torturing animals).

In sum, the epistemological version of ethical skepticism and the four varieties of the ontological version of ethical skepticism have serious diffi-culties.

One more point should be made about ethical skepticism. If one holds the view, one could not recommend any moral behavior whatever, includ-ing toleration of different moral opinions or even the obligation to be a moral skeptic. For one cannot deny the existence or knowability of moral "oughts" in one breath and affirm an absolutist "ought" in the next breath; at least one cannot do this and remain consistent.

The Principle of Tolerance

The principle of tolerance has been defined in several ways, but the sense of the principle common to most definitions is this: I (morally) ought to tolerate the moral opinions and behavior of others who disagree with me. I (morally) should not try to interfere with their opinions or behavior.

It is often thought that the principle of toleration follows from some form of moral relativism and that it is inconsistent moral absolutism. But this is not the case. The principle of toleration does not follow from cultural rela-tivism, for cultural relativism is a mere factual claim that entails no ethical claim whatever. Neither does it follow from normative relativism, for a given culture may or may not have a principle of tolerance in its code, and the specific content of that code is not determined by the doctrine of cul-tural relativism. The principle of tolerance does not follow from meta-ethical relativism, for the former is an absolutist thesis (it does not just say that "tolerance is right to us") and the latter rules out the possibility of such a thesis. Finally, it does not follow from ethical skepticism, since ethical skepticism rules out the possibility of objective moral statements or the knowability of such statements. And those who embrace the principle of tolerance recommend it as a true, rational moral principle.

On the other hand, a moral absolutist could embrace the principle of tolerance if he held that it was a moral absolute. There may be limits to its applicability, but a moral absolutist need not in principle deny the existence of such a principle. In fact, the New Testament itself seems to teach such a principle in the area of doubtful things. It seems, then, that the principle is neither entailed by any form of relativism nor is it necessarily denied by a form of moral absolutism.

We have considered four issues which frequently arise in discussions concerning God's existence. First, we considered the objection that denies God's existence because no one has had sensory experience of God. Second, we have responded to the claim that belief in God is merely a matter of psychological projection. Third, we have assessed the value of religious experience in the case for theism by focusing on two forms of argumentation from religious experience, the causal argument and the direct-perception argument. Finally, we have analyzed the claims of moral relativism by stating and responding to five different relativistic theses.

Conclusion

For those of us who seek to be followers of Jesus Christ, the central demand of the New Testament should dominate our lives—the worldwide proclamation of the gospel. That gospel tells us that Jesus of Nazareth was the incarnate Son of God who died on the cross to atone for the sins of the world and rose bodily from the dead. This message is to be presented to people primarily because it is true and not because it works, though the practical benefits of knowing Christ are certainly important. If we follow the New Testament example, we are to present the gospel as a rational message to be believed and we are to defend it against objections.

The preceding chapters have been an attempt to defend the rationality of belief in the Christian God by offering evidence that this belief is at least rationally permissible and, indeed, rationally obligatory. Chapters 1–4 considered various aspects of the world and argued that they are best explained by postulating the existence of a personal God. Chapters 5–6 focused on the historical claims of the New Testament regarding the life, teachings, and resurrection of Jesus of Nazareth. In chapters 7–8 we looked at objections which are often raised against Christian theism. Chapter 7 centered on the integration of science and theology. Chapter 8 was a survey of four issues which often arise in discussions about God's existence: the visibility of God, God and psychological projection, the value of religious experience, and the inadequacies of different forms of moral relativism. Let us review these chapters in more detail.

Chapter 1

This chapter began by surveying three kinds of cosmological arguments (the Thomist argument, the Leibnizian argument, and the kalam argument) and concentrated on the use of the last as an argument for the existence of God. The kalam argument presents a case for the claim that the universe began to exist a finite time ago by the causal agency of a personal First Cause.

Three premises were defended. First, the universe had a beginning. Four main arguments were advanced to defend this premise. First, I argued that an actual infinite cannot exist because if one accepts the existence of an actual infinite, unacceptable puzzles arise (e.g., an infinite library of red and black books could lose all the red ones and still have the same number of holdings). A beginningless universe implies that all the events in the past form an actual infinite, and thus such a state of affairs is impossible. There was a beginning. Second, even if one grants that an actual infinite can exist, one still cannot traverse an actual infinite by successive addition. In a beginningless universe, the present moment could never arise, but since it has obtained, the universe had a beginning. Third, the second law of thermodynamics implies that the universe is running out of energy available to do work, and it must have been "wound up" a finite time ago. Finally, the big bang theory in its current form states that there was an original explosion which brought the cosmos into being a finite time ago and the universe will not continue to oscillate.

The second premise stated that the beginning of the universe was caused. This was supported in two ways. First, the principle that something does not come from nothing without a cause is a rational principle verified time and again in the course of daily life. Second, we considered an objection from quantum mechanics which claims that the law of cause and effect does not hold at the subatomic level. It was pointed out that there is no clear agreement as to how quantum mechanics should be interpreted (a realist interpretation is not the clear preference). Further, statements which seem to imply that something comes from nothing (e.g., matter can come from zero energy because such a state has a balance of positive and negative energy) are better understood as a separation or modification of one state of affairs into another state of affairs and not as an origin of a state of affairs ex nihilo.

The third premise stated that the cause for the beginning of the universe was personal. The first event arose spontaneously from an ontologically prior state of affairs which was timeless, spaceless, and immutable. Physical causation has mutability and temporal sequence built into it. When the necessary and sufficient conditions for an effect are present, the effect occurs immediately. Only a personal agent could spontaneously act to generate a first event from a timeless, spaceless, immutable state of affairs. In the process of defending these four premises, objections were summarized and criticized.

Chapter 2

Chapter 2 began by spelling out the various kinds of design used in design arguments to show both the richness of the arguments and to illustrate the fact that even if there are problems with using one kind of design (e.g., biological design), the argument is not destroyed. The kinds of design we discussed were these: order (qualitative sequences [colors], regularities of spatial compresence [parts of the human eye], and regularities of temporal succession [movements of a dancer's body or the stages of organic growth]); purpose (the orderly arrangement of parts in an object which work together for some beneficial or nonbeneficial end and which points to a plan in the mind of a designer of that arrangement, actions in the world and results of those actions (such as the history of Israel as a nation); simplicity (the unity and simplicity of nature and the laws describing nature); complexity (the intricate diversity of the world and its various phenomena); beauty (in the phenomena of nature and the laws which describe those phenomena); the truthworthiness of our sensory and cognitive faculties; biological information (the genetic code); and the values of cosmic constants.

Next, three different forms of argument were presented. First, the design argument is sometimes presented as a synthetic a priori argument which begins with some synthetic a priori proposition (e.g., "meaning or information *must* come from a mind"), some fact about the world (the presence of genetic information), and infers a mind or designer for that fact of the world.

Second, there is an analogy form of the argument. This argument seeks to show a close analogy between human artifacts or machines and various aspects of the natural world. Since the former are designed, the latter are also.

Third, there are probability forms of the argument. Three different understandings of probability are used: the possibility view, the frequency view, and the evidential view. Each form of probability is used to show that some aspect of the world (e.g., the presence of life) is more rational or probable if God exists than if God does not exist.

The remainder of the chapter covered objections which have been raised against the design argument in its various forms. Four objections from David Hume were considered, a criticism against the analogy between nature and human artifacts was touched on, and evolutionary attacks on the argument were evaluated, as were objections against the use of probability in the design argument.

Chapter 3

Chapter 3 argued that the human mind is a mental substance which points to God as the cause or ground of its existence. First, substance dualism was defined as the view that in addition to a body, a person has a mind which is a substance. A substance is an entity which is a particular. It can change and have opposites (green and red), it is a fundamental existent which *has* properties but is not had by something more fundamental, and it has causal powers which can act in the world on other substances.

The next task was to defend substance dualism. First, it was pointed out that physicalism as a general worldview is inadequate because it cannot account for a host of nonphysical entities: numbers, values, theories, meanings, concepts, propositions, the laws of logic, truth, and universals. The falsity of physicalism as a worldview does not entail the falsity of mind/body physicalism (persons could still be physical even if numbers exist). But it does remove much of the motivation for mind/body physicalism which is often defended in order to preserve physicalism at the worldview level.

Second, several arguments were offered for accepting some form of dualism over physicalism as a solution to the mind/body problem: mental and physical identity does not hold between the mental and physical (e.g., thoughts have no weight), the mental is marked by private access and incorrigibility, the experience of first-person subjectivity cannot be incorporated into a physical description of the world, secondary qualities are hard to fit into a physical description of the world, intentionality is not a physical property or relation, absolute personal identity cannot be maintained on physicalist grounds, and our common-sense intuitions about morality, responsibility, and punishment do not make sense if we are merely physical.

Third, substance dualism was defended by arguing that physicalism and property dualism (epiphenomenalism) are self-refuting. They remove the very possibility of rational thought by failing to allow for five essential ingredients of rationality: intentionality, the ability of the mind to contain reasons, thoughts, and propositions, and to be influenced by these entities, the ability of the mind to have rational insight into a chain of reasoning, the presence of an enduring "I" which continues in existence during the process of thought, and the free agency necessary to choose one's beliefs for reasons other than physical causation.

Once substance dualism is granted, the question arises as to how substantial minds could arise from matter. Most physicalists attempt to solve the problem by denying the existence of the mental, or by granting only that the mental is an emergent property and not a substance in its own right. This emergent property view was analyzed and criticized. Mental properties do not emerge from matter, much less mental substances, because to do so would mean that they either come from nothing or come from potentiality in matter. The former violates the law that something cannot come from nothing. The latter frustrates physicalism as a worldview by forcing the physicalist to adopt mental potentiality as a part of the ultimate furniture of the universe. The best explanation for the existence of finite minds is the existence of an infinite Mind.

Chapter 4

Chapter 4 explored the relationship between God and the meaning of life. The question "what is the meaning of life?" was defined as this question: Are there any objective values which provide significance for the universe as a whole, human life in general, or my life in particular, and which provide a goal or purpose for the universe, human life, or my life? Since this question involves issues about the nature and existence of values, two further questions were clarified. First, what is the meaning of moral statements? Several options in metaethics were surveyed and criticized as answers to this question. Second, why should I be moral? This question is asking for what motives, but more importantly, what reasons there are for why I should adopt the moral point of view as a part of my rational plan of life.

Four views of the meaning of life were discussed. First, nihilism is the view that human existence is totally meaningless, nothing is of real value, and life is absurd. The death of God and the rise of modern science are two pillars on which nihilism rests. Several arguments were raised against nihilism: the concept of God is not vanishing from Western culture, values do in fact exist and some of them can be known (e.g., torturing babies is wrong), science is not the only arena of human knowledge, nihilism cannot be recommended as a morally obligatory worldview, and nihilism is unlivable.

Second, the optimistic humanist view agrees with nihilism about the objectivity of value and the meaning of life, but optimistic humanists do not draw a pessimistic conclusion from their position. Life can have whatever meaning we choose to give it. Three objections were raised against optimistic humanism. First, there is no rational justification for choosing it over nihilism. Second, the metaethical theories of optimistic humanism (imperativalism, emotivism, or private subjectivism) are inadequate metaethical theories. Third, nihilism is more consistent than optimistic humanism, because if there are no real values, life is objectively meaningless. Naive optimism is a fantasy world of denial.

The third view considered was the immanent purpose view. This view holds that objective values exist as components of the ultimate furniture of the universe. These values can be realized in life and the pursuit of these values gives life meaning. Several arguments were raised against the immanent purpose view. First, it cannot account for certain features of the moral life—responsibility, guilt feelings, and retribution when there is no clear human victim. Second, the existence of moral values as brute givens in an impersonal universe is puzzling to say the least. Third, even if such values exist, why would they have any reference to a little species of organisms on a tiny planet called earth? Fourth, if these values exist and can be known, then it is less odd to say that God exists and can be known, since moral knowledge and religious knowledge are similar. Fifth, without the special revelation of God in the Bible, the content of objective morality is hard to specify in detail.

The fourth view we considered was Christian theism. After stating the main features of Christian theism, four objections were examined and rejected. The chapter concluded that the most satisfying answer, intellectually and experientially, to the question of the meaning of life is Christian theism.

Chapter 5

In chapter 5, five arguments were offered for the historicity of the New Testament documents. First, several tests are used by historians to determine the historicity of a document. When many of these tests are applied to the New Testament documents, those documents do quite well. The bibliographical test establishes the textual reliability of the New Testament currently in our possession. Many of the New Testament documents were originally personal letters intended for small audiences.

Second, the New Testament writers claim to have been eyewitnesses of the events they describe. Several reasons were advanced for accepting these claims: a document should be approached with a presumption of truthtelling, the writers of the New Testament were able to tell the truth and had little to gain by lying, hostile eyewitnesses would have checked flagrant fabrication, and a consistent picture of Jesus in written form could not have been formed in the absence of eyewitness control. Objections to eyewitness influence were considered. In the process of answering these objections it was argued that the Gospels were genuine attempts at writing factual history and that historical writers in New Testament times knew how to distinguish fact from fiction.

Third, when the Gospels are seen against the backdrop of Jewish oral tradition, their historical veracity is enhanced. The Gospel materials were consciously formed as accurate representations of the teachings and deeds of Jesus, preserved, passed on with care, and guarded by apostolic authority in a manner similar to the way rabbinic students handled the teachings of a respected rabbi.

Fourth, several marks of historicity surface upon examination of the Gospel materials. Jesus' sayings are in easily memorizable form, which fits with his attempts to teach in ways which would be preserved. Other distinctive features of Jesus' sayings do not appear outside the New Testament or in other portions of the New Testament, and thus their distinctiveness would appear to come from Jesus himself. There is the presence in the Gospels of much that is irrelevant during the time when the Gospels were alleged to have been written in 50–90 (e.g., Jesus' attitude of favor toward Israel). There is a lack of much material in the Gospels that would have been relevant during the period of 50–90 (e.g., sayings of Jesus regarding charismatic gifts, circumcision, and Gentile missions). Finally, there is much in the Gospels that is actually embarrassing and counterproductive (e.g., the frequent unbelief of the disciples, Jesus' denial of being good).

Fifth, the earliness of much of the New Testament materials reduces the chances that mythical features replaced the solid historical core of those materials. In this regard, main factors were investigated regarding the dating of Paul's letters and their contents, as well as the Gospels and the speeches in Acts 1–12. It was also pointed out that the historical Jesus of the most radical New Testament critics did not see himself as a mere man, so an advanced Christology began with Jesus himself. It was not superimposed by the church several decades after his death.

Chapter 6

The thrust of chapter 6 was a defense of the bodily resurrection of Jesus from the dead. Four general areas of argumentation were considered. First, two broad kinds of evidence were given for the fact of the empty tomb. General arguments for the empty tomb were discussed (e.g., there was no veneration at Jesus' tomb); these were followed by a description of the marks of historicity in the pre-Markan empty tomb narrative and in the pre-Pauline formula in 1 Corinthians 15. The empty tomb is best explained by postulating that Jesus rose bodily from the dead.

Second, the resurrection appearances were investigated. Several features of the appearance narratives seem to be historical (e.g., the presence of women as witnesses). Further, it is unlikely that the resurrection appearances were hallucinations. The concept of one individual being resurrected before the end of the world was completely foreign to the disciples, and they would have been more likely to have understood the resurrection as some sort of translation of Jesus to heaven. In addition, the disciples did not fit the normal psychological pattern applicable to people who hallucinate. The appearances of Jesus are strong evidence for his resurrection.

Third, four key features of the early church were presented. It was pointed out that the presence of these features is explicable on the assumption of the resurrection but not otherwise. The four features are the transformation of the disciples, the change in key social structures in Judaism by the early church (sacrifices, keeping the law and the Sabbath, non-Trinitarian monotheism, and the picture of a political messiah), the sacraments which celebrate the death of One they had loved (baptism and the Lord's Supper), and the existence of the church herself.

The chapter concluded by examining the claim that the concept of the resurrection in the New Testament was significantly shaped by mystery religions or Gnostic redeemer myths.

Chapter 7

The objective of chapter 7 was to investigate the integration of Christianity and science in order to assess whether science has made belief in the Christian faith irrational.

The first area of investigation was the debate over scientific realism. Rational realism is roughly the view that science is an objectively rational discipline that is progressively giving us a true picture of the world. This was contrasted with four views labeled rational nonrealism (phenomenalism, operationism, pragmatism, and constructive empiricism) which agree in seeing science as a rational discipline which does not converge on a true picture of the world. Science helps us organize our sense impressions and control and predict nature, and gives us theories which work. Finally, the views of Thomas Kuhn were offered as an example of nonrational nonrealism. This view holds to conceptual relativism regarding the rationality of science (science is not objectively rational) and it denies that science converges on the truth. If a nonrealist view of science is correct for science as a whole or for some area within science, then the claims of science need not be a threat to theology, since the former are not to be taken as approximately true descriptions of the way the world is.

Next, several limitations to science were discussed. The claim that science is the only field that is rational and that gives truth is self-refuting. Further, several presuppositions of science lie outside the bounds of science: the reliability of the senses, the rationality of the mind, the uniformity of nature, the existence of moral, epistemic, and methodological values, and boundary conditions. Science cannot claim to be the only truth or the only rational discipline.

If one assumes a rational realist view of science, how should science and theology be integrated? Five models of integration were presented and criticized: science and theology are concerned with two distinct realms of being, they are two noninteracting approaches to the same reality, theology provides the metaphysical foundation for science, science provides the boundaries within which theology must work, and science and theology are interacting approaches to the same reality. An eclectic view which opens up the possibility of a real conflict between science and theology was suggested.

As an example of how one should approach potential areas of conflict between science and theology, the creation/evolution debate was examined. First, creationism was defended against the charge that it is not science but religion. Second, biblical issues in the doctrine of creation were discussed. Among them were different interpretations of Genesis 1 and 2 and five exegetical issues in the creation texts (the meaning of *bārā'*, and *yôm*, and the chronology, structure, and purpose of the Genesis 1 and 2 narratives). Third, three main areas of criticism against the neo-Darwinian theory of macroevolution were surveyed: the prebiotic soup, the fossil record, and the extrapolation from microevolution to macroevolution.

Chapter 8

In chapter 8, four final issues were examined. First, some people claim that it is not rational to believe in God because he cannot be seen. This objection was spelled out and six responses were offered to it.

Second, others claim that God is merely a psychological projection. In response it was argued that the atheist may be doing the projecting, but in any case, the origin of an idea should not be confused with its rational support. Even if one comes to believe in God for psychological reasons, that should not be confused with the rational support given for theism. Further, the nature of the biblical God is not one which people would want to project (he is holy and so on) and a better candidate for projection is a god of idolatrous religions. Finally, it was pointed out that what one needs usually exists (e.g., water), so if we really need God, that provides some evidence for his existence.

The third area of investigation was the evidential value of religious experience. We examined two very different forms of argumentation for theism from religious experience. The first form of argument is the causal argument. This approach starts with features of one's changed life and argues that the existence of God is the most satisfying hypothesis we have for explaining these changes. The strength of this argument lies in its ability to criticize naturalistic explanations of religious experience and present the theistic hypothesis as an equally or more viable alternative.

The second argument from religious experience is the direct-perception argument. This argument seeks to show that numinous experience bears a close resemblance to sensory perception. If we take the latter in perceptual realist terms (i.e., the objects of acts of sensory perception are things in the world and not my sense impressions of those objects), then the following argument is plausible. Sensory acts of perception are usually veridical, they bear close resemblance to numinous acts of perception, and therefore it is reasonable to take the latter as (usually) veridical. The strength of this form of the argument from religious experience turns on the strength of the analogy between sensory and numinous modes of perception.

Finally, we investigated the claim that relativism is true in ethics. This claim was broken down into five different forms of relativism: cultural relativism, normative relativism, metaethical relativism, ethical skepticism, and the principle of tolerance. Each of these forms of relativism was subjected to criticism and rejected.

Bibliography

The following are selected works for further study. They are categorized as basic (B), intermediate (I), and advanced (A). Those marked with an asterisk (*) are highly recommended.

I. Historical Apologetics

A. Philosophy of History

Clark, Gordon H. *Historiography: Secular and Religious*. Nutley, N.J.: Craig, 1971. (I)

*Dray, William H. *Philosophy of History*. Englewood Cliffs, N.J.: Prentice-Hall, 1964. (B)

Gottschalk, Louis. *Understanding History: A Primer of Historical Method*. 2d ed. New York: Alfred A. Knopf, 1969. (I)

Hook, Sidney, ed. *Philosophy and History: A Symposium*. New York: New York University Press, 1963. (A)

McIntyre, C. T., ed. *God, History, and Historians*. New York: Oxford University Press, 1977. (A)

Marsden, George, and Frank Roberts, eds. *A Christian View of History?* Grand Rapids: Eerdmans, 1975. (I)

Montgomery, John Warwick. *The Shape of the Past*. Minneapolis: Bethany Fellowship, 1975. (I)

*———. *Where Is History Going?* Reprint ed. Minneapolis: Bethany Fellowship, 1972. (B)

B. Historical Evidences

Anderson, Charles. *The Historical Jesus: A Continuing Quest*. Grand Rapids: Eerdmans, 1972. (I)

*Anderson, J. N. D. *Christianity: The Witness of History*. Downers Grove: Inter-Varsity, 1970. (B)

*Brown, Colin, ed. *History, Criticism, and Faith*. Downers Grove: Inter-Varsity, 1976. (I)

*Bruce, F. F. *The New Testament Documents: Are They Reliable?* 5th rev. ed. Grand Rapids: Eerdmans, 1960. (B)

*France, R. T. *The Evidence for Jesus*. Downers Grove: Inter-Varsity, 1986. (I)

Gruenler, Royce Gordon. *New Approaches to Jesus and the Gospels: A Phenomenological and Exegetical Study of Synoptic Christology*. Grand Rapids: Baker, 1982. (A)

Guthrie, Donald. *New Testament Introduction*. Downers Grove: Inter-Varsity, 1970. (A)

Hengel, Martin. *The Son of God*. Translated by John Bowden. Philadelphia: Fortress, 1976. (A)

*McDowell, Josh. *Evidence That Demands a Verdict*. San Bernardino, Calif.: Here's Life, 1972. (B)

*Marshall, I. Howard. *I Believe in the Historical Jesus*. I Believe series. Grand Rapids: Eerdmans, 1977. (A)

————. *The Origins of New Testament Christology*. Issues in Contemporary Theology series. Downers Grove: Inter-Varsity, 1976. (A)

*Mitton, C. Leslie. *Jesus: The Fact Behind the Faith*. Grand Rapids: Eerdmans, 1974. (B)

Montgomery, John Warwick. *History and Christianity*. Downers Grove: Inter-Varsity, 1964. (B)

*Moule, C. F. D. *The Birth of the New Testament*. 3d rev. ed. San Francisco: Harper and Row, 1981. (A)

————. *The Origin of Christology*. Cambridge: Cambridge University Press, 1977. (A)

————. *The Phenomenon of the New Testament*. London: SCM, 1967. (A)

Stanton, G. N. *Jesus of Nazareth in New Testament Preaching*. Cambridge: Cambridge University Press, 1974. (A)

C. Extrabiblical Evidence for Jesus

*Bruce, F. F. *Jesus and Christian Origins Outside the New Testament*. Grand Rapids: Eerdmans, 1974. (I)

*Habermas, Gary R. *Ancient Evidence for the Life of Jesus: Historical Records of His Death and Resurrection*. Nashville: Nelson, 1985. (I)

D. Dating the Gospels

*Ellis, E. Earle. "Dating the New Testament." *New Testament Studies* 26 (July 1980): 487–502. (I)

*Robinson, John A. T. *Can We Trust the New Testament?* Grand Rapids: Eerdmans, 1977. (B)

*———. *Redating the New Testament*. Philadelphia: Westminster, 1976. (A)

Staudinger, Hugo. *The Trustworthiness of the Gospels*. Edinburgh: The Handsel Press, 1981. (I)

Wenham, John W. "Gospel Origins." *Trinity Journal* (old series) 7 (Fall 1978): 112–34. See the reply by Douglas Moo in *Trinity Journal* (new series) 2 (1981): 24–36, and the rejoinder by Wenham. (A)

E. Miracles

1. Philosophical Issues

Brown, Colin. *Miracles and the Critical Mind*. Grand Rapids: Eerdmans, 1984. (I)

*Geisler, Norman L. *Miracles and Modern Thought*. Grand Rapids: Zondervan, 1982. (B)

Lewis, C. S. *Miracles: A Preliminary Study*. New York: Macmillan, 1947. (I)

2. First-Century Issues

Drane, John W. "The Religious Background." In *New Testament Interpretation: Essays on Principles and Methods*, edited by I. Howard Marshall, pp. 117–25. Grand Rapids: Eerdmans, 1978. (I)

*Kim, Seyoon. *The Origin of Paul's Gospel*. Grand Rapids: Eerdmans, 1982. (A)

Machen, J. Gresham. *The Origin of Paul's Religion*. Grand Rapids: Eerdmans, 1925. (I)

*Mosley, A. W. "Historical Reporting in the Ancient World." *New Testament Studies* 12 (October 1965): 10–26. (I)

Sabourin, Leopold. "Hellenistic and Rabbinic 'Miracles.'" *Biblical Theology Bulletin* 2 (October 1972): 281–307. (I)

F. The Resurrection

*Bode, E. L. *The First Easter Morning*. Rome: Biblical Institute Press, 1970. (A)

*Craig, William Lane. *The Son Rises*. Chicago: Moody, 1981. (I)

*Habermas, Gary R. *The Resurrection of Jesus: An Apologetic*. Grand Rapids: Baker, 1980. (B)

Ladd, George E. *I Believe in the Resurrection of Jesus*. Grand Rapids: Eerdmans, 1975. (I)

Lapide, Pinchas. *The Resurrection of Jesus: A Jewish Perspective*. Translated by Wilhelm C. Linss. Minneapolis: Augsburg, 1983. (I)

*McDowell, Josh. *The Resurrection Factor*. San Bernardino, Calif.: Here's Life, 1981. (B)

*Morrison, Frank. *Who Moved the Stone?* Grand Rapids: Zondervan, n.d. (B)

O'Collins, Gerald. *The Resurrection of Jesus Christ*. Valley Forge: Judson, 1973. (I)

Osborne, Grant R. *The Resurrection Narratives: A Redactional Study*. Grand Rapids: Baker, 1984. (I)

Tenney, Merrill C. *The Reality of the Resurrection*. New York: Harper and Row, 1963. (B)

Wenham, John W. *Easter Enigma: Are the Resurrection Accounts in Conflict?* Grand Rapids: Zondervan, Academie Books, 1984. (I)

Wilckens, Ulrich. *Resurrection*. Translated by A. M. Stewart. Atlanta: John Knox, 1978. (A)

II. General Apologetics

Boa, Kenneth. *God, I Don't Understand*. Wheaton: Victor, 1975. (B)

Boa, Kenneth, and Larry Moody. *I'm Glad You Asked*. Wheaton: Victor, 1982. (B)

*Craig, William Lane. *Apologetics: An Introduction*. Chicago: Moody, 1984. (I)

————. *The Existence of God and the Beginning of the Universe*. San Bernardino, Calif.: Here's Life, 1979. (B)

Dyrness, William A. *Christian Apologetics in a World Community*. Downers Grove: Inter-Varsity, 1983. (I)

*Geisler, Norman L. *Christian Apologetics*. Grand Rapids: Baker, 1976. (I)

Little, Paul. *Know Why You Believe*. Wheaton: Scripture, 1967. (B)

Montgomery, John Warwick. *Faith Founded on Fact*. New York: Nelson, 1978. (I)

*Purtill, Richard L. *Thinking About Religion: A Philosophical Introduction to Religion*. Englewood Cliffs, N.J.: Prentice-Hall, 1978. (B)

Sire, James W. *The Universe Next Door: A Basic World View Catalog*. Downers Grove: Inter-Varsity, 1976. (B)

III. Arguments for the Existence of God

A. General

*Davies, Brian. *An Introduction to the Philosophy of Religion*. Oxford: Oxford University Press, 1982. (I)

Evans, C. Stephen. *Philosophy of Religion*. Contours of Christian Philosophy series. Downers Grove: Inter-Varsity, 1985. (B)

*Ewing, A. C. *Value and Reality*. London: George Allen and Unwin, 1973. (A)

*Geisler, Norman L. *Philosophy of Religion*. Grand Rapids: Zondervan, 1974. (I)

Grisez, Germain. *Beyond the New Theism: A Philosophy of Religion*. Notre Dame: University of Notre Dame Press, 1975. (A)

Hick, John H., ed. *Arguments for the Existence of God*. Philosophy of Religion series. New York: Herder, 1971. (I)

Maynell, Hugo. *God and the World*. London, 1971. (I)

Miller, Ed L. *God and Reason: A Historical Approach to Philosophical Theology*. New York: Macmillan, 1972. (B)

Plantinga, Alvin. *God and Other Minds: A Study of the Rational Justification of Belief in God*. Contemporary Philosophy series. Ithaca, N.Y.: Cornell University Press, 1967. (A)

Plantinga, Alvin, and Nicholas Wolterstorff, eds. *Faith and Rationality: Reason and Belief in God*. Notre Dame: University of Notre Dame Press, 1984. (A)

Swinburne, Richard. *The Coherence of Theism*. Oxford: Clarendon Press, 1977. (A)

*―――. *The Existence of God*. Oxford: Clarendon Press, 1979. (A)

Trueblood, D. Elton. *Philosophy of Religion*. New York: Harper and Row, 1957. (A)

*Yandell, Keith. *Christianity and Philosophy*. Grand Rapids: Eerdmans, 1984. (I)

B. Cosmological Argument

Burrell, Donald R., ed. *The Cosmological Arguments: A Spectrum of Opinion*. Garden City, N.Y.: Doubleday, Anchor Books, 1967. (A)

*Craig, William Lane. *The Kalam Cosmological Argument*. New York: Macmillan, 1979. (A)

Reichenbach, Bruce R. *The Cosmological Argument: A Reassessment*. Springfield, Ill.: Charles C. Thomas Publishers, 1972. (I)

Rowe, William L. *The Cosmological Argument*. Princeton: Princeton University Press, 1975. (A)

C. Teleological Argument

Clark, Robert E. D. *The Universe: Plan or Accident?* Grand Rapids: Zondervan, 1949. (B)

*Horigan, James E. *Chance or Design?* New York: Philosophical Library, 1979. (B)

McPherson, Thomas. *The Argument from Design*. London: Macmillan, 1972. (B)

Tennant, F. R. *Philosophical Theology*, vol. 2, *The World, the Soul, and God*. Cambridge: Cambridge University Press, 1956. (A)

D. Moral Argument

*Adams, Robert. "Moral Arguments for Theistic Belief." In *Rationality and Religious Belief*, edited by C. F. Delaney, pp. 116–40. Notre Dame: University of Notre Dame Press, 1979. (A)

Green, Ronald M. *Religious Reason: The Rational and Moral Basis of Religious Belief*. New York: Oxford University Press, 1978. (A)

*Helm, Paul, ed. *Divine Commands and Morality*. Readings in Philosophy series. New York: Oxford University Press, 1981. (A)

Lewis, C. S. *The Abolition of Man*. New York: Macmillan, 1947. (B)

―――. *Mere Christianity*. New York: Macmillan, 1943; rev. ed., 1952. (B)

*Mitchel, Basil. *Morality: Religious and Secular*. Oxford: Clarendon Press, 1980. (I)

Owen, H. P. *The Moral Argument for Christian Theism*. London: Allen and Unwin, 1965. (I)

E. Religious Experience

Evans, C. Stephen. *Subjectivity and Religious Belief*. Grand Rapids: Eerdmans, 1978. (B)

James, William. *The Varieties of Religious Experience*. New York: Modern Library, 1902. (I)

Taylor, A. E. "The Argument from Religious Experience." In *Arguments for the Existence of God*, edited by John H. Hick, pp. 153–64. New York: Herder, 1971. (B)

Underhill, Evelyn. *Mysticism*. New York: New American Library, 1955. (I)

*Wainwright, William J. "Mysticism and Sense Perception." In *Contemporary Philosophy of Religion*, edited by Stephen M. Cahn and David Shatz, pp. 123–45. New York: Oxford University Press, 1982. (A)

F. The Meaning of Life

Britton, Karl. *Philosophy and the Meaning of Life*. Cambridge: Cambridge University Press, 1969. (A)

*Chaney, David R., and Steven Sanders, eds. *The Meaning of Life: Questions, Answers and Analysis*. Englewood Cliffs, N.J.: Prentice-Hall, 1980. (B)

*Evans, C. Stephen. *Existentialism: The Philosophy of Despair and the Quest for Hope*. Grand Rapids: Zondervan, Academie Books, 1984. (B)

Klemke, E. D., ed. *The Meaning of Life*. New York: Oxford University Press, 1981. (B)

Murphy, Jeffrie G. *Evolution, Morality, and the Meaning of Life*. Philosophy and Society series. Totowa, N.J.: Rowman and Littlefield, 1982. (I)

IV. Science

A. Problems with the Rationality and Truthfulness of Science

Byl, John. "Instrumentalism: A Third Option." *Journal of the American Scientific Affiliation* 37 (March 1985): 11–18. (B)

Clark, Gordon H. *The Philosophy of Science and Belief in God*. Nutley, N.J.: Craig, 1964. (B)

Harré, R. *Varieties of Realism*. New York: Basil Blackwell, 1986. (A)

Hübner, Kurt. *Critique of Scientific Reason*. Translated by Paul R. Dixon and Hollis M. Dixon. Chicago: University of Chicago Press, 1983. (A)

Kuhn, Thomas. *The Structure of Scientific Revolutions*. 2d ed. Chicago: University of Chicago Press, 1970. (I)

Laudan, Larry. "Explaining the Success of Science: Beyond Epistemic Realism and Relativism." In *Science and Reality*, edited by James T. Cushing, C. F. Delaney, and Gary Gutting. Notre Dame: University of Notre Dame Press, 1984. (I)

*———. *Progress and Its Problems: Toward a Theory of Scientific Growth*. Berkeley: University of California Press, 1977. (I)

*Newton-Smith, W. H. *The Rationality of Science*. International Library of Philosophy. Boston: Routledge and Kegan Paul, 1981. (A)

Putnam, Hilary. *Reason, Truth, and History*. Cambridge: Cambridge University Press, 1981. (A)

van Fraassen, Bas C. *The Scientific Image*. Oxford: Clarendon Press, 1980. (A)

B. Religion and Science

*Jaki, Stanley L. *The Road of Science and the Ways to God*. Chicago: University of Chicago Press, 1978. (A)

Morris, Henry M. *The Biblical Basis for Modern Science*. Grand Rapids: Baker, 1984. (B)

Peacocke, A. R. *Creation and the World of Science*. Oxford: Oxford University Press, 1979. (I)

*———, ed. *The Sciences and Theology in the Twentieth Century*. Notre Dame: University of Notre Dame Press, 1981. (A)

Ramm, Bernard. *The Christian View of Science and Scripture*. Grand Rapids: Eerdmans, 1954. (B)

*Quinn, Philip. "The Philosopher of Science as Expert Witness." In *Science and Reality*, edited by James T. Cushing, C. F. Delany, and Gary Gutting, pp. 32–53. Notre Dame: University of Notre Dame Press, 1984. (I)

C. Physicalism and Reductionism

Ayala, Francisco, and Theodosius Dobzhansky. *Studies in the Philosophy of Biology: Reduction and Related Problems*. Berkeley: University of California Press, 1975. (A)

Churchland, Paul M. *Matter and Consciousness: A Contemporary Introduction to the Philosophy of Mind*. Cambridge, Mass.: MIT Press, 1984. (I)

Clark, Stephen. *From Athens to Jerusalem*. Oxford: Clarendon Press, 1984. (I)

*Lewis, H. D. *The Elusive Self*. Philadelphia: Westminster, 1982. (I)

*Lucas, J. R. *The Freedom of the Will*. Oxford: Clarendon Press, 1970. (A)

MacKay, Donald M. *Human Science and Human Dignity*. Downers Grove: InterVarsity, 1979. (B)

*Maddell, Geoffrey. *The Identity of the Self*. Edinburgh: The University Press, 1981. (A)

Moreland, J. P. *Universals, Qualities, and Quality-Instances: A Defense of Realism.* Lanham, Md.: University Press of America, 1985. (A)

Popper, Karl, and John C. Eccles. *The Self and Its Brain.* Berlin and New York: Springer International, 1977. (A)

*Robinson, Howard. *Matter and Sense.* Cambridge: Cambridge University Press, 1982. (A)

Smith, Vincent E. *Philosophical Problems in Biology.* Jamaica, N.Y.: St. John's University Press, 1966. (A)

*Swinburne, Richard. *The Evolution of the Soul.* Oxford: Clarendon Press, 1986. (A)

Thorpe, W. H. *Purpose in a World of Chance: A Biologist's View.* New York: Oxford University Press, 1978. (A)

D. Evolution

Blocher, Henri. *In the Beginning: The Opening Chapters of Genesis.* Translated by David G. Preston. Downers Grove: Inter-Varsity, 1984. (B)

*Denton, Michael. *Evolution: A Theory in Crises.* London: Burnett Books, 1985. (B)

Frair, Wayne, and Percival David. *A Case for Creation.* Chicago: Moody, 1967. (B)

*Geisler, Norman L., and J. Kerby Anderson. *Origin Science: A Proposal for the Creation-Evolution Controversy.* Grand Rapids: Baker, 1987. (B)

Gillespie, Neal. *Charles Darwin and the Problem of Creation.* Chicago: University of Chicago Press, 1979. (I)

*Gish, Duane T. *Evolution: The Challenge of the Fossil Record.* El Cajon, Calif.: Master, 1985. (B)

Kofahl, Robert E., and Kelly L. Segraves. *The Creation Explanation.* Wheaton: Harold Shaw, 1975. (B)

*Lester, Lane, and Raymond G. Bohlin. *The Natural Limits to Biological Change.* Grand Rapids: Zondervan, Academie Books, 1984. (I)

*Morris, Henry M. *Scientific Creationism.* El Cajon, Calif.; Master, 1974. (I)

Morris, Henry M., and Gary Parker. *What Is Creation Science?* San Diego: Creation-Life, 1982. (I)

Newman, Robert, and Herman Eckelmann. *Genesis One and the Origin of the Earth.* Downers Grove: Inter-Varsity, 1977. (B)

Pitman, Michael. *Adam and Evolution.* London: Rider and Company, 1984. (I)

*Shapiro, Robert. *Origins.* New York: Summit, 1986. (A)

Shuster, George N., and Ralph E. Thorson, eds. *Evolution in Perspective: Commentaries in Honor of Pierre Lecomte du Noüy.* Notre Dame: University of Notre Dame Press, 1970. (A)

*Thaxton, Charles B., Walter L. Bradley, and Roger L. Olsen. *The Mystery of Life's Origin: Reassessing Current Theories.* New York: Philosophical Library, 1984. (A)

*Thurman, L. Duane. *How to Think About Evolution.* 2d ed. Downers Grove: Inter-Varsity, 1978. (B)

Wilder-Smith, A. E. *The Creation of Life.* Wheaton: Harold Shaw, 1970. (A)

————. *Man's Origin, Man's Destiny*. Wheaton: Harold Shaw, 1968. (B)

Youngblood, Ronald, ed. *The Genesis Debate*. Nashville: Nelson, 1986. (B)

V. The Problem of Evil

A. The General Issue

*Geisler, Norman L. *The Roots of Evil*. Grand Rapids: Zondervan, 1978. (B)

Hick, John H. *Evil and the God of Love*. Rev. ed. San Francisco: Harper and Row, 1977. (I)

Plantinga, Alvin. *God, Freedom, and Evil*. New York: Harper and Row, 1974. (A)

Silvester, Hugh. *Arguing with God*. Downers Grove: Inter-Varsity, 1971. (B)

B. The Morality of the Old Testament

Wenham, John W. *The Goodness of God*. Downers Grove: Inter-Varsity, 1974. (I)

*Wright, Christopher J. *An Eye for an Eye: The Place of Old Testament Ethics Today*. Downers Grove: Inter-Varsity, 1983. (I)

Index